How to Become a Successful Store Leasing Broker

HOW TO BECOME A SUCCESSFUL STORE LEASING BROKER

CALVIN L. GREENBERG

Prentice-Hall, Inc.
Englewood Cliffs, N.J.

PRENTICE-HALL INTERNATIONAL, INC., *London*
PRENTICE-HALL OF AUSTRALIA, PTY. LTD., *Sydney*
PRENTICE-HALL OF CANADA, LTD., *Toronto*
PRENTICE-HALL OF INDIA PRIVATE LTD., *New Delhi*
PRENTICE-HALL OF JAPAN, INC., *Tokyo*

© 1971, BY

PRENTICE-HALL, INC.
ENGLEWOOD CLIFFS, N.J.

ALL RIGHTS RESERVED. NO PART OF THIS BOOK MAY BE REPRODUCED IN ANY FORM OR BY ANY MEANS, WITHOUT PERMISSION IN WRITING FROM THE PUBLISHER.

LIBRARY OF CONGRESS
CATALOG CARD NUMBER: 73-152844

"This publication is designed to provide accurate and authoritative information in regard to the subject matter covered. It is sold with the understanding that the publisher is not engaged in rendering legal, accounting, or other professional service. If legal advice or other expert assistance is required, the services of a competent professional person should be sought.
... *From the Declaration of Principles jointly adopted by a Committee of the American Bar Association and a Committee of Publishers and Associations.*"

PRINTED IN THE UNITED STATES OF AMERICA
ISBN 0-13-402263-7
B & P

Dedicated to the many playful hours lost by commercial leasing men, and the foolish hope that they may someday be recaptured.

List of Illustrations in Book

Exhibit 4-1.	Advertising Insert to Prospect	42
Exhibit 4-2.	Where to Send Publicity Items	43
Exhibit 4-3.	Ice-Cream Companies—Good Prospect Sources . . .	46
Exhibit 4-4.	Where Prospects May Be Found	46
Exhibit 4-5.	Various Lines of Business	47
Exhibit 4-6.	General Services Administration Regional Offices . .	48
Exhibit 4-7.	Coin-Op Dry Cleaning Companies	50
Exhibit 4-8.	Small Business Administration Field and Regional Offices	50
Exhibit 5-1.	Percentage Rental Rates	64
Exhibit 5-2.	Leasing Schedule (Community or Regional) . . .	67
Exhibit 5-3.	Developing Shopping Centers	68
Exhibit 5-4.	Store Locations	68
Exhibit 6-1.	Rentals per Front Foot Table (Per Annum) . . .	72
Exhibit 6-2.	Minimum Cash Investment for Establishing Certain Businesses	72
Exhibit 6-3.	Minimum Numbers of Persons Necessary to Keep Neighborhood Retail Stores Operating	74
Exhibit 6-4.	Necessary Listing Information	74
Exhibit 6-5.	Retail-Store-for-Sale Advertising Brochure	76
Exhibit 6-6.	Memorandum of Store Listing	77
Exhibit 6-7.	Exclusive Agreement (From Owner to Agent) . . .	80
Exhibit 9-1.	The Bonanza Formula	96
Exhibit 10-1.	Franchise Questionnaire Form	101
Exhibit 10-2.	Street and Traffic Information	103
Exhibit 10-3.	Types of Franchises Listed	106
Exhibit 10-4.	Index of Franchises by Type	107

Exhibit 10-5. Index Franchises by Name 113
Exhibit 10-6. Index of Franchises by State 118
Exhibit 11-1. Franchising Location and Leasing Information . . 126
Exhibit 11-2. Additional Franchise Sources to Be Contacted . . . 166
Exhibit 12-1. Store Location Report 172
Exhibit 12-2. Types of Chain Businesses Listed 173
Exhibit 12-3. Index of Chains by Type 173
Exhibit 12-4. Index of Chains by State 182
Exhibit 13-1. Leasing Formula 193
Exhibit 13-2. Additional Chain Store Sources to Be Contacted . . 248
Exhibit 14-1. Government Leasing and Purchasing Agencies (District Offices of Dept. of the Army Corps of Engineers) 253
Exhibit 14-2. State Leasing and Purchasing Agencies 254
Exhibit 14-3. Post Office Regional Real Estate Offices 256
Exhibit 14-4. Post Office Lease 258
Exhibit 14-5. Post Office Agreement to Lease 265
Exhibit 14-6. Post Office Lease Bidder's Qualifications Form . . . 270
Exhibit A-1. Brokerage Agreement 281
Exhibit A-2. Brokerage Agreement 283
Exhibit B-1. Listing Letter 286
Exhibit B-2. Presentation of Listing 287
Exhibit B-3. Typical Solicitation Forms 288
Exhibit B-4. Typical Publicity Pieces for Securing Taxpayers . . 289

TABLE OF CONTENTS

List of Illustrations in Book	. . . .	**7**
CHAPTER 1	**The Secret Gold Mine of the Real Estate World** . .	**17**

Easy to Learn, Dignified, Good Hours (17) ● *You Can Do What Others Have Done* (18).

CHAPTER 2	**My Success Formula**	**21**

Moneymaking Methods Reference Checklist (21).

CHAPTER 3	**How to Open an Office for Less Than $600** . . .	**23**

Initial Fixture and Expense Requirements (23) ● *A Library Is a Must* (24) ● *Sources of Information for the Commercial Leasing Broker* (25) ● *Free State Leasing Information Sources (Booklets)* (25) ● *Additional Sources, Listed by Firms* (28) ● *Additional Sources, Listed by Retail Trade Organizations* (32) ● *Urban Renewal Is a Great Source* (36) ● *Urban Renewal Regional Offices to Contact* (37) ● *Individual Cities and Towns Which Have Urban Renewal Lands* (37).

CHAPTER 4	**How to Attract Clients**	**41**

Advertising Insert to Prospect (42) ● *An Agent Must Be Well Known* (43) ● *Where to Send Publicity Items* (43) ● *Write Articles for Publicity* (44) ●

Remember Christmas, Give Gadgets (44) ● *Location Is of Prime Importance* (45) ● *Signs Are Cheap and a Must* (45) ● *Commercial Supplies—Prospect Sources* (45) ● *Ice-Cream Companies—Good Prospect Sources* (46) ● *Where Prospects May Be Found* (46) ● *Various Lines of Business* (47) ● *The Government Is a Prime Leasing Source* (48) ● *General Services Administration Regional Offices* (48) ● *Don't Neglect the Coin-Op Business* (49) ● *Coin-Op Dry Cleaning Companies* (50) ● *Small Business Administration Services* (50) ● *Small Business Administration Field and Regional Offices* (50).

CHAPTER 5 **Techniques for Negotiating Leases** 53

Types of Leases (53) ● *Ordinary Taxpayer Leases vs. Shopping Center (Percentage) Leases* (53) ● *Shopping Center Leases* (54) ● *The Three Classes of Building Repairs* (56) ● *Sample Supermarket Lease Specifications* (58) ● *Electric Facilities* (60) ● *Plumbing* (61) ● *Heat, Ventilating, and Air-Conditioning* (62) ● *General Provisions* (62) ● *Parking Area* (63) ● *Painting* (63) ● *Percentage Rental Rates* (64) ● *Size and Leasing Requirements of Various Retail Stores* (67) ● *Site Requirements* (68) ● *Factors to Consider in Developing a Shopping Center* (68).

CHAPTER 6 **More Negotiating Techniques** 71

How to Figure Rental Costs (71) ● *Rentals per Front Foot Table* (72) ● *Minimum Cash Investment for Establishing Certain Businesses* (72) ● *Minimum Numbers of Persons Necessary to Keep Neighborhood Retail Stores Operating* (74) ● *Necessary Listing Information* (74) ● *Brochure Content* (75) ● *Retail-Store-for-Sale Advertising Brochure* (76) ● *Forms and Brochures as Leasing Aids* (77) ● *Memorandum of Store Listing* (77) ● *How to Use the Telephone* (78) ● *Exclusive Agreement (From Owner to Agent)* (80).

CHAPTER 7 **How to Secure Any Lease You Want** 83

Methods of Approach—Securing Leases (83) ● *The Secret Method of Leasing* (85) ● *Always Be a Professional* (86).

CHAPTER 8 **The Sale-Leaseback Technique** 89

Be an Expert—Know the Techniques (89) ● *Three Basic Sales Methods* (91) ● *How the Various Options Work* (92) ● *Outright Sale* (92) ● *Sale-Leaseback* (92) ● *Leasehold Arrangement* (93).

Table of Contents / 13

CHAPTER 9 Commercial Leasing Bonanzas 95

Rent Guarantee Policies (95) ● *Work on "Expired Buildings" (96)* ● *The Bonanza Formula (96)* ● *How Much Money Can Be Made? (97).*

CHAPTER 10 The Fabulous Franchise Source 101

Find Out Franchise Requirements (101) ● *Franchise Questionnaire Form (101)* ● *Site Evaluation Method (102)* ● *Street and Traffic Information (103)* ● *Types of Franchises Listed (106)* ● *Index of Franchises by Type (107)* ● *Index of Franchises by Name (113)* ● *Index of Franchises by State (118).*

CHAPTER 11 Franchising Location and Leasing Information . . 125

Sample Franchising Location and Leasing Information Form (126) ● *Additional Franchise Sources to Be Contacted (166).*

CHAPTER 12 Chain Stores and Their Availability 171

How to Submit Chain Locations (171) ● *Store Location Report (172)* ● *Types of Chain Businesses Listed (173)* ● *Index of Chains by Type (173)* ● *Index of Chains by State (182).*

CHAPTER 13 Chain Stores—Location and Leasing Information . 193

Leasing Formula (193) ● *Additional Chain Store Sources to Be Contacted (248).*

CHAPTER 14 Sources for Leasing and Purchasing Federal Properties 253

Government Leasing and Purchasing Agencies (253) ● *Property Owned by Individual States (254)* ● *State Leasing and Purchasing Agencies (254)* ● *Post Office Regional Real Estate Offices (256)* ● *Post Office Lease (258)* ● *Post Office Agreement to Lease (265)* ● *Post Office Lease Bidder's Qualifications Form (270).*

APPENDIX

APPENDIX A The Basics of Commercial Leasing Law 277

Types of Property and Ownership (277) ● *How Real Property May Be Acquired (278)* ● *The Prime Importance of Commission Agreements (279)* ● *Terms of Commission Agreement (280)* ● *Brokerage Agreement (281), (283).*

APPENDIX B Listing and Selling Pointers 285

Contact Property Owners for Listings (285) ● *Listing Letter* (286) ● *Continue Selling New Listings* (286) ● *Presentation of Listing* (287) ● *Typical Solicitation Forms* (288) ● *Typical Publicity Pieces for Securing Taxpayers* (289).

APPENDIX C Glossary of Terms 291

Index 299

How to Become a Successful Store Leasing Broker

THE SECRET GOLD MINE OF THE REAL ESTATE WORLD

1

Are you really happy in your present job? Do you feel that you are being paid what you are worth? Does your job offer an unlimited future? Do you own your own home? Do you drive a Fleetwood Cadillac? Do you own a yacht? If the majority of your answers are "no," then this book is for you. All the aforementioned items are possible for you just as they were for me. This book will show you how to achieve a great many of the good things of life. All you have to do is read and follow the advice contained in it and the opportunity will be available to you.

Basically, the book covers a relatively little know occupation, commercial store leasing. This field is not crowded and probably will not be in the foreseeable future, because many people fail to realize that often a store rental commission may be greater than the commission one receives for actually selling a building. Another plus is the time element. The hours are 10 AM to 5 PM, five days, with weekends off. These are real bankers' hours. Enter this field and enjoy these hours; life is short.

EASY TO LEARN, DIGNIFIED, GOOD HOURS

Who can be successful as a commercial store leasing broker? You can! Almost anyone who can read and understand this simple, nontechnical book can achieve the benefits derived from this business. What more can you ask for? Good hours, free weekends to be with your family and friends, a dignified profession, and a well-above-the-average income. I have achieved all of these things and so can you.

Another feature of this business is that you are your own boss. Whether you work for someone else or open your own office, you will find that your time is your own. You can work *when* you wish and *how* you wish. This is the nature of the business.

One of the truly big features of commercial store leasing is the money. The commissions are excellent. The growth of this field is fantastic and your opportunities to achieve success are amazingly good. Just as thousands of others have been successful in it, so can you. You owe it to yourself and your family to enter this field in order to insure a secure future.

YOU CAN DO WHAT OTHERS HAVE DONE

My enthusiasm for this business is not necessarily based on my own success, but even more so upon the success of others. I can vividly recall an experience of several years ago concerning a residential real estate salesman that I knew. This acquaintance of mine was selling one-family homes and earning about $10,000 a year. The prospects of increasing his take-home pay were negligible because of the many variable factors in home sales that curb the opportunity to increase income. For example, the weather is a big factor. If it rains on Sunday, then the whole week is lost. Also, Sunday is really the only time that you show houses available for sale. This fellow decided to supplement his income by working evenings and renting stores.

He spent several weeks gathering information on vacant stores and then placed a $3 ad in a local newspaper. The ad was simple:

HAVE STORES—WILL RENT

It also included his name and telephone number. From this ad he leased three stores and earned $1,700 in commissions. The following week he repeated the ad and rented two stores, earning $1,400 in commissions. To cut the story short, five years have now gone by and this man has never earned less than $35,000 per annum since entering the store leasing field.

I know of another young fellow who started leasing stores while still in college. His business has grown so large that the man has bought, leased, and sold properties in every state in the union. This person is a European with a thick accent that might have hampered him in another line of work.

A friend of mine was earning $10–12,000 a year while employed by a toy company. The prospects of increasing his salary were not too good. This man decided to change jobs and entered the store leasing field. After about three years, he had tripled his previous income. I would like to stress that this book contains the information that it took my friends five years to become familiar with. You will not, after reading this book, have to wait five years to know the tricks of the business. All of the important aspects are well covered and simply explained. The basis of success is know-how and that has been included.

This is a "bread and butter" book written for the person who wishes to improve his job or income but cannot absorb a financial loss if things do not work out. I refer specifically to the various classes of job holders, including those in the $4,000 a year class to those in the $20,000 a year class. In commercial leasing, the sky is the limit.

This book will provide you with the 11 secrets of my success. These secrets *can* and *will* greatly increase the earning power of both the beginner and veteran real estate leasing broker.

MY SUCCESS FORMULA

2

This book will show you how to best lease commercial store properties—whether you are a veteran leasing broker, a property owner, a managing agent, a residential real estate salesman, or a beginner in real estate. All of the methods covered in this book have been tried and proven; they are not theory. This is a practical book containing methods that will produce immediate results. After years of trial and error, I've developed an 11-step set of techniques which has worked well for me. In the chapters that follow, these steps are covered in detail. If you will follow these steps, you will have an excellent chance to make top money.

A brief explanation of these moneymaking methods is seen in the following reference checklist:

1. This book reveals to you how and why people enter the secret gold mine of the real estate world. This field boasts short hours and generally great benefits. (See Chapter 1.)
2. I fully explain how you may open an office with only $600. This is actually a fraction of what it would cost you to open any other type of retail business. I fully explain the cost breakdown of the new office. (See Chapter 3.)
3. I explain quite simply how and where your business will come from. I show you the most economical methods of attracting clients. I show you systems that will make new clients beat a path to your door. (See Chapter 4.)
4. I explain and show the workability of my special techniques for profitable leasing. (See Chapters 5 and 6.)
5. Through methods acquired over a period of years, and now passed along to you, a system of securing practically any lease you want is available to you. (See Chapter 7.)

6. I cover one of the more sophisticated forms of leasing, the sale-leaseback technique. In plain, everyday language, this exciting leasing method is explained. (See Chapter 8.)
7. I advise you *when* and tell you *how* to take advantage of situations that can create a financial bonanza. Every so often this type of situation will be presented to you. I tell you how to handle things at that time. (See Chapter 9.)
8. This book covers quite fully how you may benefit from the franchise explosion. Thousands of companies are desperately seeking retail locations throughout the United States. I tell you where to go, who to see, and exactly what the firms are looking for. I created this valuable source because I needed the information myself and could not find it anyplace. (See Chapters 10 and 11.)
9. Even though franchise firms are grabbing locations, they do have competition. The established chain stores are also on an expansion binge. Again I tell you what to offer, where to offer, when to offer, and who to offer to. You will refer to these chapters constantly. (See Chapters 12 and 13.)
10. This book contains information relative to another unlimited source of business—the federal government. I tell you how to do business with the government. (See Chapter 14.)

HOW TO OPEN AN OFFICE FOR LESS THAN $600

3

In writing this book, I have tried to convey a basic knowledge of the commercial leasing business. I have attempted to show that the business does not require a great deal of knowledge and know-how. It is my belief that when the reader has mastered this book, he, although not an expert, will be ready to take his place in the business world. At this point, the reader should be able to earn a good living. The investment required is gaining a thorough knowledge of this book and spending less than $600 for fixtures and supplies.

The actual initial fixture and expense requirement is as follows:

Ashtrays	$5.00
Trade books, magazines, etc.	90.00
Used mimeograph and supplies	50.00
Stamps	5.00
1 used desk	25.00
6 used chairs	18.00
1 used conference table	25.00
Stationery, business cards, etc.	20.00
8 picture frames	8.00
1 used typewriter	35.00
2 wastebaskets	5.00
1 used bookshelf	15.00
Maps	5.00

Miscellaneous items, including telephone installation, desk blotters, etc.	20.00
Directories	90.00
Used rug or carpet	$40.00
Lights (fluorescent), usually supplied by landlord	—
Partitions (if needed), usually supplied by landlord	—
Painting premises, usually supplied by landlord	—
1 used filing cabinet	15.00
1 classified ad	3.00
10 signs (for store windows)	25.00
1 Rollex file	5.00
1 month's advance rent	65.00
TOTAL CASH OUTLAY	$569.00

Some people may feel that used furniture presents a shabby appearance. Nothing could be further from the truth. Many firms that sell new furniture take in used furniture in trade. This used furniture is repaired, when required, and in some cases is in excellent condition. It is relatively easy to acquire used furniture in matching sets, because there is so much used furniture available.

It may seem strange that I list picture frames as an item to purchase but do not include pictures. Landlords, in many cases, supply the pictures. Within one month, the average renting agent should have dozens of pictures supplied to him by landlords.

The big question asked by the beginning renting agent is usually, "Will I make money from the start?" The answer is "yes and no." It should take two to three months to reach productive capacity, but results may come quickly. Productive capacity is the period during which you develop an adequate customer file and a substantial listing file. At this point, money can be made. In fact, you should quickly make up for the first lean months after you have built up a reasonably adequate listing file.

The cost of opening an office is listed on these pages, but I must warn you that it is an initial opening cost. The new leasing broker must be prepared to finance himself for between two and three months. It is my opinion that commercial leasing presents an opportunity to participate in a field offering ample rewards with minimum risk.

A LIBRARY IS A MUST

Of prime importance to any office is the acquiring of a library. You cannot go to a bookstore and ask for a real estate library. I doubt if any bookstore in the country could be of help. The sources for acquiring these books are varied and can be frustrating to find unless you know where to look. You may now reap the benefits of long years of trial and error spent in determining what reference sources should be included in a proper library for a commercial store leasing broker.

I have listed some questions that will aid you in understanding the balance of this chapter.

1. Is it necessary to have a real estate library?
2. How much will it cost to set up a real estate library?
3. Will any books cost me money?
4. What do I know about the Small Business Administration and its publications?

SOURCES OF INFORMATION FOR THE COMMERCIAL LEASING BROKER

In order to operate a commercial leasing business, it is necessary to have many types of information available. This information enables the broker to be able to discuss locations and various businesses in an intelligent and up-to-date manner. With the exception of several books, all of the other literature is available free.

The books to be purchased are:

1. *Directory of Leading Chain Stores.* Available to the trade only. Available from *Chain Store Age*, 2 Park Ave., New York, N.Y. Cost is $50.
2. *Directory of Shopping Centers.* Available from the National Research Bureau, Inc., 415 N. Dearborn St., Chicago, Ill. Cost is $40.

A commercial real estate man has an opportunity to lease to all types of businesses throughout the entire country. The broker must be knowledgeable, in order to serve his clients properly. Much of the information is available from free sources. I have tried to include as many free sources of information as possible.

Free State Leasing Information Sources (Booklets)

Alabama	State Chamber of Commerce, Montgomery, Alabama. Free 62-page booklet of "Comparative Statistics" is available.
Alaska	Department of Commerce, P.O. Box 2259, Juneau, Alaska. Free "Business License Directory" and a copy of "Alaskan Business Statistics."
Arizona	Development Board, 1500 W. Jefferson, Phoenix, Arizona. Many free booklets available upon request.
Connecticut	State of Connecticut, State Office Building, Hartford, Connecticut. 128-page booklet available, "Connecticut Market Data," covering regional, state, and town statistics.

Florida	Development Commission, Tallahassee, Florida. Free population and sales estimates for Florida and selected southeastern cities.
Georgia	Georgia Department of Commerce, 100 State Capital, Atlanta, Georgia. Free copy of "General Business" available.
Hawaii	Chamber of Commerce, Dillingham Bldg., Honolulu 13, Hawaii. "A Brief Review of Hawaii for the Businessman" and "Hawaii Industrial Development for Island Growth" available.
Idaho	Department of Commerce and Development, State House, Boise, Idaho, for free copies of "Idaho Image."
Indiana	Indiana Department of Commerce, 336 State House, Indianapolis, Indiana. Free copies of "Indiana Business Review" available.
Iowa	Development Commission, 200 Jewett Bldg., Des Moines, Iowa, for free 45-page booklet, "Iowa Market." Sales tax figures are also available.
Kansas	Kansas Industrial Development Commission. Literature is available regarding the effects of the tourist trade upon retail business. Request the leaflet, "Travel Topics."
Kentucky	Department of Commerce, New Capital Annex Office Bldg., Frankfort, Kentucky. Free copy of "Deskbook of Kentucky Economic Statistics."
Louisiana	Department of Commerce and Industry, Baton Rouge, Louisiana. Free copy of "Survey of Buying Power."
Maine	Department of Economic Development, Augusta, Maine. Available free are "Sales and Use of Tax Assessments by Types of Businesses" and "Retail Sales Taxation by Economic Areas." Also available, "Recreational Regions and Principal Towns and Cities."
Maryland	Department of Economic Development, Annapolis, Maryland. No literature is available, but help is given with individual problems.
Massachusetts	Department of Commerce, 150 Causeway St., Boston, Massachusetts. Almost completely free monographs are available of the City of Boston.
Minnesota	Department of Business Development, State Capital, St. Paul, Minnesota. No literature available, but will try to satisfy individual requests.
Missouri	Division of Commerce and Industrial Development, Jefferson City, Missouri. Free 155-page book which provides a wealth of information "Missouri Location Facts." Also, Commerce and Industrial Division, Eighth floor, Jefferson Bldg., Jefferson City, Missouri provides free copy of "Management Decisions."
Montana	Montana State Planning Board, Sam W. Mitchell Bldg., Helena, Montana. Free copy of "Retail Trade Area Statistics."

How to Open an Office for Less Than $600 / **27**

Nebraska	Division of Nebraska Resources, State Capital, Lincoln, Nebraska. Free copy of "Business in Nebraska" available.
New Hampshire	State Department of Resources and Economic Development, State House Annex, Concord, New Hampshire. Request free copy of "County and City Retail Buying Income."
New Jersey	Department of Conservation and Economic Development, 520 E. State St., Trenton, New Jersey. All types of population and business reports available. Many are free; some are priced very moderately.
New Mexico	Department of Development, State Capital Bldg., Santa Fe, New Mexico. Many fine free publications available, such as "Rich in Profit Potential," "100 Site Locations in New Mexico," and "Favorite Tax Climate for Industry."
New York	Department of Commerce, 112 State St., Albany, New York. Free copies of "A Business of Her Own" and "Your Business." Also, "Market Measures for Cities and Villages."
North Carolina	Department of Conservation and Development, Raleigh, North Carolina. Free magazines and business literature.
North Dakota	No literature available from state; however, information is available from Greater North Dakota Association.
Ohio	Department of Industrial and Economic Development, 155 Noltigh St., Columbus, Ohio. Free copies of "Statistical Abstract of Ohio" are available plus other publications. Write, State of Ohio Capital, Industrial and Economic Division.
Oregon	Greater Portland Chamber of Commerce, 142 Free St., Portland, Oregon. Free copy of "Fingertip Facts About Greater Portland, Oregon." Also available is booklet, "Greater Portland." A list of Portland real estate brokers is also provided.
Rhode Island	Development Council & Research Division, Roger Williams Bldg., Hayes St., Providence, Rhode Island. Provides free copy of "Rhode Island Retail Sales, Subject Sales Tax."
South Carolina	South Carolina Retail Council, 900 Assembly St., Columbus, South Carolina. Distributes free literature regarding retail business.
Tennessee	Department of Conservation and Commerce, Nashville, Tennessee. Free copy of "Tennessee Industrial Development News" available.
Texas	Texas Information Division, Austin, Texas. Available free, "Visitor Tours—Texas Industry."
Utah	Utah Publicity Council, State Capital, Salt Lake City, Utah. A number of free booklets available upon request.
Virginia	Division of Industrial Development and Planning, 803 State Office Building, Richmond, Virginia. Provides free copy of "Virginia Economic Review."

West Virginia	Earle L. Elmore, Managing Director, West Virginia Chamber of Commerce, P.O. Box 2789, Charleston, West Virginia.
Wisconsin	State of Wisconsin, Department of Resource Development, Madison, Wisconsin. Att: Phillip Sundal. Will help with information for specific needs.

Additional Sources, Listed by Firms

Accounting Corp. of America	1929 1st Ave. San Diego, California. Free booklet, "Operating Results and Ratios," available.
A.C. Nielson Co.	2101 Howard St., Chicago, Illinois. Free copy of "Nielson Review of Retail Grocery Store Trends."
American Appraisal Co.	1 Cedar St., New York, N.Y. Has available, "Clients' Service Bulletin." This is a free bulletin published bimonthly and deals with valuation problems.
American Cyanamid Co.	Wayne, New Jersey. Excellent magazine available for people interested in the food business.
Batten, Barton, Durstine & Osborne	338 Madison Ave., New York, N.Y. Provides free copy of "The Confusion Factor in Grocery (Supermarket) Shopping."
Bureau of Business and Economic Research	Montana State University, Missoula, Montana. Free copy of "The Law of Small Business" available.
Bureau of Business Management	University of Illinois, Urbana, Illinois. Free copy of "Selling Furniture by Television."
Carpet Institute	350 Fifth Ave., New York, N.Y. Distributes free copy of "Meet Mrs. Carpet Customer."
Chamber of Commerce of U.S.	Washington, D.C. Provides free booklet, "So You're Going into Business."
Chicago Sun Times	250 Park Ave., New York, N.Y. Issues an excellent book, "Shopping Center Directory." You will need an advertiser to get one for you. 93-page book listing shopping centers, size, cost, parking, tenancy, when opened, location, etc.
Cities Service Oil Co.	60 Wall St., New York, N.Y. Free copy of "Credits and Collections" available.
Columbia Records	799 7th Ave., New York, N.Y. Free copy of "Your Future Sound."
Curtis Publishing Company	Research Department, Philadelphia 5, Pennsylvania. Provides free copy of "Market for Fishing and Hunting Equipment."
Dun & Bradstreet, Inc.	Public Relations Division, 99 Church St., New York, N.Y. Has available free copies of:
	"How Does Your Business Compare with Others in Your Line?"

How to Open an Office for Less Than $600 / 29

	"Operating Results and Ratios." "Profitable Management for Main Street." "Important Ratios for 72 Lines of Business."
E.I. duPont de Nemours & Co.	Wilmington, Delaware. Free copy of "The Story of Business: Large and Small."
Enco Foundation for Highway Traffic Control, Inc.	Saugatuck, Conn. Free copies available (supply limited) of "Shopping Centers," by Eugene J. Kelly.
Federal Reserve Bank of Minneapolis	73 South 5th St., Minneapolis, Minnesota. Distributes free copy of "Shopping Centers and Population Growth in the Twin Cities Area."
Federal Reserve System	Washington, D.C. Provides free copy of "Retail Furniture Report Monthly."
First National Bank of Arizona	411 North Central, Phoenix, Arizona. Free copy of "A Survey of Shopping Centers in Greater Phoenix, Arizona" available.
Mercantile Trust Co.	Saint Louis 66, Missouri. Ask to be added to free weekly mailing list of "Weekly Business Summary."
Minneapolis Honeywell Regulator Co.	Wayne and Windrim Aves., Philadelphia 44, Pennsylvania. Free booklet, "Small Business Automation," available.
National Cash Register Co.	Merchants Service, Main and K Streets, Dayton 9, Ohio. Provides free copies of: "Operating Results and Ratios." "Getting Ahead in Retail Selling." "Success in the Restaurant Business." "Expenses in Retail Business." "Profiting by Adequate Records." "Ten Principles of Modern Selling." "Variety Stores."
New York Life Insurance Co.	Career Information Service, Madison Square Station, New York 10, N.Y. Provides free copies of: "Should You Be a Pharmacist?" "Should You Go into Retailing?"
New York State Dept. of Commerce	112 State St., Albany 7, New York. Ask for free copy of "Shopping Centers and New York's Retail Economy," *New York State Commerce Review*, Vol. 12, No. 9, 1958.
New York Times	Times Square, New York, N.Y. Request free copy of booklet of classified advertisements, "Business Opportunities." Also available on request is the booklet, "Your Guide to Employment Agencies."
Orchids of Hawaii	305 7th Ave., New York, N.Y. Free promotion calendar available.

30 / *How to Open an Office for Less Than $600*

Pitney-Bowes, Inc. 69 Walnut St., Stamford, Connecticut. "Free Postal Rates and Information Chart" available.

Polaroid Cambridge 39, Massachusetts. Free literature available illustrating "82 ways Polaroid Camera Helps Businessmen."

The Small Business Administration Washington 55, D.C. The following free booklets are available on request:

"Are You Kidding Yourself About Profits?" ✓
"Attracting Customers to Your Small Store."
"Business Ethics and Small Marketers."
"Credit and Collection Controls for Small Markets."
"Methods for Improving Off-Season Sales."
"Profitable Buying for Small Retailers."
"Public Relations for Small Business Owners." ✓
"Reducing Stock Shrinkage in Small Firms."
"Stock Management in Small Firms."
"Traps to Avoid in Small Business Management."

Also write Small Business Administration, 42 Broadway, New York 4, N.Y. and request to be placed on mailing list to receive new aids and other free Small Business Administration publications. ✓

S.B.A. Checklist for Going into Business
"Laundry and Dry Cleaning."
"Bookstore Operation."
"Job Printing Shop."
"Woodworking Shops."
"Soft Frozen Dessert Stands."
"How Trade Associations Help Small Business." ✓
"Getting Your Product on a Qualified Products List."
"How to Analyze Your Own Business."
"Business Life Insurance."
"Corporation Life Insurance."
"Partnership Life Insurance."
"Store Location." ✓
"Basic Library Reference Sources." ✓
"Variety Stores."
"Automatic Laundries."
"Food Stores."
"Frozen Foods and Lockers."
"Gift and Art Shops."
"Shopping Centers." ✓
"Retail Store Hours."
"Voluntary and Cooperative Chains."
"Plumbing and Heating Jobs."
"Furniture Retailing."
"Training Commercial Salesmen."
"Sporting Goods."

"Small Store Opportunities in Planned Shopping Centers."
"How Urban Renewal Projects Affect Small Business."
"Facts About Small Business Financing."
"Hours of Operation in Retail Stores."
"Case Studies of Small Retail Stores."
"Site Evaluation for Small Retailers."
"Unusual Small Businesses in Louisiana."
"Advertising Volume and Expenditures."
"Operating Cost and Ratios—Retail."
"Retailing."
"The Nursery Business."
"Buying for Retail Stores."
"Record Keeping Systems—Small Stores and Service Trade."
"Restaurants and Other Eating Places."
"Basic Library Reference Sources for Business Use."
"Bakery Products."
"Advertising—Retail Store."
"Training Retail Salespeople."
"Grocery, Meat, and Produce Stores."
"Men's and Boys' Clothing."
"Jewelry Retailing."
"Hardware Retailing."
"Drugstores."

Supermarket Institute 500 N. Dearborn St., Chicago, Illinois. Free copy of "Facts About Supermarkets Opened in 1958" available.

Swimming Pool Age 425 4th Ave., New York, N.Y. Provides free copy of "Swimming Pool Industry Market Report."

Syracuse University College of Business Administration, Syracuse 10, New York. Free copy of "Planned Shopping Centers vs. Neighborhood Shopping Centers," by Edgar R. Neff, "Business Research Center Marketing Series," No. 3, 1956.

U.S. Dept. of Agriculture Agriculture Marketing Service, Washington 25, D.C. Free copy of "Cost Control in Retailing Food Stores by Use of Wholesalers Accounting Services" available.

U.S. Federal Trade Commission Washington 25, D.C. Free copy of "Trade Practice Rules for Pleasure Boat Industry."

University of Miami Coral Gables 46, Florida. Provides free copy of "Determination and Evaluation of Retail Areas Serviced by Suburban Shopping Centers" by R. P. Wolff, *Bureau of Business and Economic Research Bulletin*, 1955.

University of Oregon Department of Planning and Development, 560 State Office Building, Portland, Oregon. Free copy "Oregon

32 / *How to Open an Office for Less Than $600*

	Economic Statistics" available; also sales management information in its "Survey of Buying Power" booklet is available on request.
Washington Board of Trade	1616 K St., N.W., Washington 6, D.C. Provides free copy of "Metropolitan Area Population Estimates as of January 1, 1958" compiled by Economic Development Committee.

RETAIL TRADE ORGANIZATIONS A GREAT HELP

One of the leading sources of free information available to the new retailer or experienced merchant comes from the various trade associations. Trade associations serve as advisors to respective trades. Actually, the trade association is a clearing house for information. Below you will find a partial list of trade associations and the type of business each represents.

Additional Sources, Listed by Retail Trade Organizations

American Institute of Laundering	Joliet, Illinois.
Associated Third Class Mail Users	100 Indiana Ave., N.W., Washington, D.C.
Automatic Laundry Assn. of Massachusetts	Maurice Miller, Secretary, 19 Church St., Rockland, Massachusetts.
Automatic Laundry Assn. Inc., of Southern Calif.	Mr. William F. Anderson, La Cienega Launderette, 1266 S. La Cienega Blvd., Los Angeles 35, California.
Coin Laundry Operators Assns. of Florida	G. O. McMillin, Secretary-Treasurer, P.O. Box 7156, Tampa 3, Florida.
Coin-Operated, Self-Service Laundry Assns., Inc.	Mr. Donald E. Paquette, Exec. Secretary, 2130 Dime Building, Detroit 26, Michigan.
Direct Mail Advertising Assns.	3 E. 57th St., New York 22, N.Y.
Education and Training of Sales Personnel	American Management Assn., 1515 Broadway, New York 36, N.Y.
	American Marketing Assn., 27 E. Monroe St., Chicago 3, Illinois.
	American Society of Training Directors, 2020 University Ave., Madison 5, Wisconsin.
	National Sales Executive, Inc., 630 3rd Ave., New York 17, N.Y.

How to Open an Office for Less Than $600 / **33**

	National Society of Sales Training Executives, 410 S. Michigan Ave., Room 842, Chicago 5, Illinois.
	Sales Promotion Executives Assn., 389 Fifth Ave., New York 16, N.Y.
Food Distribution	American Institute of Food Distribution, 420 Lexington Ave., New York 17, N.Y.
	Cooperative Food Distributors of America, 141 W. Jackson Blvd., Chicago, Illinois.
	Food Merchandisers of America, 1511 K Street, N.W. Washington, D.C.
	Independent Grocers' Alliance, 131 S. Wabash Ave., Chicago, Illinois.
	National-American Wholesale Grocers' Assns., Inc., 60 Hudson St., New York, N.Y.
	National Assn. of Food Chains, 1925 Connecticut Ave., Washington, D.C.
	National Voluntary Groups Institute, 77 W. Washington St., Chicago, Illinois.
	Supermarket Institute, 500 N. Dearborn St., Chicago, Illinois.
	U. S. Wholesale Grocers Assns., Inc., 1511 K St., Washington, D.C.
Food Retailing	Cooperative Food Distributors of America, 140 S. Dearborn St., Chicago, Illinois.
	National Assn. of Retail Grocers of the U.S., 360 N. Michigan Ave., Chicago, Illinois.
	National Assn. of Retail Meat & Food Dealers, 510 N. Dearborn St., Chicago, Illinois.
	National Assns. for the Specialty Food Trade, 550 Fifth Ave., New York, N.Y.
	National Food Assns. of Food Chains, 1725 I St., N.W. Washington, D.C.
	Supermarket Institute, 500 N. Dearborn St., Chicago, Illinois.
Furniture Retailing	American Institute of Decorators, 41 E. 57th St., New York.
	Art & Antique Dealers League of America, 138 E. 55th St., New York, N.Y.
	Carpet Institute, 350 Fifth Ave., New York, N.Y.

34 / *How to Open an Office for Less Than $600*

Chrome Furniture Institute,
1421 Chestnut St., Philadelphia, Pennsylvania.

Home Furnishing Industry Committee,
666 N. Lake Shore Drive, Chicago, Illinois.

Gas Appliance Manufacturers' Assn.,
60 E. 42nd St., New York, N.Y.

Grand Rapids Furniture Exposition Assn.,
1004 Michigan National Bldg., Grand Rapids, Michigan.

Institute of Appliance Manufacturers,
Shoreham Hotel, Washington, D.C.

Lamp & Shade Institute of America,
15 E. 26th St., New York, N.Y.

Mirror Manufacturers Assn.,
2217 Tribune Tower, Chicago, Illinois.

National Appliance & Radio Television Dealers Assn.,
1141 Merchandise Mart Plaza, Chicago, Illinois.

National Appliance Service Assn.,
2201 Grand Ave., Kansas City, Missouri.

National Assn. of Bedding Manufacturers,
Merchandise Mart Plaza, Chicago, Illinois.

National Assn. of Furniture Manufacturers,
666 Lake Shore Drive, Chicago, Illinois.

National Assn. of Summer Furniture Manufacturers,
216 E. 49th St., New York, N.Y.

National Home Lamp Council,
10 S. La Salle St., Chicago, Illinois.

National Office Furniture Assn.,
327 S. La Salle St., Chicago, Illinois.

National Retail Furniture Assn.,
666 Lake Shore Drive, Chicago, Illinois.

National Wholesale Furniture Assn.,
666 Lake Shore Drive, Chicago, Illinois.

Oriental Rug Importers Assn.,
295 5th Ave., New York, N.Y.

Georgia Laundry and Cleaners Assns.
Mr. Louis Klauber, Executive Secretary,
1053 W. Peachtree St., N.E., Atlanta, Georgia.

Gift, Art Manufacturers & Retailing
Allied Exhibitors, Inc.,
3832 Wilshire Blvd., Los Angeles, California.

American Glassware Assns.,
19 W. 44th St., New York, N.Y.

Associated Ceramic Importers of America,
7901 Empire State Bldg., New York, N.Y.

Associated Glass & Pottery Manufacturers,
Box 26, Knox, Pennsylvania.

Brack Shops Assn.,
527 W. 7th St., Los Angeles, California.

California Art Potters Assn.,
1170 S. Alameda St., Lynwood, California.

China, Glass & Pottery Assns. of America,
111 4th Ave., New York, N.Y.

China, Pottery & Glassware Assns.,
232 S. Central Ave., Los Angeles, California.

Crockery Board of Trade of New York, N.Y.,
71 W. 23rd St., New York, N.Y.

Eastern Manufacturers & Importers Exhibit, Inc.,
220 5th Ave., New York, N.Y.

15th Floor Merchandise Club,
Merchandise Mart, Chicago, Illinois.

Indiana Quick Service Laundry Assn.	William Watkins, Secretary, Watkins Launderette, 1027 John St., Anderson, Indiana.
Laundry & Cleaners Allied Trade Assn.	95 Liberty St., New York, N.Y.
Mail Order Assns. of America	612 N. Michigan Ave., Chicago, Illinois.
The Mail Order Business Board	P.O. Box 75, Mora, Minnesota.
Michigan Automatic Laundry Assn.	William Olson, Secretary-Treasurer, Lakeside Launderette, Muskegon, Michigan.
National Assn. of Coin Laundry Equip. Operators, Inc.	Du Pont Circle Buildings, Washington, D.C.
National Assns. of Variety Stores	803 Merchandise Mart, Chicago, Illinois.
National Institute of Dry Cleaning	Silver Springs, Maryland.
National Retail Merchants Assns.	100 W. 31st St., New York, N.Y.
Plumbing and Heating Field	American Society of Heating, Refrigeration, and Air-Conditioning Engineers, 62 Worth St., New York, N.Y.
	American Society of Mechanical Engineers, 29 W. 39th St., New York, N.Y.

36 / *How to Open an Office for Less Than $600*

	Better-Heating-Cooling Council, 250 Park Ave., New York, N.Y.
	Mechanical Contractors Assns. of America, 45 Rockefeller Plaza, New York, N.Y.
Sporting Goods Trade Assns.	American Fishing Tackle Manufacturers Assns., 20 N. Wacker Drive, Chicago, Illinois.
	Archery Manufacturers and Dealers Assns. 23 E. Jackson Blvd., Chicago, Illinois.
	Athletic Goods Manufacturers Assns., Rm. 805, Merchandise Mart, Chicago, Illinois.
	The Athletic Institute, Rm. 805, Merchandise Mart, Chicago, Illinois.
	Bicycle Institute of America, Inc., 122 E. 42nd St., New York, N.Y.
	Bicycle Institute-Merchant Member Group, 122 E. 42nd St., New York, N.Y.
	Bicycle Manufacturers Assn., 122 E. 42nd St., New York, N.Y.
	Billiard & Bowling Institute of America, 23 E. Jackson Blvd., Chicago, Illinois.
	Cycle, Parts & Accessories Assn. c/o Burt P. Pharis, Carlisle Tire and Rubber Co., Division of Carlisle Corp., Carlisle, Pennsylvania.
	Golf Ball Manufacturers Assn., Rm. 805, Merchandise Mart, Chicago, Illinois.
	Hardware Golf Assns., 4415 W. 72 Terrace, Prairie Village, Kansas.
	Hobby Industry Assns. of America, 1528 Walnut St., Philadelphia, Pennsylvania.
	Manufacturers' Representatives Assn., Rm. 914, 600 S. Michigan Ave., Chicago, Illinois.
	Marine Manufacturers Safety Equipt. Assn., 23 E. Jackson Blvd., Chicago, Illinois.
Variety Stores Assns., Inc.	25 W. 43rd St., New York, N.Y.

URBAN RENEWAL IS A GREAT SOURCE

One of the largest commercial projects ever undertaken is the present urban renewal program. This program is not wholly confined to commercial properties, but because of the tremendous scope of the plan, the commercial segment is, in itself, quite large.

Urban renewal is a term used to describe the efforts by municipal authorities, with the help of the federal government, to eliminate blighted and slum areas. The program seeks to prevent slum areas, remodel and rebuild structures, and clear and provide for redevelopment of entire neighborhoods.

Much of the urban renewal program is concerned with commercial development and redevelopment and offers outstanding opportunities for leasing agents. In general, the agent should contact local urban renewal agencies and inquire regarding available properties. There may be a sponsor, a man willing to purchase and build the property, or the broker may have to secure his own sponsor.

For more specific information relative to urban renewal, it is suggested that one of the regional offices be contacted:

Region 1. 346 Broadway, New York 13, N.Y.—
New York, Maine, New Hampshire, Vermont, Massachusetts, Connecticut, Rhode Island.

Region 2. Widner Building, Philadelphia 7, Pa.—
Pennsylvania, New Jersey, Maryland, Delaware, District of Columbia, West Virginia, Virginia.

Region 3. 360 North Michigan Ave., Chicago 1, Ill.—
Michigan, Ohio, Indiana, Illinois, Wisconsin, Iowa, Minnesota, N. Dakota, S. Dakota, Nebraska.

Region 4. Federal Center, 300 W. Vickery Blvd., Fort Worth 4, Texas—
Kansas, Missouri, Arkansas, Louisiana, Oklahoma, Texas, Colorado, New Mexico.

Region 5. 989 Market St., San Francisco 3, California—
Washington, Oregon, California, Idaho, Nevada, Arizona, Utah, Montana, Wyoming, Alaska, Hawaii, Guam.

Region 6. 1608 Ponce de Leon Ave., Santuci 17, Puerto Rico—
Puerto Rico, Virgin Islands.

The individual cities or towns having urban renewal lands available are as follows:

Greater Gadsden Housing Authority
P.O. Box 970
Gadsden, Alabama

Montgomery Housing Authority
1020 Bell St.
Montgomery, Alabama

Sylacauga Housing Authority
Betsy Ross Lane
Sylacauga, Alabama

Little Rock Housing Authority
201 E. Roosevelt Rd.
Little Rock, Arkansas

Fresno Redevelopment Agency
410 Abby St.
Fresno, California

Community Redevelopment Agency of the City of Los Angeles
617 S. Olive St., Rm. 1010
Los Angeles, California

Merced Redevelopment Agency
P.O. Box 309
Merced, California

Richmond Redevelopment Agency
P.O. Box 1786

Richmond, Virginia
Sacramento Redevelopment Agency
1006 4th St.
Sacramento, California

San Bernardino Redevelopment Agency
306 Blackstone Bldg.
San Bernardino, California

San Francisco Redevelopment Agency
525 Golden Gate Ave.
San Francisco, California

New London Redevelopment Agency
281 State St.
New London, Connecticut

Rockville Redevelopment Agency
5 W. Main St.
Rockville, Connecticut

Santa Rosa Urban Renewal Agency
528 4th St.
Rockville, Connecticut

District of Columbia Redevelopment Land Agency
919 18th St.
Washington 6, D.C.

American Housing Authority
P.O. Box 228
Americus, Georgia

City of Augusta Redevelopment Agency
Augusta, Georgia

Cordele Urban Renewal Dept.
P.O. Box 507
Cordele, Georgia

Macon Housing Authority
1130 Oglethorpe St.
Macon, Georgia

Savannah Housing Authority
P.O. Box 507
Savannah, Georgia

Waynesboro Housing Authority
P.O. Box 351
Waynesboro, Georgia

Dept. of Urban Renewal
City of Chicago
320 N. Clark St.
Chicago, Illinois

Dept. of Redevelopment
City of Mishawaka
112½ Lincoln Way E.
Mishawaka, Indiana

South Bend Redevelopment
129 W. Colfax Ave.
South Bend, Indiana

Dept. of Redevelopment
417 S. 5th St.
Terre Haute, Indiana

City of Waterloo
Rm. 218, City Hall
Waterloo, Iowa

Urban Renewal Development
310 S. 6th St.
Louisville, Kentucky

Malden Redevelopment Authority
17 Leyden St.
Plymouth, Massachusetts

Plymouth Redevelopment Authority
17 Leyden St.
Plymouth, Massachusetts

City Hall, Room 205
Battle Creek, Michigan

Detroit Housing Commission
2211 Orleans St.
Detroit 7, Michigan

City of Grand Rapids
City Hall
Grand Rapids, Michigan

City of Sagman
Dept. of Planning
City Hall
Saginaw, Michigan

St. Paul Housing & Redevelopment Authority
55 E. 5th St.
St. Paul 1, Minnesota

Land Clearance for Redevelopment Authority of St. Louis
St. Louis 3, Missouri

Borough of Belmar
P.O. Box 90
Belmar, New Jersey

East Orange Housing Authority
City Hall
East Orange, New Jersey

Edison Housing Authority
Management Office
N. Edison Gardens
Metuchen, New Jersey

The City of Orange
325 Mechanic St.
Orange, New Jersey

City Hall
Mount Vernon, New York

Urban Renewal Agency of Rome
112 W. Liberty St.
Rome, New York

City Hall
Tonawanda, New York

Redevelopment Commission of Charlotte
1617 Johnston Building
Charlotte 2, North Carolina

City of Cincinnati
Room 141, City Hall
Cincinnati 2, Ohio

Dept. of Urban Renewal
206 Municipal Building
Dayton, Ohio

City of Middleton
City Building
Middleton, Ohio

Redevelopment Authority of Dauphin County
341 S. Cameron St.
Harrisburg, Pennsylvania

Meadville Redevelopment Authority
898 Park Ave., Rm. 15
Meadville, Pennsylvania

Redevelopment Authority of the County of Delaware
Court House Annex
Medra, Pennsylvania

Monessen Redevelopment Authority
512 Schoonmaker Ave.
Monessen, Pennsylvania

Urban Redevelopment Authority
of Pittsburgh
200 Ross St.
Pittsburgh 19, Pennsylvania

York Redevelopment Authority
32 W. King St.
York, Pennsylvania

Puerto Rico Urban Renewal
& Housing Corp.
P.O. Box 397
Rio Piedras, Puerto Rico

Redevelopment Agency of Newport
City Hall
Newport, Rhode Island

Providence Redevelopment Agency
410 Howard Building
Providence 3, Rhode Island

Morristown Housing Authority
P.O. Box 2047
Morristown, Tennessee

Union City Housing Authority
P.O. Box 387
Union City, Tennessee

Harrisonberg Redevelopment &
Housing Authority
286 Kelley St.
Harrisonberg, Virginia

Newport News Redevelopment &
Housing Authority
P.O. Box 77
Newport News, Virginia

S. Norfolk Redevelopment &
Housing Authority
P.O. Box 5005
S. Norfolk, Virginia

Huntington Urban Renewal Authority
P.O. Box 324
Huntington 8, W. Virginia

Urban Renewal Authority of Wheeling
Rm. 500, Riley Lou Bldg.
Wheeling, W. Virginia

Madison Redevelopment Authority
Rm. 409, City County Bldg.
Madison 9, Wisconsin

HOW TO ATTRACT CLIENTS

4

In selling real estate or in leasing, it is important to create visual aids, such as proper atmosphere. The office, though it may be only one small room, must be dignified and give off a glow that creates confidence. I do not recommend new, modern furniture. The mood of the office should be old and solid. The furniture can be secondhand, but it should be clean and in good repair. Wood furniture rather than metal or plastic is suggested because it conveys the feeling of solidarity. The floors of the office, and this is very important, should be carpeted. For the new man in business, I recommend used carpets or rugs. These may be purchased from any large rug cleaner. The cost is low and the effect is perfect.

The walls should be painted flat white or a light pastel shade. They should have mounted on them large, framed photographs of stores, shopping centers, etc. These pictures will put a prospective tenant into the proper mood. The pictures may be secured from brochures or be snapshots that you take yourself. The pictures, in effect, create the mood of doing business.

Display your license prominently. The license tells a client that you are qualified to act. In time, you will qualify for various professional groups in your field, and these impressive, diploma type papers should be properly framed and displayed. Above all, you must strive to maintain the professional dignity of the commercial leasing man. In maintaining the professional dignity of the business, the agent is creating a degree of confidence that will certainly, over a period of time, earn additional money for him. Business is, in the final analysis, only a game, and each partici-

EXHIBIT 4-1. Advertising Insert to Prospect.

(These publicity items appeared in *Realty*, *National Real Estate Investor*, and *Real Estate Weekly*.)

Balter & Greenberg

Balter & Greenberg, Jamaica, New York Realtors, announce that they were the brokers who arranged sale of the taxpayer at 4021-4023 Glenwood Road and 1574-76 Albany Avenue in Brooklyn.

The property, containing six stores on plot of 40x90, was sold for all cash over one mortgage. The sellers were Witten Building Corporation represented by the law firm of Rubinton & Coleman.

The purchaser is an investing client of Balter & Greenberg, Inc.

Brooklyn Parcel Sold

A one-story building with eight stores at 4001 13th Avenue, Brooklyn, has been sold for $155,000 in cash over a first mortgage by Steven Associates, a Brooklyn realty investing concern. The purchaser of the building and its plot of 100- by 60 feet was Sidney Berger. The broker in the transaction was Lee Weisinger of Balter & Greenberg, Inc. The lawyer for the seller was Edward A. Segal. Gene Wolin, represented the buyer.

SHOPPING CENTER IN QUEENS BOUGHT

Investor Gets Grand Union Building in Laurelton

The Grand Union Shopping Center at the intersection of Merrick Road and Laurelton Parkway, Queens, has been purchased by an investing client of Balter & Greenberg, commercial property brokers of Jamaica.

Balter & Greenberg, Inc. is broker in the sale of the first drive-in cleaning establishment ever built in Queens, located at 35-15 Bell Blvd. in Bayside ...

Balter & Greenberg, Inc., announces the sale of the colonial taxpayer at Northern Blvd. and 157th St., Flushing, N.Y. The taxpayer was built on a plot 103 by 90 feet and contains 6 stores.

BALTER & GREENBERG, INC.

Balter & Greenberg, Inc. leading investment firm, announced the recent sale of 12 commercial buildings for aggregate sales of $4,837,000.

11 STORE BUILDINGS BOUGHT FOR MILLION

The A. S. W. Holding Corporation, a real estate investing company, has bought 11 store buildings in the metropolitan area in a transaction involving about $1,000,000. The one-story taxpayers were acquired from the Greenwich Real Estate, a realty holding company.

The properties, which are in Queens, Brooklyn, the Bronx and Nassau County, were sold through Balter & Greenberg, Inc., brokers of Jamaica, Queens, who were represented

BALTER & GREENBERG

Balter & Greenberg, Inc., Queens investment brokers, announce the sale of the seven store shopping center located at 147-14A Northern Blvd., Flushing, N.Y. The seller was "3400 Estates, Inc.," represented by Burry & Katzman. The purchaser, D. Woldman, was represented by I. Linder, Esq.

The improvement is 100 x 60 located on 115 x 100 plot and contains five stores. The property was purchased for all cash over a $100,000 mortgage.

BALTER & GREENBERG, INC.

Balter & Greenberg, Inc. Queens realtors announce the sale of a taxpayer located at 349 Knickerbocker Avenue, Brooklyn, N.Y.

TAXPAYERS WE HAVE SOLD IN NEW YORK CITY

147-14A Northern Blvd., Flushing, N.Y.
35-15 Bell Blvd., Bayside, N.Y.
157-02 Northern Blvd., Flushing, N.Y.
801 Flatbush Avenue, Brooklyn, N.Y.
5510 Fifth Ave., Brooklyn, N.Y.
542 Fifth Avenue, Brooklyn, Jackson Hts., N.Y.
86-26 Roosevelt Avenue, Jackson Hts., N.Y.
118-02 Rockaway Blvd., Ozone Pk., N.Y.
204-06 Jamaica Avenue, Hollis, N.Y.
3046 Avenue I, Brooklyn, N.Y.
511 Marcy Avenue, Brooklyn, N.Y.
639 Marcy Avenue, Brooklyn, N.Y.
3046 Avenue X, Brooklyn, N.Y.
87-27 Britton Avenue, Jackson Hts., N.Y.
112-48 Sutphin Blvd., Jamaica, N.Y.
117-34 Sutphin Blvd., Jamaica, N.Y.
686 Grand Street, Brooklyn, N.Y.
349 Knickerbocker Avenue, Brooklyn, N.Y.
4021 Glenwood Road, Brooklyn, N.Y.
4001 13th Avenue, Brooklyn, N.Y.
128-04 Liberty Avenue, Richmond Hill, N.Y.
218-82 Hempstead Ave., Queens Village, N.Y.
1409 35th Street, Brooklyn, N.Y.
2118 Avenue U, Brooklyn, N.Y.
9103 Avenue L, 111th Avenue, Ozone Pk., N.Y.
127-13 111th Avenue, Ozone Pk., N.Y.
Merrick Road & 234th Street, Laurelton, L.I.
349 Knickerbocker Avenue, Brooklyn, N.Y.
1409 35th Street, Brooklyn, N.Y.

BALTER & GREENBERG

Balter & Greenberg, Inc., New York investment firm, announced the sale of the taxpayer located at 9101 and 9103 Avenue L, corner of East 91 Street, Brooklyn, N.Y. The taxpayer is built on a plot 131 x 100. Terry Realty Company was the seller and John and Maria Bivanos were the purchasers. Harry A. Kornfeld, Esq. was attorney for the seller. Manual Manos, Esq. represented the purchaser.

Balter & Greenberg, Inc., investment brokers, announced the sale of the store and office building located at 801-803 Flatbush Avenue corner Caton Avenue, Brooklyn, N.Y. The property assessed for $135,000 was sold for all cash above financing. This property has long been tenanted by one of Brooklyn's most famous bakeries, Sutters.

The property was purchased by an investing client of Calvin L. Greenberg. The seller, Joseph Rosenblum was represented by Leepson & Rabman.

Clippings courtesy of Real Estate Weekly, 614 E. 14th St., New, N.Y.; Realty, 264 W. 40th St., New York, N.Y.; National Real Estate Investor, 132 W. 31st St., New York, N.Y.

pant must wear the proper costume and have the necessary props. There is no secret for success; all that is necessary is a small amount of luck, a goodly amount of perspiration, a proper application of the rules, and a certain amount of creativeness.

Continuing along with visual aids, I feel that the real estate leasing broker can truly add to his prestige by placing his name before the public. This must be done constantly. The easiest way to place your name before the public, is to purchase advertising space, but this is costly. I personally feel that free publicity is better in two ways. First, it will cost you nothing, and second, the public will buy something that someone else says about you or your work before it will buy what you say about yourself or your ability. Publicity is easily achieved by writing reports about your deals or about any ideas you may have. Having your ideas printed in local newspapers or trade papers will save you years of work in building up a name. In a matter of months, you can educate the public and make your name a familiar one.

AN AGENT MUST BE WELL KNOWN

In order for an agent to be successful, he must be well known. A well-known agent is a definite lure to prospective tenants and is constantly sought by landlords and owners. It is a simple procedure to get your name before the public. When you close a deal or if you have a new idea regarding commercial leasing, compose an interest-arousing article and send it along to the local newspapers. The proper form for the article does not require a lengthy explanation. Copy the form that is used in the newspapers. The article should be double-spaced and on plain, white paper. See Exhibits 4-1 and 4-2.

The list of taxpayer sales is included in this advertising insert because it provides a psychological advantage. The owner, receiving this mailing, feels that he is doing business with a complete commercial organization. I wish to add that the sale of taxpayers is a lucrative by-product of store leasing. The sale of taxpayers brings the store leasing broker into close contact with taxpayers and shopping center owners—the only people who ever have vacant stores.

EXHIBIT 4-2. Where to Send Publicity Items.

List of Newspapers and Their Addresses*

Daily News, 220 E. 42nd St., New York, N.Y.
Long Island Press, 92–24 168th St., Jamaica, New York.
New York Post, 75 West St., New York, N.Y.
New York Times, 229 W. 43rd St., New York, N.Y.

EXHIBIT 4-2 (Contd.)

Real Estate Weekly, 614 E. 14th St., New York, N.Y.
Realty, 264 W. 40th St., New York, N.Y.
United Press, 220 E. 42nd St., New York, N.Y.

plus

The papers in your local area or the papers in the area where the deal was consummated.

NOTE: Address all envelopes to the attention of the real estate editor.

---

* This is a metropolitan New York area group of papers. Local lists may be made up by checking the classified section of your telephone book.

WRITE ARTICLES FOR PUBLICITY

One of the more eye-catching publicity methods is to have the newspapers print an article containing your views. How is this done? Basically, by taking a segment of the leasing field, researching this segment in the local public library, and writing your article. It is not necessary that the article be a new contribution to the field. Check through books and articles on the subject chosen. Look for little-known facts and highlight them. Make your article lengthy, because publications have a tendency to cut down on the size of articles submitted to them. Let me give you an example.

One of the most interesting and controversial subjects in the leasing profession is parking fields. There is an abundance of material on the subject, so much so that you can either defend today's parking fields or offer suggestions for improvement. All information is available in books and articles previously written. Do not steal another man's work, but give your views in your own words, which may coincide with the articles you have read.

A number of old-line realty firms feel that large advertising space taken in the telephone company's *Red Book* is of much importance. The *Red Book* is good and it does a definite job. However, I do not recommend the *Red Book* for the beginner. It is quite expensive and, in addition, it creates a fixed expense which should be avoided as much as possible by the neophyte. Your name in the classified section of the telephone book, as a small listing, will suffice. Also, there will be no loss of prestige.

REMEMBER CHRISTMAS, GIVE GADGETS

Christmas is a very important time of the year, in that it provides the commercial leasing man with an opportunity to give or send out gadgets that place his name before the public. One of the oldest and best gadgets is the calendar. An attractive calendar will always be kept and serves the purpose of continually placing your name in front of the public. Actually, there are thousands of gadgets, but somehow no one has ever been able to replace the calendar as the number one item.

LOCATION IS OF PRIME IMPORTANCE

The location of your office is important for creating sales. If you are difficult to reach, people will avoid you. You must locate yourself in the middle of the commercial hub of your town. This serves three purposes: first, you are centrally located; second, you will be, if centrally located, near all transportation; third, you must be in the downtown store area so that you can get to know the local storekeepers and also be in a position to be able to show a store to a client easily. I do not recommend a store, but suggest office space. A commercial leasing expert rarely gets any off-street traffic. The vast bulk of new customers will seek you out directly because of classified advertisements you have inserted in the local papers. The dignity that an office lends is of far greater value than the one or two stray clients that may come into a store.

SIGNS ARE CHEAP AND A MUST

Another helpful aid toward leasing stores is signs. When you see a vacancy in a building, contact one of the existing tenants and inquire as to the identity of the landlord. Call him and inquire regarding the possibility of placing a "for rent" sign in the window. Signs are cheap, and you can have them made for you by a neighborhood sign painter. When your office is well established, you can have the signs silk-screened. Silk-screening is cheaper, but only when purchased in volume. In order for the signs to be of permanent value, they must be uniform. The uniformity should be both by word and color. After a time, you will be associated with your sign. The sign is your emblem.

COMMERCIAL SUPPLIES—PROSPECT SOURCES

Ice-cream salesmen are constantly in touch with luncheonette and restaurant owners and, generally, know when these men sell their stores and when they are looking for new or additional locations. (See Exhibit 4-3.)

The agent should forward the size, rent, occupancy date, adjacent tenants, etc. information to the sales department of the local ice-cream companies.

46 / How to Attract Clients

EXHIBIT 4-3. Ice-Cream Companies—Good Prospect Sources.*

Ice-cream companies are the best sources for leasing luncheonettes and restaurants from a typical urban area—New York City and its suburbs.

Abbott's
369 Raymond Blvd.
Newark, New Jersey

Armel
532 Craven St.
Bronx, New York

Breyer's
34–09 Queens Blvd.
L.I.C., New York

Carvel
430 Nepperhan Ave.
Yonkers, N.Y.

Ciro's
524 Southern Blvd.
Bronx, New York

Foremost
596 Market St.
Newark, New Jersey

Hershey's Ice Cream
2114 Jericho T'pke.
Garden City, N.Y.

Karl Droge Ice Cream
6508 6th Ave.
B'klyn, New York

Lili's French Ice Cream
888 Jamaica Ave.
B'klyn, New York

Marchiony Ice Cream
291 Broadway
Huntington Station
Long Island, New York

Marchiony Ice Cream Corp.
67 Washington Ave.
B'klyn, New York

Maurice French Ice Cream, Inc.
1221 Utica Ave.
B'klyn, New York

Meadow Gold
777 Kent Ave.
B'klyn, New York

Philadelphia Dairy
596 Market St.
Newark, New Jersey

Pioneer
221 Glen Cove Rd.
Mineola, New York

Reid's
551 Waverly Ave.
B'klyn, New York

Ricciardi
551 Waverly Ave.
B'klyn, New York

Schrafft's
50 W. 23rd St.
New York, N.Y.

Sealtest Foods, Div. of Krafto Corp.
34–09 Queens Blvd.
L.I.C., New York

Louis Sherry
30–30 Northern Blvd.
L.I.C., New York

Smith Bros.
1759 2nd Ave.
New York, N.Y.

*This list is for the New York City area. Lists for other areas may be compiled through the use of the telephone *Red Book*. You may also do the same thing with other lines of business.

Exhibit 4-4 is a list of 29 prospect-soliciting ideas, each of which can give you an almost constant source of new clients looking for stores. These sources, combined with creative thinking, can give you an unlimited supply of clients.

EXHIBIT 4-4. Where Prospects May Be Found.

1–Adjacent tenants
2–Tenants down the street
3–Co-brokers
4–Newspaper advertising
5–Canvassing
6–Direct mail
7–Chain stores
8–Firms whose leases are expiring
9–Government agencies

EXHIBIT 4-4 (Contd.)

10–Signs	20–Civic affairs
11–Attorneys	21–Trade directories
12–Banks	22–Trade papers
13–Recommendations	23–Realty news in local papers
14–Telephone solicitation	24–Property owners
15–Salesmen	25–Insurance brokers
16–Friends, relatives	26–Municipal records
17–Realty publications	27–Fixture companies
18–Old prospects	28–Telephone *Red Book*
19–Clubs, organizations	29–Social affairs

Exhibit 4-5, following, is purely a memory refresher. It is a list of many businesses that may be found in commercial buildings. A glance at this list may be very helpful in selecting a proper line of business. I, myself, after many years as a broker, constantly find myself checking this list of various lines of business. I would like to stress that the list, while adequate, is not by any means complete. It, however, should serve as a handy reference. This list may create a deal for you by suggesting a particularly adequate line for a location.

EXHIBIT 4-5. Various Lines of Business.

Auto School	Clubs	Furrier
Auto Agency	Coin-Op	Gas Station
Auto Seat Covers	Confectionery	Gift Shop
Bakery	Corsets	Glassware
Bank	Dance Studio	Greeting Cards
Barber	Delicatessen	Grocery
Beauty Salon	Druggist	Health Foods
Billiards	Electrical Appliances	Hardware
Books	Film	Hats
Bowling	Finance Company	Hobby
Boy's Clothes	Fish	Hosiery
Bridal	Fishing Equipment	Housewares
Caterer	5 Cents to $1	Infants' Wear
Chiropractor	Florist	Interior Decorators
Christian Science	Fruit and Vegetable	Jewelers
Cleaner	Funeral Parlor	Juvenile Furniture

EXHIBIT 4-5 (Contd.)

Knitting	Pawnbroker	Shoes
Lamp Shades	Perfume and Cosmetics	Soda Fountains
Launderettes		Sporting Goods
Laundry	Pet Shop	Sportswear
Leather Goods	Photographer	Stationery, Commercial
Lingerie	Pianos	
Liquor	Poolrooms	Suit Rental
Meat	Poultry	Tailor
Men's Wear	Prepared Foods	Tavern
Millinery	Real Estate	Tires
Mirrors	Restaurant	Toys
Music	Savings and Loans	Travel Bureau
Office Furniture	Schools	Upholstery
Optician	Sewing Machines	Wallpaper
Paint	Shoe Repair	Women's Wear

Today, knowledge and goodwill have become rather important items. The commercial leasing broker can, because of his new-found importance, get by with just leasing stores. He has become a supporting pillar in the scheme of American business. His advice is eagerly sought by prospective tenants. It is important that this advice be true and accurate. The broker must realize that his advice can either help or, in extreme cases, cause financial havoc. Good advice can be instrumental in creating additional business.

THE GOVERNMENT IS A PRIME LEASING SOURCE

One of the finest sources of new leasing business is the United States Government. Write to the General Services Administration in Washington D.C. and request to be placed on its mailing list. Also, mention the area in which you will be working. The General Services Administration will advise you when it is interested in leasing space in your area. A complete list of specifications and requirements will be forwarded to you. Your client than may make a bid through you, as the leasing broker. (See Exhibit 4-6.)

EXHIBIT 4-6. General Services Administration Regional Offices.

	Regional Area Served
Region 1	
Post Office and Courthouse Bldg.	Maine, New Hampshire, Vermont,
Boston 9, Massachusetts	Massachusetts, Rhode Island, and Connecticut

EXHIBIT 4-6 (Contd.)

Region 2	*Regional Area Served*
30 Church St. New York 7, N.Y.	New York, New Jersey, Delaware, and Pennsylvania
Region 3	
7th and D Streets, S.W. Washington 25, D.C.	District of Columbia, Maryland, Virginia, and West Virginia
Region 4	
1776 Peachtree St., W.W. Atlanta 9, Georgia	Tennessee, North Carolina, Florida, South Carolina, Georgia, Mississippi, and Alabama
Region 5	
219 South Clark Street Chicago 4, Illinois	Illinois, Ohio, Wisconsin, Michigan, Indiana, and Kentucky
Region 6	
2306 East Bannister Road Kansas City 14, Missouri	North Dakota, South Dakota, Minnesota, Iowa, Nebraska, Kansas, and Missouri
Region 7	
1114 Commerce Street Dallas 2, Texas	Texas, Oklahoma, Louisiana, and Arkansas
Region 8	
Denver Federal Center, Bldg. 41 Denver, Colorado	Wyoming, Utah, Colorado, New Mexico, and Arizona
Region 9	
49 4th Street San Francisco 3, California	California and Nevada
Region 10	
Federal Office Building 909 1st Avenue Seattle 4, Washington	Washington, Oregon, Montana, and Idaho

DON'T NEGLECT THE COIN-OP BUSINESS

Another fine source for leasing is the relatively new business of coin-operated dry cleaning. This business, only several years old, has expanded with tremendous rapidity. Almost every new shopping center has a coin-op. It is not necessary for the broker to seek out clients interested in leasing space for a coin-op. Any one of the equipment companies will gladly supply customers. The equipment salesman will take his clients out and show them your locations. The salesman has no interest in your commission, but is very interested in selling his equipment. The easiest way

50 / *How to Attract Clients*

to sell it is to be able to show the prospect a nice store location in which he can place the equipment. For fast results contact the equipment companies, giving size, occupation, rent, adjacent tenants, sewer conditions, etc. information.

Exhibit 4-7 applies to the New York City area, but local lists may be made up by using your local *Red Book* to find equipment dealers in your area.

EXHIBIT 4-7. Coin-Op Dry Cleaning Companies (Metropolitan N.Y.C. Area)

All-State Laundry Equipt. Co., 1 Pondfield Rd., Bronxville, New York
American Laundry Machinery, 5050 Section Rd., Cincinnati, Ohio
American Permac, 1 Commercial Ave., Garden City, New York
Cleanex Machinery Corp., 544 4th Ave., Mt. Vernon, New York
Cummings-Landau Laundry Machinery, 305 Ten Eyck St., Brooklyn, New York
Hoffman Machinery Distributors of New York, 433 E. 148th St., Bronx, New York.
Market Equipment Corp., 392 Bedford Park Blvd., Bronx, New York
N.Y. Valetone Sales Corp., 133 E. Jericho T'pke., Mineola, New York
Speed Queen Commercial Laundry Equipment, 127–19 101st Ave., Richmond Hill, New York
Wascator & Wascomat, 461 Dougherty Blvd., Inwood, New York
Zee Sales & Service, Inc., 208 Tapscott St., Brooklyn, New York

SMALL BUSINESS ADMINISTRATION SERVICES

Quite often you will have clients who are interested in going into business but lack certain technical information. One of the finest sources of this type of information is the Small Business Administration. The S.B.A. maintains field offices in a number of trade centers. Consult the U.S. Government section of the local telephone book for locations not already listed in Exhibit 4-8.

The members of any Small Business Administration field office will be glad to assist you in connection with business problems. See Exhibit 4-8 for S.B.A. locations.

EXHIBIT 4-8. Small Business Administration Field and Regional* Offices.

Birmingham, Alabama	Anchorage, Alaska
3rd Floor	307 E. Penthouse
New First Fed. Savings and Loan Bldg.	Federal Building
2030 1st Ave., N.	P.O. Box 1253

* Regional offices underscored.

EXHIBIT 4-8 (Contd.)

Phoenix, Arizona
Central Towers Bldg.
2727 N. Central Ave.

Little Rock, Arkansas
3209 Federal Office Bldg.
700 W. Capital Ave.

Los Angeles, California
312 W. 5th St.

San Francisco, California
525 Market St.

Denver Colorado
Railway Exchange

Hartford, Connecticut
44 Gillett St.

Washington, D.C.
First Fed. Savings and Loan Bldg.

Jacksonville, Florida
47 West Forsyth St.

Miami, Florida
301 Huntington Bldg.
168 S.E. 1st St.

Atlanta, Georgia
90 Fairlie St., N.W.

Honolulu, Hawaii
Finance Factors Bldg.
195 S. King St.

Boise, Idaho
214 Sonna Bldg.
910 Main St.
P.O. Box 933

Chicago, Illinois
Rm. 430, Banker's Bldg.
305 West Adams St.

Indianapolis, Indiana
Rm. 721
Farm Bureau Insurance Bldg.
130 E. Washington St.

Des Moines, Iowa
Suite 850
Insurance Exchange Bldg.
5th and Grand Ave.

Wichita, Kansas
215 Board of Trade Bldg.
120 S. Market St.

Louisville, Kentucky
1900 Commonwealth Bldg.
Fourth and Broadway

New Orleans, Louisiana
Rm. 303, Fed. Office Bldg.
610 South St.

Augusta, Maine
116 State St.

Baltimore, Maryland
611 Calvert Building
Fayette and St. Paul Sts.

Boston, Massachusetts
Sheraton Building
470 Atlantic Ave.

Detroit, Michigan
232 W. Grand River Ave.

Minneapolis, Minnesota
Lewis Building
603 2nd Ave., S.

Jackson, Mississippi
U.S.P.O. and Courthouse Bldg.
Capital and West Sts.
Rm. 322

Kansas City, Missouri
Home Savings Bldg.
1006 Grand Ave.

St. Louis, Missouri
Rm. 2469
Federal Bldg.
1520 Market St.

Helena, Montana
Mailing Address:
P.O. Box 1690
Rm. 205, Power Block

Omaha, Nebraska
Rm. 7425 Fed. Bldg.
215 N. 17th St.

Concord, New Hampshire
DuBois Building
72 North Main St.

EXHIBIT 4-8 (Contd.)

Albuquerque, New Mexico
U.S. Courthouse, Rm. 102
5th and Gold Sts.

New York, N.Y.
42 Broadway

Syracuse, New York
Chimes Building
500 S. Salina St.

Charlotte, North Carolina
1116 Independence Bldg.
102 W. Trade St.

Fargo, North Dakota
American Life Bldg., Rm. 300
207 North 5th St.

Cleveland, Ohio
Standard Bldg.
1370 Ontario St.

Oklahoma City, Oklahoma
U.S.P.O. Bldg.
3rd and Robinson Sts.
Rm. 807

Tulsa, Oklahoma
Rm. 519, Mayo Bldg.
420 S. Main St.

Portland, Oregon
309 Pittock Block
921 S.W. Washington St.

Philadelphia, Pennsylvania
Jefferson Building
1015 Chestnut St.

Pittsburgh, Pennsylvania
Fulton Bldg.
107 6th St.

Santurce, Puerto Rico
San Alberto Condominic Bldg.
1200 Ponce de Leon Blvd.

Providence, Rhode Island
Rm. 611, Smith Building
57 Eddy St.

Columbia, South Carolina
1801 Assembly St.

Sioux Falls, South Dakota
Leaders Bldg.
109½ North Main Ave.

Knoxville, Tennessee
301 W. Cumberland Bldg.
301 W. Cumberland Ave.,
Rm. 233

Nashville, Tennessee
Sudekum Bldg., Suite 410
6th Ave. and Church St.

Dallas, Texas
Fidelity Bldg.
1000 Main St.

Houston, Texas
2202 Federal Office Bldg.
515 Rusk Ave.

Lubbock, Texas
Rm. 212
Veterans Admin. Bldg.
1616 19th St.

Marshall, Texas
Marshall National Bank
101 E. Austin St.

San Antonio, Texas
412 Kallison Bldg.
434 S. Main Ave.

Salt Lake City, Utah
520 Kearnes Bldg.
136 S. Main St.

Montpelier, Vermont
79 Main St.

Richmond, Virginia
P.O. Box 8565
1904 Byrd Ave.

Seattle, Washington
Smith Tower, Rm. 1206

Charleston, West Virginia
U.S. Courthouse and Fed. Bldg.
500 Quarrier St.

Clarksburg, West Virginia
Old P.O. Bldg.
227 West Pike St.

Madison, Wisconsin
Commercial State Bank Bldg.
114 North Carroll St.

TECHNIQUES FOR NEGOTIATING LEASES

5

One of the important aspects of the store leasing business is the negotiation of leases. I do not expect you to become an attorney, but you must be in a position to negotiate on behalf of a tenant. The major terms and most conditions of a lease should be negotiated prior to its being drawn up.

TYPES OF LEASES

Before going into the actual lease negotiations, I will discuss one of the many types of leases in use today, the shopping center lease. A shopping center is a shopping area complex of multiple stores, parking facilities, etc., with one or more major tenants to pull the buying power. The small centers rely heavily on supermarkets. The major centers stress department stores and acres of parking.

Ordinary Taxpayer Leases vs. Shopping Center (Percentage) Leases

The individual merchants have what is referred to as an "ordinary taxpayer lease," while many chain stores have percentage leases. The percentage lease provides for a guaranteed minimum rental against a previously agreed upon percentage of the business, and the tenant pays the greater amount. For example: a tenant leases a store at an agreed rental of $3,600 per annum against 6%. If the tenant does $50,000 worth of business per annum, the rental is still $3,600, because the 6% would amount to only $3,000, the tenant paying either the percentage rental or the minimum, whichever is greater.

Unlike the smaller taxpayers, the shopping centers have leases drawn up well in advance. The builder or developer is often told by the mortgagee what type of tenancy to lease, and what type of lease to draw. The mortgagee is concerned with having enough well-rated chains in the center so that if any vacancies should occur, the rentals from the prime tenants will be sufficient to assure payment of the financing.

Because of the size of many shopping centers and the number of tenants contained therein, the landlord may have a form lease. This is a lease that is similar for all his tenants, not in every, but most clauses. This type of lease provides for easier management by the landlord.

A major shopping center lease is, of course, drawn up prior to the construction of the shopping center. It will differ somewhat from those drawn up for existing structures. Each lease will contain a set of specifications outlining the work to be performed by the landlord; all other work, naturally, will be done by the tenant. For the small, unrated tenant, the landlord will ordinarily supply a ceiling, three walls, a moderate store front, a lavatory, and a heating unit. In some cases, basements are supplied. In others, the depth of the store is increased and basements eliminated. The tenant is generally given 20 to 25 electrical outlets, and either a wood or concrete floor. The tenant allows the landlord a reasonable time to complete his share of the construction. The outside date selected for this purpose is usually 12 to 18 months. An outside date is of prime importance, because upon signing of the lease, the tenant posts monies, and the agent must see to it that his client's monies are not tied up indefinitely. There have been many instances in which a builder has been unable to secure financing for the project and the tenant's monies have been tied up indefinitely.

The exact location of the tenant's store should be clearly marked on a building plan and made a part of the lease. The tenant is entitled to know exactly where his store will be and who his neighbors will be. The wrong type of neighbors can hurt what might otherwise be a successful operation. For example, a service store may be located adjacent to a supermarket, but never next to a wearing apparel store.

The number of car spaces allotted for customer parking is of great importance to the tenants. This prevents the landlord from overbuilding and creating parking problems. This particular phase is constantly stressed by the chain stores.

The ordinary taxpayer lease differs from the shopping center lease in many respects. In the shopping center lease, the important clauses are condemnation, fire, use, and parking. Ordinarily, a landlord would be required to rebuild or cancel a tenant's lease where substantial fire damage has occurred. The tenant, however, has leased a store for one or all of the following:

1. Number of chains in the center.
2. Amount of parking.
3. Number of stores in the center.

It can now be seen that condemnation or fire would eliminate one or all of the three reasons listed above. This situation could greatly reduce the value of a tenant's store. The managing agent must protect his client by securing for him the right to cancel his lease in the event that a substantial change is effected in the center.

Almost without exception, shopping center leases contain a clause whereby the tenant agrees to pay a proportionate share of any increase in taxes after the first full assessment. Actually, this is a fair request and is acceptable. Before accepting the clause, however, the tenant should make sure he does not have a graduated lease. This type lease provides for rent increases over periodic intervals. In many instances, the competent broker will be able to work out a situation wherein the tenant can deduct a tax increase from a percentage overage, if one exists.

At this point, I must note that the managing agent is employed sometimes by the tenant and, at other times, by the builder or property owner. Whoever hires the agent, is entitled to his best efforts. It should be remembered that no agent can serve two masters at the same time, and serve both well.

An important part of all leases is the right of assignment. When a tenant signs a lease, he generally expects to do business until his lease expires. Various conditions, however, may cause a change in his plans. Sometimes it is sickness, or other times the merchant may be lucky enough to receive a handsome offer to sell his business. In any event, the merchant may not be able to sell or transfer his lease, unless his lease says that it may be sold or assigned without the landlord's consent. I cannot stress the importance of this clause too heavily. Lack of the proper clause can give an unscrupulous landlord an opportunity to demand either an exorbitant increase in rent or a large sum of money in order to approve the transfer of the lease. The broker must be careful regarding this clause, even when doing business with a reputable landlord. Regardless of who the landlord may be, one never knows when the building may be sold or when the owner may die, his heirs taking ownership.

The average store lease will contain provisions for additional rent. I speak specifically of an increase in taxes, water charges, sewer charges, assessments, and liability insurance. These are common provisions, and should not be objected to by the agent. Occasionally, in a shopping center, there may be charges for basement space, maintenance of parking areas and removal of rubbish in the larger centers. These additional charges should not be questioned, but the broker should feel that it is his obligation to advise the tenant, making sure that he has figured these additional rental charges into his overhead. Though the charges are equitable, they may be a burden to a merchant, nevertheless, and should be weighed carefully.

Electricity is virtually always paid for by the tenant. The landlord will generally supply from 20 to 25 outlets. Any additional electrical work is to be done by the tenant at the tenant's own expense.

Repairs are generally divided into three classes:

(1) Interior.
(2) Exterior.
(3) Structural.

Interior repairs: the inside of the store, including bathroom, plumbing, painting, minor electrical work, floors, and ceiling, but excluding structural or major repairs. The tenant is usually responsible for the storefront plate glass and interior repairs.

Exterior repairs: in most cases they coincide with structural **repairs**, including roof, outside walls, parking lot, and major repairs.

Basements: some taxpayers and certain shopping centers contain basements, while others do not. Ordinarily, the store without a basement is 15 to 25 feet greater in depth. The stores with basements usually have them in the same dimensions as the store. There are a few exceptions where builders have built half-basements; that is, basements running only one-half the total length of the store. When I use the word basement, I specifically refer to storage space, unfinished, 7'6" to 8'6" in height. These areas are suitable for storage only. Less than 1% of all basements are selling basements. A selling basement is one that is suitable for the retail sale of merchandise. It is finished, ordinarily, and has at least a height of 9'0", complies with fire department regulations, and is properly ventilated. The merchant must know what type of basement he is receiving and if the basement will meet his own particular requirements. The lease should contain the actual address of the store and contain the words "store and basement." Do not take it for granted that the basement is included with the store, because often it is not. In fact, some of the larger shopping centers charge additional rent for basement space.

The use clause is very important. Actually, it is one of the really important parts of a lease. This is the clause that designates what the tenant may sell and to what use space may be put. For a great number of years, stores were more or less restricted as to what items they carried. In recent years, however, most businesses have taken to carrying additional lines to such a point that use clauses actually overlap. The important protection this clause renders is coverage of what the tenant may sell.

In conjunction with the use clause, there is the restrictive clause. This may give the tenant the exclusive right to sell certain items. It prevents tenants' use clauses from overlapping with one another. Basically, the tenants are usually given the exclusive rights to sell only the items which form a major part of their respective business. It is important that the burden of policing be placed upon the landlord.

Heat and water clauses are contained in all shopping center and taxpayer leases. The usual procedure regarding heat is that the landlord supplies the facilities, and the tenant keeps the heating apparatus in good working order and provides the fuel. Cold water lines are supplied by the landlord, but hot water lines and boiler are generally installed by the tenant, if needed.

Options are becoming scarce. Many landlords frown upon the granting of options, because an option is a one-way contract—it completely favors the tenant. Therefore, if an option is requested, the landlord will invariably insist upon a substantial increase in rent, in the event that the option is exercised. It is my opinion that the landlord is entitled to a substantial increase for an option period. The tenant is taking no chances, because instead of signing a long-term lease, he hedges by signing a short-term one and maintains the right to stay or not to stay for the option period, as he sees fit.

Advertising signs are of importance in today's business world. The tenant should have the areas in which he wishes signs placed designated in the lease. It is also suggested that sketches be submitted and made part of the lease. In order to avoid any problems at a later date, the tenant must see to it that the lease explains fully not only where the signs are to be placed but also what type of signs are to be mounted there.

Alterations are in the same category as signs. Sketches should be made and approved by the landlord. Do not let your client make any structural alterations without consulting the landlord; almost without exception, this is a violation of a commercial lease. It must be remembered further that any alterations of a permanent nature, or which are attached to the real estate, become a part of the real estate and belong to the landlord.

Security is generally posted by the individual tenants. The chains, by virtue of their strong financial position, are not required to post security. The average taxpayer-owner will request one to three months' security. The major shopping centers will demand three to six months' security. I have never objected to a tenant posting security, but I do feel he should be permitted to incorporate and thus limit his liability under the lease. Quite often, the question of the interest on security has come up and the broker has done well to suggest that it be waived. There are more important clauses in the lease. The tenant also gives the landlord the right to assign or transfer the security, in the event of a sale of the property. Some landlords will accept stocks or bonds as security, thus giving the tenant an opportunity to collect interest or dividends on his money.

An important word of advice that can be given regarding leases is that all agreements should be in writing. Do not allow your clients to accept any oral agreements.

A touchy point in some leases, especially net leases, is the fire clause. Trouble usually arises regarding the last few years of a lease. A landlord may not wish to have the same type of building erected as that destroyed or partially destroyed in a fire. The tenant who is responsible for the fire insurance and replacement, if the building is demolished, may not want to replace an old building with a new one. It is true that the tenant carries fire insurance, but the insurance money paid on an old building may not cover a new type of building's cost. On the fire clause, both sides may disagree. The managing agent must do his best to arbitrate, because there is really no single solution.

A clause to be noted is the one concerning the possibility of an increase in insurance rates brought about as a result of the tenant's use or occupancy. Dry cleaning stores and paint stores are the most common offenders. However, the clause is not unreasonable.

In order to negotiate a supermarket lease, the agent must be in a position to discuss the specifications, since these form a most significant part of the lease. In the great majority of cases, buildings for supermarkets are erected after a lease is signed and suitable financing arrangements have been made. The following pages will list a set of specifications generally used today by many major supermarkets.

SAMPLE SUPERMARKET LEASE SPECIFICATIONS

The purpose of these specifications is to outline the lessee's (tenant's) requirements in a general way. Based upon this general outline, the lessor's (landlord's) architect will prepare plans and specifications complying with all codes and ordinances having jurisdiction in the area involved.

The completed plans and specifications prepared by the lessor's architect will be submitted to the lessee for approval, prior to commencement of construction.

A new building of size and type required by the lease agreement will be constructed, in accordance with a fixture layout, which will be submitted by the lessee to the lessor prior to completion of preliminary architectural drawings. All materials used in building construction will be new and of the best respective quality available for this type of structure. The lessor will submit a first survey of the property included in this agreement, with elevations and property delineated by a licensed surveyor.

The lessor will turn over the leased premises in a broom-clean tenantable condition, including a cleaned and polished storefront. The building certificate of occupancy will be obtained, together with certificates for electricity and plumbing work, and copies of same will be submitted to the lessee prior to acceptance of the building. A temporary certificate of occupancy will also be acceptable, if the building is open for business prior to the securing of the final certificate of occupancy. The lessor will furnish the lessee with a complete set of "as-built" drawings reflecting all changes made in the structure after the issuance of the approved plans and specifications.

The lessor will legally notify the lessee when the building is completed and ready to turn over to the lessee. Upon receipt of this notification, the lessee will inspect the premises with the lessor and notify the lessor immediately as to his acceptance or nonacceptance of the premises.

Doors for delivery purposes, over and above legally required exit doors, will be required by the lessee. One delivery door will be provided with a special back, allowing for installation of a meat rail by the tenant.

A 350-square-foot garbage room of brick or concrete block construction, outside the building proper, will be provided. This garbage room is to have a hot water line with hose bibb and floor drainage. Two gravity roof ventilators will also be provided by the lessor with necessary ductwork.

Adequate floor drains for the entire cellar area and for condensate lines from refrigerator boxes are to be provided.

Stairs between main floor and mezzanine will be equipped with non-slip surfaces. Location of stairwells will be as required by authorities having jurisdiction and as approved by lessee.

Toilet facilities will be as required by law and will include the following items:

(a) Clothes hooks by tenant.
(b) Soap dispensers.
(c) Metal toilet partitions with paper holders.
(d) One mirror to each rest room.
(e) Legal-size cot for female rest room—by tenant.
(f) Floors and 4-foot wainscot will be ceramic tile—color selected by tenant.

All interior exposed concrete floors will be dustproofed.

Windows, other than storefront, will be steel security type sash.

If city water is utilized for cooling purposes, a cooling tower from manufacturer approved by lessee will be used. The use of a supply and diffusion well system for cooling purposes will be subject to prior approval of lessee.

Where the lease agreement does not provide for a cellar, the lessor will provide a utility trench system for drainage of fixtures, in accordance with the lessee's requirements. This utility trench will be provided with steel cover and frame constructed with the adjacent concrete floor.

Ground floor will be 4 inches minimum thickness, steel troweled to a smooth finish. Integral waterproofing such as "antihydro" will be provided in the concrete mixture for the cellar floor, if a water condition exists. Ground floor slabs are to be reinforced with approved reinforcing. A 6-inch bed of clean gravel is to be provided under the entire floor slab.

The entire sales floor will be finished with $\frac{1}{8}$-inch vinyl asbestos tile; colors are to be selected by the lessee's designer.

Flooring for work areas will be long-leaf, yellow pine over sleepers (bakery, meat, fish, and appetizer areas).

Foundation walls are to be poured concrete. The interior face of exterior walls require plaster or dry wall finish, to be coated with an approved type of mastic damp-proofing. Interior wall finishes to be $\frac{1}{2}$-inch Sheetrock, fanned out from masonry walls throughout entire ground floor with tape and three-coat spackling.

Column spacing to be approximately 40'×40' bays.

Minimum ceiling height requirements:

(a) Ceiling height under mezzanine, if any, to be 9'6" clear.
(b) Sales area to be 15 feet clear.

Storefront, exit, and entrance doors will be of "Kawneer" standard extruded sections or approved equal.

"Stanley," or like quality, door hinges will be provided for all in-swinging doors; out doors to be "Stanley" automatic "Magic Carpet" or equal.

Roof insulation will be 4S "Infra" accordion aluminum. Roofing is to be 20-year bonded type with copper through wall flashing.

Electric Facilities

The lessor will provide all electric facilities necessary for a complete operating supermarket, which, in general, include the following:

(a) 1,200-ampere, 208-volt, three-phase, four-wire electric service with all equipment necessary and required by the power company to provide for the entire light and power load required by the lessee. Ampere may be higher depending upon equipment.
(b) Main distribution panel and light and power panels will be located by the lessee.
(c) Salesroom lighting will be continuing, two-lamp, 96-inch, slim-line fixtures on light foot centers with G.E. ballasts. Lighting layout will be as designed by the lessee's designer. Recessed incandescent ceiling fixtures (not to exceed 35) will be furnished and installed by the lessor. Bulbs for all light fixtures will be supplied and installed by the lessor. The lessor is to hang all fixtures.

(d) Interior rear areas will be lighted with industrial 48-inch, three-lamp fixtures on 15-foot centers, with G.E. ballasts furnished and installed by the lessor. The lessee will furnish lessor with layout. Six circuits will be provided for the lessee's signs with time clocks approved by the lessee.
(e) The lessor will provide adequate panels for all of the lessee's fixtures. Branch circuit panels will be square D, Bulldog, or equal circuit-breaker type panels.
(f) Light panels will be provided with 20 circuits, in addition to the total required for the lessee's lighting requirements.
(g) The power distribution panel will be three phase, four wires, and 208 volts, circuits to be protected by circuit breakers (square D or approved equal).
(h) The maximum voltage drop in any lighting circuit will not exceed 2 volts and no wire size will be less than #12 RH. All feeder run over 40 feet will be at least #10 RH.
(i) The lessor will provide all wiring necessary for tenant's fixtures as located on tenant's fixture layout, to be submitted to the lessor's architect.
(j) Adequate parking lighting will be provided by the lessor prior to opening the store. Light standard to be Pfaff or Kendall tapered aluminum, 30 feet high, with color-corrected mercury vapor luminaires, quantity to be at least:

  (1) 2 twin arm standards, plus;
  (2) 3 single arm standards, plus;
  (3) 3 davit arm standards.

Plumbing

The lessor will provide all plumbing, plumbing fixtures, and materials necessary for a complete operating supermarket which will, in general, include but not be limited, to the following:

(a) A complete drainage system for building and parking area with interior leaders.
(b) All legally required plumbing facilities with flushometers by the lessor.
(c) Two slop sinks condensate drainage; locations as directed by the lessee.
(d) One 2×4 galvanized, produce, double-compartment sink and three 2×4, 14-gauge stainless steel, meat, double-compartment sinks.
(e) One gallon, Duo-Temp Rudd hot water system, or equal.
(f) Complete drainage roughing system for all of the lessee's facilities requiring drains. Final drain connections to be provided by the lessor.
(g) Gas lines and flue through roof for lessee's oven.
(h) All water piping for compressors and water tower connections. Water tower to be provided, rigged, and installed by the tenant, on steel provided by the lessor.
(i) Three grease traps.
(j) All cold water lines to be wrapped.

Heat, Ventilating, and Air-Conditioning

The lessor will provide all heating, ventilating, and air-conditioning necessary for a complete operating supermarket which will, in general, include the following:

(a) Complete combination heating and air-conditioning system providing capacity to maintain the entire leased premises at 70° in zero weather and cooling capacity to maintain the leased premises at 20° differential when the outside temperature is 100°.
(b) Heating, ventilating, and air-conditioning ducts to be concealed in suspended ceiling. Roof to be insulated above ducts.
(c) Location of anemostats to be subject to the lessee's approval.
(d) Entire combination heating and air-conditioning system, and ventilating to be thermostatically controlled. Location of thermostats will be approved by the lessee.
(e) All legally required ventilation including ductwork, fans, controls, etc.
(f) Guarantee for a period of one (1) year to be furnished by the lessor's contractor.
(g) Separate 5-ton, Typhoon, low-temperature air-conditioning unit for meat room.

General Provisions

(1) The lessor will furnish and install 5,000 square feet of marlite where directed by lessee.
(2) The lessor will furnish and install approximately 250 lineal feet of interior partition with ½-inch Sheetrock, each side taped, spackled, and painted as specified above. Adjustments of actual quantity installed will be made at $18 per lineal foot (for amount over 250 lineal feet).
(3) The lessor will furnish and install three (3) 1¾ stainless-steel-covered doors with vision panel each and 1½ pair of Bonomer 8-inch spring hinges each.
(4) 10'6" suspended ceiling to be provided by lessor for meat room.
(5) South elevation to be 12-inch Waylite block stack, bonded and painted with Colorcoat or approved equal.
(6) Sales area ceiling to be aluminum T bar grid system with $2' \times 4'$ acoustical panels and integral lighting system, such as tenant's (actual location) store.
(7) Front facade to be in accordance with architect's layout with 18-inch brick bulkheads, ¼-inch plate glass to extend from bulkhead to ceiling elevation; no single light of glass to be over 100 square feet. Spandrel walls to be same brick as bulkhead. Brick not to exceed $200 per M in value.
(8) Storefront to have mullions and top, bottom, and division bars, all of $1\frac{3}{4}'' \times 4''$ extended aluminum Kawneer selections.
(9) Rear walls to be 12-inch concrete block painted with Colorcoat or equal.

(10) Two vestibules, same construction as storefront to be provided with a total of eight doors; four(4) "in" and four(4) "out."
(11) Two loading doors will be 6'×7', roll-up type. Additional service doors to be 1¾-inch B label with BB butts.
(12) Canopy will be 6 inches wide across entire front and at return, north side of tenant's store; fascia and gravel stop to be aluminum, gravel stop extended and fascia .032 gauge.
(13) Paving to walk at entries.

Parking Area

The lessor will provide a parking area in accordance with the lease agreement. The parking area will be laid out approximately as per attached plot diagram.

Customer parking areas will be asphaltic concrete consisting of 4-inch stone bars, compacted with a 10-ton roller and penetrated with oil, with 2-inch compressed asphalt top. Include eight (8), 8-inch pipe standards filled with concrete 6 feet above grade and 4 feet below grade, with 2'× 2'×4' footing.

Painting

The lessor will provide all interior painting of the leased premises. Colors will be designated by the lessee's decorator.

The entire sales area of the leased premises will receive one priming coat and two additional coats of lead and oil paint. Rear and storage will receive two coats of lead and oil paint.

* * * * * *

I do not expect a broker to memorize the supermarket specifications, but rather to be familiar with them. In this way, he will know when a landlord or tenant is unreasonable and act accordingly.

While I have explained what the managing agent must look for in a lease, and what pitfalls he must try to avoid on his client's behalf, I do not want to give the impression that he should be at odds with the legal profession. Nor do I wish to have him attempt to give legal advice. My suggestion is that prior to the meeting between landlord and tenant, the managing agent should iron out these points with his client's attorney. There always has, and probably always will be, to some degree, strained relations between realty agents and lawyers. In recent years, strides have been made to coordinate agent and attorney, but there is much room for further improvement and understanding. I, however, do feel that an attorney should restrict himself to strictly legal matters and leave the business leasing advice to men who are qualified to give this advice: commercial leasing agents.

Exhibit 5-1 which follows has already been covered, to a degree, in this chapter. I refer to percentage leases. What is a percentage lease? It is a lease that affords protection for the landlord and tenant. The tenant is protected in that he is paying a relatively low minimum guaranteed rental. If business is bad, the tenant will not be in trouble because of a high rental, which may have been caused by his overestimating the gross potential of the store. The landlord, on the other hand, is also protected. The minimum rental will be low, but high enough to meet all expenses of the landlord. Naturally, if the store does a good gross business, then the landlord will make additional monies. This type of lease is, to my mind, the fairest form of rental arrangement possible between landlord and tenant. The amount of money to be made by both landlord and tenant is governed by the actual amount of gross business the store is capable of doing.

During your study of Exhibit 5-1, it will be noted that I do not give a definite percentage for a definite line of business. There is a spread to the percentages. At the bottom of the exhibit, you will note that the percentages vary in different parts of the country. The chart also points out that the type of operation will vary the percentages. The range in different areas is considerable. For these reasons, the percentage rate table in this book is to be used as a guide only. A rate that may apply to a downtown main street location may be way off for a regional shopping center.

It should be mentioned at this time that there are several different types of percentage leases: (1) *Straight percentage*—this is an unusual type of percentage lease, where the rental increases when gross business increases with no minimum. (2) *Variable scale*—in this type, the percentage is not consistent and changes with the amount of business done. (3) *Minimum*—a base rental is required to cover all the owner's expenses. If business increases, the rent increases. If the business falls down, the rent will drop, but never below the minimum. (4) *Maximum*—this type may contain any of the features of the other leases, but it has a ceiling regarding maximum rent.

Be careful—many tenants will lean heavily upon their agent's advice, and this counsel should be carefully weighed. Each percentage lease is practically custom built to location, merchant, and retail situation.

Developing a shopping center is not too difficult if the proper rules are followed. You must decide if the parcel can accommodate a neighborhood, community, or regional center.

EXHIBIT 5-1. Percentage Rental Rates.

	Independent	Local Chain	Regional Chain	National Chain
Auto Accessories	4–5%	4% (*franchise*)	4%	3%

Techniques for Negotiating Leases / 65

EXHIBIT 5-1 (Contd.)

	Independent	Local Chain	Regional Chain	National Chain
Bakeries	8–10%	6–8%	6%	6%
Banks	(Local only 1/10 and 2/10 of 1%)			
Barber	10–12%	8–10%		
Beauty Salon	12%	6–10%		
Bowling	10–15%	12%	10%	8%
Cafeterias	7–10%	6%	4–5%	5%
Camera	8–15%	6–10%		
Candy	9–12%	7–8%		6%
Car Wash	8–15%			
Cigar Stores	7–12%			6%
Confectionery	7–9%			
Cosmetics	6–9%	7–7½%		
Dairy	7–10%	6%	5%	
Delicatessen	5–6%	4%		
Department Stores	6%	5%	3–6%	2–5%
Discount	1½–3%	1½–2%	1–1¼%	1–1¾%
Drive-in Restaurant	7–10%	6–8% (franchise)	5%	5%
Drug	3–6%	1½–6%	2½–5%	2½–5½%
Dry Cleaning	10%	8–10%		
Family Apparel	5–7%	5–6%	4–5%	
Family Shoes	8–10%	8–9%	4–8%	4–8%
Floor Covering	6–8%	6%	5%	
Florist Shops	6–12%	4–10%		
Furniture	6–7%	5%		2½–5%
Furriers	8–9%			
Gifts	14–20%	10%		
Hardware	8–10%	6–8%	4–5% (franchise)	
Hobby, Toys	10–12%	8–10%		
Household	3½–5%	2½–5%		
Ice Cream	8–10%	5–8%	5%	
Ice Vending	10–12%	12%		
Jewelry	4–10%	4–6%	3–5%	3–4%
Laundromat	12–15%	10%		

EXHIBIT 5-1 (Contd.)

	Independent	Local Chain	Regional Chain	National Chain
Liquor (Package)	4–5%	3%		
Luggage	7–8%	6%		
Maternity	6½–7%	6%		
Men's Apparel	5–7%	6%	5%	4%
Men's and Boy's Shoes	8–9%	7%	7%	6%
Millinery, Hosiery	10–15%	9–12%	9–10%	
Optometrist	10–12%	8–10%		
Paint and Wallpaper	6–8%	5–6%	4–5%	3–5%
Parking Garage	40–50%	25–50%	25–50%	25–50%
Photography	10–12%			
Radio and T.V.	6–8%			
Records	8%	6%		
Reducing Salons	10–12%	8%		
Restaurant	10%	8–10%	8–10%	4½–10%
Sewing Machines	6–7%		4%	4–5%
Service Stations	3%	1–3%	1–3%	1–2½%
Shoe Repair	10–15%	15%		
Sporting Goods	8–10%			10%
Stationery, Books	8–10%			6%
Supermarkets	1½–2%	1–2%	1–2%	1–2%
Taverns	5–7%			10%
Variety	4–5%	4–5% (*franchise*)	4–5%	3–4%
Women's Apparel	7–10%	4–6%	4–5½%	3–6%
Women's Shoes	5–8%	5%		4½–8%

NOTE: The variance in percentage is caused by areas, such as: (1) New England, (2) Southeast, (3) Midwest, (4) West Coast. In each different sector, there may be a different rental rate.

Another factor is the type of shopping area, such as: (1) Neighborhood, (2) Regional, (3) Downtown, (4) Outlying, (5) Community. Yet another factor is the various types of tenancy under each category, such as: (1) Local chain, (2) Independent, (3) National chain, (4) Regional chain.

The following exhibit, 5-2, should be helpful in guiding you as to size and lease requirements. If the stores do not blend with proper sizes you will have a bad balance. A bad balance can concentrate too much business in one area and too little business in another area.

EXHIBIT 5-2. Leasing Schedule (Community or Regional).

Minimum to Average Size and Length of Lease

TYPE	SIZE	LENGTH OF LEASE
Auto Accessories	2,400'	10 years
Bakery	2,400'	15 years
Bank	3,000'	15 years
Barber	1,000'	5 years
Beauty Salon	1,500'	10 years
Books	1,000'	10 years
Children's Wear	1,000'	10 years
Cleaner, Chain	800'	5 years
Cleaner, O.P.	3,000'	10–15 years
Department Store	100,000'	20 years plus options
Delicatessen	800'	10 years
Drug, Chain	4,200'	15 years
Drug, Individual	2,500'	15 years
Finance	1,500'	10 years
Food, Take Out	700'	5 years
Furniture	4,000'	15 years
Gas Station (Land Area)	20,000'	10–15 years
(Building Area)	5,000'	
Haberdashery	1,500'	10 years
Jewelry	1,000'	5 years
Junior Department Store	30,000'	20 years plus options
Lingerie, Hosiery	600'	5 years
Luncheonette	2,000'	15 years
Paint, Wallpaper	4,000'	15 years
Restaurant	3,000'	15 years
Stationery, Dry	900'	15 years
Supermarket	20,000'	15 years
Variety	20,000'	15 years plus options
Women's Wear, Popular	3,000'	10 years plus options

EXHIBIT 5-2 (Contd.)

Women's Wear, Specialty	1,500'	10 years
Yard Goods	2,000'	10 years

Site Requirements

Auto accessibility, two main arteries, stoplights, zones, surveying, topography, competition, price, change of highways, etc. are some of the factors which must be considered here.

Exhibit 5-3 should be helpful in guiding you as to size and lease requirements.

Different types of stores are found in different types of locations. In order to simplify matters, Exhibit 5-4 has been provided.

EXHIBIT 5-3. Developing Shopping Centers.

Factors	Neighborhood	Community	Regional
Land	5 acres	15 acres	40 acres
Bldg. Area	20–40,000'	150,000'	400,000'
Parking Area	3 acres min.	11 acres	30 acres
No. of Cars	360 min.	1,400 min.	3,500
Driving Time	5–10 minutes	15 minutes	25 minutes
No. of Stores	4 to 10	approx. 20	40 or more
Tenancy	AAA–1 Mkt. and Svce. Stores	Junior dept. store plus all neighborhood and chain varieties.	Major dept store plus community and neighborhood.

One type may develop into another; the above figures are minimum.

EXHIBIT 5-4. Store Locations.

Choice Locations Usually Contain:

(A) Discount Stores
(B) Hat Stores
(C) Clothing Stores
(D) Gift Stores
(E) Variety Stores
(F) Department Stores

Are Generally Found in or Near:

(A) Good transportation
(B) Office buildings
(C) Low-income neighborhoods
(D) Regional shopping centers
(E) Main thoroughfares
(F) Main highways

EXHIBIT 5-4 (Contd.)

Service Locations Usually Contain:

(A) Delicatessen
(B) Supermarket
(C) Drugstore
(D) Coin-Op Cleaner

(E) Luncheonette
(F) Chain Cleaner
(G) Food Store
(H) Beauty Salon

Are Generally Found in or Near:

(A) One-family developments
(B) Smaller shopping developments
(C) Apartment house developments

The perfect location is sometimes called a 100% location. From that point, we work down to 90% locations, 80% locations, etc., until we find a location that is worthless for a retail merchant. This type of location also has its usefulness, in that it may be suitable for manufacturing or industrial use.

MORE NEGOTIATING TECHNIQUES

6

When you lease store space, it is customary for the builder or landlord to quote the rental of a store as so much per foot. Generally, only larger store units are figured on a square-foot basis. Almost all other store units are on a per-front-foot basis. Just exactly what does this mean When the price per front foot is multiplied by the actual front footage of the store, the result will be the yearly rental; for the monthly rental, divide by 12.

HOW TO FIGURE RENTAL COSTS

Let me give an example. If a store measures 13'×60', and the landlord is asking $200 per front foot, what is the monthly rental? First, the 60-foot depth does not figure in at all. The tenant is charged for the actual frontage of the store, only. Now, to arrive at the monthly rental, multiply the price per front foot ($200) by the actual store frontage (13 feet). This will give us $2,600, which is the yearly rental. Then divide the $2,600 by 12 and you get $216.66, which is the monthly rental. In order to simplify the actual arithmetic, I have prepared a chart which will give the yearly rent. To arrive at rental, move down the per-front-foot column to the correct rent, then to the right, stopping under the correct size. This is the yearly rent. A handy reference table is shown in Exhibit 6-1. The chart will take care of most situations; however, where there are fractions involved, it will be necessary to interpolate. For example, a 12-foot frontage at $200 per annum will cost $2400. A 12-foot, 6-inch frontage will cost $2500 or half the difference between 12 fee and 13 feet.

EXHIBIT 6-1. Rentals per Front Foot Table (Per Annum).

Rent per Front Foot	10'	11'	12'	13'	14'	15'	16'	17'	18'	19'	20'
$100	1,000	1,100	1,200	1,300	1,400	1,500	1,600	1,700	1,800	1,900	2,000
$110	1,100	1,210	1,320	1,430	1,540	1,650	1,760	1,870	1,980	2,090	2,200
$120	1,200	1,320	1,440	1,560	1,680	1,800	1,920	2,040	2,160	2,280	2,400
$175	1,750	1,925	2,100	2,275	2,450	2,625	2,800	2,975	3,150	3,325	3,500
$200	2,000	2,200	2,400	2,600	2,800	3,000	3,200	3,400	3,600	3,800	4,000
$225	2,250	2,475	2,700	2,925	3,150	3,375	3,600	3,825	4,050	4,275	4,500
$250	2,500	2,750	3,000	3,250	3,500	3,750	4,000	4,250	4,500	4,750	5,000
$275	2,750	3,025	3,300	3,575	3,850	4,125	4,400	4,615	4,950	5,225	5,500
$300	3,000	3,300	3,600	3,900	4,200	4,500	4,800	5,100	5,400	5,700	6,000
$325	3,250	3,575	3,900	4,225	4,550	4,875	5,200	5,525	5,850	6,175	6,500
$350	3,500	3,850	4,200	4,550	4,990	5,250	5,625	6,000	6,375	6,670	7,000
$375	3,750	4,125	4,500	4,875	5,250	5,625	6,000	6,375	6,800	7,125	7,500
$400	4,000	4,400	4,800	5,200	5,600	6,000	6,400	6,800	7,200	7,600	8,000
$425	4,250	4,675	5,100	5,525	5,950	6,375	6,800	7,225	7,660	8,075	8,500
$450	4,500	4,950	5,400	5,850	6,300	6,750	7,200	7,650	8,075	8,550	9,000
$475	4,750	5,225	5,700	6,175	6,650	7,125	7,600	8,075	8,500	9,025	9,500
$500	5,000	5,500	6,000	6,500	7,000	7,500	8,000	8,500	9,000	9,500	10,000

NOTE: Price per front foot times actual front footage equals yearly rental; for monthly rental divide by 12.

I am concerned with the average small business and the minimum cash required to open one of these various lines. I would like to stress that I am not referring to the entire cost of opening a business. Exhibit 6-2 which follows is incomplete in that it refers to cash required to cover stock and fixtures being placed into a store. As a general rule, approximately 25% of the total expense is required in cash, while the remaining 75% may be secured by a chattel mortgage on the fixtures.

I must further suggest that the agent advise his client that there will be additional expenses. I refer to the amount of cash needed for reserve. Different lines of business have varying seasons and cash reserve will vary, depending upon how close to a "season" a store is opened. I would suggest that at least $2,500 be set aside as a cash reserve against what is popularly known as "unforeseen contingencies."

EXHIBIT 6-2. Minimum Cash Investment for Establishing Certain Businesses.

Beauty Salon	$ 6,000
Coin-Op Cleaner	12,500
Electrical Appliance	10,000

EXHIBIT 6-2 (Contd.)

General Merchandise	8,000
Grocery	8,000
Hardware	12,000
Laundromat	10,500
Laundry	3,500
Men's Furnishings	9,000
O.P. Cleaning (Unit)	12,000
Paint and Wallpaper	10,000
Plumbing and Heating	1,500
Real Estate	500
Restaurant	250 per seat
Retail Bakery (No Baking on Premises)	4,500
Retail Drug	10,000
Service Station	5,000
Shoe Repair (Rented Machinery)	1,000
Small Factory	5,000
Sporting Goods	10,500
Women's Wear	8,000

NOTE: These figures all include a sufficient cash reserve and normal credit.

Another question very often asked is, "How many people are needed for my type of business?" Again, the answer will depend on the size and fixed expenses of the individual enterprise. We will, however, continue our work on the basis of a minimum investment and, consequently, will require a minimum number of people.

When we calculate the number of people necessary for a business survival, we follow a simple formula. We take the total population of the immediate drawing area and divide this number by the competition. (See Exhibit 6-3 for the minimum number of persons necessary for neighborhood retail stores.)

The population figures are secured from the post office. The post office will advise regarding the number of families in the area. We then multiply the number of families by $3\frac{1}{2}$, in order to arrive at total population. For example, let us say that you are contemplating opening a drugstore. After you have gotten the total population figure, it must then be divided by the number of other drugstores in the area. If the answer is the same or greater than the minimum requirement, the store will probably be successful. This is no guarantee, but at least the store has enough potential to be successful.

Some stores fail for reasons other than lack of proper population backing. A prime reason for failure is undercapitalization. Another reason for failure may be the operator himself. Particularly in a service business, the operator must be able to handle people. Personality is an important factor. The individual operator must be wary of chain competition. If the individual feels that he can give enough personal service to offset the low chain prices, he can compete. If he can't, he should not attempt to fight a chain store with strong advertising power. Where there are only neighborhood stores, the formula is accurate.

EXHIBIT 6-3. Minimum Numbers of Persons Necessary to Keep Neighborhood Retail Stores Operating.*

Type of Store	No. of Persons per store
Bank	5,000
Barber Shop	1,500
Beauty Salon	1,500
Cleaner (Coin-Op)	2,500
Drug	2,500
Food	1,500
Gas Station	800
Hotel	7,500
Laundry (Coin-Op)	1,500
Paint and Wallpaper	4,000
Real Estate	1,000
Restaurants	1,500
Supermarkets	3,000
Theatres	2,000
Undertakers	2,500
Women's Wear	2,500

* These figures apply to neighborhood shopping areas only.

When you list a store, it is necessary that you have a correct form with the right information. I suggest the following:

EXHIBIT 6-4. Necessary Listing Information.

AREA: Manhattan, 225 W. 14th St.   OCCUPANCY: Immediate

SIGN: Yes

RENT: $300 mo. (2) years
$325 mo. (3) years   OWNER: Jane Doe

EXHIBIT 6-4 (Contd.)

KEYS: With grocer
DATE: January 4th
SECURITY: 2 mo. rent
LEASE: 5 years

BASEMENT: Yes/Full
HEAT: Tenant/Gas
TELEPHONE: MO 7-2163

Other Tenants: Cleaner, grocer, luncheonette.
Remarks: Front parking for 30 cars.

I have filled in the form in order to give you a little better idea as to the purpose for which it will be used. The date is the day that the store was actually listed by you. That is the day that the owner gave you the okay to rent. The area is the general town or local area that the store is located in and specific address. Some rental agents file their forms by areas, while others prefer to file by rent groups. I have found that, for myself, rental grouping is preferable. Security is self-explanatory. It is the amount of security money required by the landlord. The rent unit, as written in this particular form, designates the asking rental as $300 per month for the first two years of the lease and $325 per month for the next three years of the lease. Under the lease, you will note that the landlord is looking for a five-year lease. Occupancy is also self-explanatory. The store will be available for a new tenant on the date written in the form. Under the heading of heat, the explanation is that it is paid for by the tenant and that the type of heat is gas. The keys unit is important in that it tells where the keys to the vacancy are available. Going a little further into the keys situation, I usually suggest that the landlord leave the keys with one of the tenants in the building. This makes it simpler to show the store, since the keys are always available. A list of other tenants must be included, because it not only presents a complete picture of all existing tenancy but also gives you an idea of what is missing or will fit into the building. It is impossible to remember all of the buildings that you will have listed, so try to put features that will help you recall the individual building under remarks. The unit "sign" designates whether or not you have your sign in the store window. On the whole this information form is simple, but it gets the job done. Multiple copies of the form can either be typed or mimeographed. The latter is the better method.

BROCHURE CONTENT

Actually, the brochure must be simple, state the facts, and be designed for easy reading.

Exhibit 6-5 contains most of the basic elements. These are:

EXHIBIT 6-5. Retail-Store-for-Sale Advertising Brochure.

100% RETAIL LOCATION

LOCATION: Main Ave., Skyview Pl., Horizon City, N.Y.

SIZE: 80' × 100' plus 5,000' mezz. (full base).

RENTAL: $28,000 per annum NET (taxes $4,000).

[PHOTO OF PROPERTY]

The available retail space was formerly occupied by Seaboard Retail Stores, Inc. Seaboard has moved approximately one block away in order to take larger space. Directly behind this location is one of Horizon City's largest customer parking areas. Horizon City is one of the finest shopping towns in America. Immediately adjacent to this location can be found the following tenants: B. Altman, Bonwit Teller, Saks Fifth Ave., Wallach's, Fanny Farmer, S.S. Kresge, Barricini, Sears Roebuck, Peck & Peck, W. & J. Sloane, Best & Co., Macy's, Singer Sewing, Horn & Hardart, Lamston, Nestle Co., Howard Clothes, Schrafft's Loft Candy, F.W. Woolworth, W.T. Grant, National Shoes, Thom McAn, A.S. Beck, Safeway Supermarket, and others.

Horizon City has all types of homes to draw upon for its shopping area. The population consists of large estates, fine large homes, modest cottages, modern well-run apartment buildings and public housing developments. Horizon City is only 30 miles from Grand Central Station. Commutation time is 40 minutes. Horizon City draws its shopping population from all of Pilgrim County. Horizon City's shopping area, in drawing from Pilgrim County, is drawing from one of the wealthiest counties in America.

FOR FURTHER DETAILS AND APPOINTMENT FOR INSPECTION, CONTACT _____
Center 7-8376

More Negotiating Techniques / 77

Location: Give address.

Size: Give dimensions and note if there is a basement or mezzanine.

Neighborhood: List the top retail stores by name.

Remarks: Mention what the retail draw is and where it comes from. Also include income bracket of potential customers.

Photo: Always include a photo. This gives a good idea of the store front and the area.

Ending: Give your name, telephone number, and who to contact.

If there is sufficient interest in the property, then a floor plan should be given to the prospect.

FORMS AND BROCHURES AS LEASING AIDS

As a rule, the most expensive stores are found in the better shopping areas. The landlords in the prime areas are seeking prime tenants. Your brochure should first go out to the chain stores. However, before discussing a retail unit with the chains, I would suggest that you make sure initially that the asking rental is comparable with that of other stores in the immediate area. Then, make up your brochure and send it out to the chain stores that are not already in the area and which you feel would be successful at this location.

Another purpose that a brochure serves is as an answering device when you have inserted a newspaper advertisement and the response is large. The last, and probably the greatest use of brochures, is in the presentation of new shopping centers. I will not cover the shopping center brochures, because they are usually paid for by the builder and designed by experts in the field.

Within a relatively short time, you should have a goodly number of vacant stores in your listing book. From time to time, you will want to check to see if some or all of these stores are still available. This problem is covered with another form. The following, Exhibit 6-6, shows the memorandum-of-store-listing form.

Memorandum courtesy of Mines Press, 342 W. 14th St., New York, N.Y. 10014

EXHIBIT 6-6. Memorandum of Store Listing.

Memorandum of Store Listing   Date:
Property:

78 / *More Negotiating Techniques*

EXHIBIT 6-6 (Contd.)

Store Size:

Is the above listed store still available?
Have there been any changes in the above listing?
In the event we do not hear from you to the contrary, we shall assume that the above listing is correct and we will continue to show it accordingly.

John Jones Realty
120 N. Main St.
New York, N.Y.
WI 7-0830

To

(Form #61 w/changes—The Mines Press, N.Y.C.)

As you, the reader, progress through this book, you will find that I continually stress the use of forms as a sales method. The form provides a multitude of services. It, of course, simplifies your method of operation and enables you to do your job quickly and simply. It also serves an economic function, in that it eliminates much of your typing. This means that you can carry on your work without the services of a secretary. At a later date, when your business increases to the point at which you require additional sales help, the form will again serve you well. A new salesman can quickly be taught many of the basic fundamentals of the business through the use of forms. Even with the addition of one salesman, the forms will still enable you to operate without the services of a secretary.

Other companies also operate with forms, particularly form letters. My suggestion is that whenever you receive a form letter or an individual letter that sends a message, you should file this letter away for the future. Generally, with very few changes, you may be able to fashion the letter to serve you.

HOW TO USE THE TELEPHONE

One of the most important methods used in selling is the telephone. It is my feeling that without a telephone a commercial renting agent could not survive. As a salesman, you will find the telephone to be a tremendous weapon in helping you do business. The telephone is, however, a double-edged sword. If used improperly, it may hurt instead of help. When using the telephone, be brief. Most renting agents make the error of being too lengthy. A salesman, when telephoning, should highlight the facts and nothing more. A businessman cannot listen to a lot of time-wasting talk. At the beginning, the neophyte salesman should try to write out his sales approach. Then, the more important facts should be underlined, in order to make them outstanding (they should be touched upon briefly). This should constitute the entire sales approach. The telephone conversation may be followed up with a meeting, but keep the telephone conversation brief.

The methods of abusing the telephone are few but expensive, in that they kill deals. Do not call when you have nothing to say. Do not continue a conversation after you have made your point. Do not be funny over the telephone. Always adopt the attitude that the other party is busy. I might also mention that if you chatter endlessly, you not only defeat yourself in not making deals but also run up a big telephone bill. The telephone can be a very expensive instrument when used improperly.

Quite a few salesmen are gadget conscious. A great many like to hook up recording machines and record telephone conversations. In most cases there is no ulterior motive, but the results can be disastrous. I can think of nothing that will antagonize a client more quickly than finding out that his voice has been recorded without his permission. I might also suggest that you do not record a conversation with a client unless you are unconcerned about losing him.

There is another gadget that I do not recommend. This is the loudspeaker. There are small telephone-amplifying machines on the market that are handy, in that they amplify the voice. This permits the speaker the use of his two free hands. This little machine is quite useful in its place. However, it must not be used when talking with a client. The use of the amplifier is readily recognized because of the hollow tone it has. The main objection to the machine is that it reminds one of a recorder, and anything related to a recorder is out. If you are interested in using the telephone and having both hands free, I recommend a shoulder rest. This little gadget is readily purchased at any stationery store and may be installed quickly.

I have kept away from the question of "how to sell," until I had stressed sales aids that I felt were important prerequisites to "how to sell." There are few fancy sales tricks that a salesman must know. I do not feel it is necessary to stress what to do, but rather, what not to do. The so-called secret of the presentation is quite simple. When describing why a location is suitable, eliminate the use of any adjectives. Never say a location is "good," but rather say "I like this location because," and then give the facts instead of adjectives. Leasing stores is a simple business and does not require any great salesmanship, flowery phrases, or presenting of a situation with dressed up effects.

If the information contained in this chapter is faithfully followed, you will be well on your way to leasing a store. However, the most important part of your salesmanship has not been touched upon. The magic words have not been discussed, as yet. These are the words: "A one-hundred dollar deposit will tie up the store for you." No matter what a salesman does or how he does it, it is practically impossible to close a deal unless the client is asked for money. You must help a man make up his mind, and the best way to do this is to ask for a deposit. The deposit is merely goodwill money, giving the prospective tenant an option, and is subject to the drawing up of a lease.

The following exhibit, 6-7, serves a dual purpose. This agreement may be used for either sales or leasing; by substituting the word "sell" where it applies in place of "rent," the agreement may be changed to serve as an exclusive one for the sale of a store property.

EXHIBIT 6-7. Exclusive Agreement (From Owner to Agent).

John Smith Realty Co.
127 Main St.
New York, N.Y.

Gentlemen:

In consideration of your agreement to endeavor to secure a tenant and to list for rent premises _____, the undersigned hereby gives you the sole and exclusive right to lease these premises for the period of this agreement. This agreement shall continue in effect until terminated by either party, giving to the other written notice of termination at least one month prior to the date fixed in the notice of termination, but it is agreed that in no event shall any such termination take effect prior to _____ 19____.
If, during the period of this agreement, you obtain a tenant willing to lease the premises for a price not less than $_____, or at such lower rental and on such terms as may be acceptable to the undersigned, or if the undersigned agrees to lease the same directly or through any other person, at any rent, the undersigned will pay a commission of ____% of the gross rental for the premises. The same commission will be paid you if, within a period of three months after this agreement is terminated, the undersigned leases or agrees to lease the premises, irrespective of the terms of rental, to any person with whom you had negotiated prior to termination.

We agree to pay to you upon request, up to but not in excess of $_____ for promotional advertising expenses. You are authorized to place your "For Rent" sign upon the property, and it is agreed that no other sign will be displayed while this agreement is in effect.

EXHIBIT 6-7 (Contd.)

This sole and exclusive right will be binding upon the heirs, executors, administrators, and assigns of the undersigned.

Very truly yours,

_____ (Seal)

_____ (Seal)

Date:

Accepted
John Smith Realty Co.

by _____ partner

HOW TO SECURE
ANY LEASE YOU WANT

7

Believe it or not, it is possible to secure, with a few exceptions, any lease you want. The commercial leasing field is so vast that actually, it would be difficult not to secure a lease that you wish.

METHODS OF APPROACH—SECURING LEASES

There are two ways to approach the securing of a lease. Either you may find a location for a client or, in reverse, you may find a client. Suppose we attempt to secure a location for a client.

We will assume that the prospective tenant requires the following:
  (A) Free-standing building, costing $30,000 on 100′×100′ plot.
  (B) Location must be near a shopping center and have a good traffic pattern.
  (C) Location to be used for drive-in food.

Our first job is to prepare a listing which will apprise the landowner of the value of the deal you will be presenting, therefore we must determine the cost of land. I shall arbitrarily set a value of $40,000 on the land. The building is known to cost $30,000. Other factors to consider will be the strength of the tenant. Let us assume the tenant is a small chain with a net worth of $300,000. Within the scope of such a net worth, the lending institutions would lend approximately 80% of the cost of land and building. The bank rates, which fluctuate, would be about 8% for interest and 3% for amortization.

Our presentation to the property owner would be as follows:

Cost of Land	$40,000
Cost of Building	30,000
Total Cost	$70,000

FIRST MORTGAGE: $56,000 at 8% interest and 3% amortization (mortgage is 80% of cost of land and building); carrying cost $6,160 per annum.

EXPENSES:

Interest and Amortization	$6,160
* Taxes (Estimated)	3,000
* Insurance (Estimated)	500
* Water and Sewer (Estimated)	100

* The estimating is done by comparing with neighboring properties

Repairs	500
Total Expenses	$10,260

Cash in Job: $14,000

NOTE: A builder will usually try to recapture his investment in six years. Consequently, the tenant's rent would be $2,333, the yearly profit, plus the fixed expense of $10,260 or a total rent of $12,593 per annum.

Now the second or brokerage step commences. If the land is priced over and above the neighboring properties, then we must negotiate with the owner. If the tenant desires to pay less than the rentals paid for similar properties, then we must advise the tenant. If both landlord and tenant are out of line, then we have a weak situation. However, where the tenant only is out of line, secure another tenant. Where the landlord is out of line, then seek another landlord. It is entirely possible to switch either landlord or tenant, provided you are dealing with a rated tenant and a good location. Good-rated tenants and prime commercial locations will, in most cases, provide satisfactory dealings.

I cannot stress the importance of working with rated tenants and prime locations. As you go about, take notice that the majority of commercial vacancies occur in depressed areas. Throughout the nation, the prime commercial properties are almost 100% leased.

In other instances, it will be necessary to prepare presentations of existing buildings, as opposed to vacant land upon which buildings must be erected. Where there is an existing building, the same formula as previously shown may be used—the only difference being, we use the market value of the property in place of estimated cost of land and building. The assessed value may be secured from the local Town Hall. This, together

How to Secure Any Lease You Want / 85

with the town's equalization rate, will provide you with the market value. Substitute the market value in the previously mentioned formula for land and building cost and proceed in the same manner. Basically, we have been discussing buildings with single tenancies.

The taxpayer or shopping center is handled in a different manner. Certain lines of business are easy to secure, while others are difficult to obtain. Give a tenant a good position in a good taxpayer and you will secure your lease without any problems. I am listing below some tenancies with comments:

THE SECRET METHOD OF LEASING

BAKERY (Chain or Individual)— Very difficult, because they must have a truly high-quality location. I suggest avoiding this line of business.

BEAUTY SALON (Individual or Chain)—All that they require for success is adequate parking and a chain supermarket.

DEPARTMENT STORE (Chain)— Very difficult to consummate a lease. Avoid this type of tenancy, but as soon as a department store signs a lease for a location, you should start bringing your tenants to the builders. Do not wait until construction has commenced. Leases may be signed one to two years in advance of actual construction.

DISCOUNT STORE (Chains—Large)— Same as department stores.

DRUG (Chain)— If the department store and the supermarket are signed, you will have no trouble with the drug tenant.

DRY CLEANER (Chain)— Show them a location with a supermarket and they are yours.

GAS STATION (Chain)— If the center is located on two main highways and proper zoning is available, then you cannot miss. However, make sure that a minimum of $100' \times 100'$ is available for this purpose.

GIFTS AND CARDS (Individual)— If the center contains a supermarket chain plus 12–15 stores, the same situation will prevail as with luncheonettes.

LAUNDROMAT—	If you have a supermarket already signed, the laundromat will offer no resistance.
LUNCHEONETTE (Individual)—	This type of tenancy is, without a doubt, the easiest to lease. The competition is so keen that bonuses are offered by the applicants. The brokerage commission is also paid by the tenant.
PAINT AND HARDWARE (Chain)—	Very easy to place if the center contains a department store.
SHOE STORES (Chain)—	Have you ever felt like a king? If this is your desire, call a shoe chain and ask them if they would be interested in a shopping center containing a chain department store. The answer will probably be yes without even asking where the location is.
SUPERMARKET (Chain)—	If the plot is large and the backing fair, they will fight to be first.

If you are beginning to get the idea that you can secure leases easily, then your assumption is correct. You must, however, be on top of the situation at all times. Watch your local newspapers for reports of buildings to be built or plans filed. Drive around and look for signs and for new construction sites. Talk with architects, engineers, and builders. If you are alert, you will be the first broker to bring tenants and probably the first to secure leases.

I have, in this chapter, designated some types of tenancy as difficult to achieve and have recommended that you avoid these lines. The thought behind this advice is that a broker does not sell real estate, but time. This precious commodity must be used where it will return the most money. Consequently, difficult tenancies should be avoided.

ALWAYS BE A PROFESSIONAL

It is also wise to remember that the name of the game is commissions. Do not become overanxious and prostitute yourself.

A leasing agent is constantly asked for rebates by some owners. The threat is always the same, loss of the deal. Many old-time realty men operated on the theory that "half a loaf is better than none." I have learned that they are wrong. If you have a client who is actively seeking a location, he can be sold on any one of several. There is no such thing as only one location which is suitable for a client. If the landlord wants half of your commission, be firm and do not agree to prostitute yourself.

Remember that if you get into the practice of continually giving away 50% of your commissions, you will have to make twice as many deals. Once in a while, you will find yourself unable to switch a client from a location and you will lose a deal. Remember that you can't be a winner every time. Also, it is much cheaper to lose a deal occasionally than to give away a portion of your commission constantly. I mention the question of "the kickback" to landlords because it is probably the single biggest evil that store leasing agents must cope with. It may be easily overcome, but if you give in to this evil, it will swallow you up. I should add that for every landlord who seeks part of your commission, there are many more who do not.

Never assume that your client is aware of even outstanding facts. Always stress and impress upon him even the most obvious things. In doing so, you may be pointing out a fact that your client overlooked or, at worst, you may be emphasizing a salient point. Repetition can, on occasion, be a bore, but it does help to close deals. It pays to repeat yourself.

THE SALE-LEASEBACK TECHNIQUE

8

Selling commercial properties is no longer a hit-or-miss proposition. The seller today, must go through a system of estimating the various sales methods and systems in order to determine how these different options will affect his profit. All of the methods suggested later in this chapter must be tested taxwise. The government is a partner in any transaction and this interest may be large or small, depending upon the mode of transfer. The sale of property has become greatly involved, and I feel that a real estate agent or salesman is morally obligated to advise his client to contact an accountant. Now, if you have given your client the very fine advice "see an accountant," then why should you as the broker be acquainted with the tax facts concerning sales? The only way that I can answer this is to say that first aid can be of some importance before calling a doctor. There have been many instances where the proper application of first aid has saved a life. In more or less the same way, in a realty transaction, the proper application of even limited tax knowledge can also secure a listing from an owner who otherwise may not be interested in selling.

BE AN EXPERT—KNOW THE TECHNIQUES

However, the managing agent, in order to aid an owner's thinking regarding a sale, should be in a position to give general tax information and advise how the property may be sold. There is no other way to approach an owner. In addition to the sales presentation, or certainly as a part of the same, the agent is morally obligated to present to the seller an accurate picture, give general tax information, and advise how the property should be sold or leased. In order to achieve these ends, he must be aware of the problems involved and supply the answers.

Throughout this book, I have stressed "be an expert." However, few rules can be completely firm or ironbound. There must be a certain amount of flexibility to a formula. The managing agent, by the very nature of his business, will find himself confronted with commercial properties that he has leased which are being offered for sale. Quite often, the property becomes saleable only after he has leased existing vacancies. In this way, listings are created.

It has long been a feeling of mine that the commercial store leasing broker is the individual most suited for handling the sale of commercial properties. Why? Because the best method of determining the true value of a building, is to try, in your mind, to picture the building as being completely vacant; then determine, by experience or comparables, what the rental value would be if the property was to be rented today. The commercial store leasing broker is involved in this type of problem every day of the year and, consequently, I feel that he, as managing agent, is the most reliable man for solving this type of problem. With a good background of leasing knowledge, it is not difficult for him to determine if a building is "overrented" or "underrented."

There are instances where a landlord will make deals in order to secure an advantageous mortgage. Suppose it is the practice of local banks to lend mortgages at three times the rent roll, then a building with a $10,000 rent roll would be in a position to secure a mortgage in the amount of $30,000. However, if the tenant has a rental of $8,000 and the landlord wishes to secure the same $30,000 mortgage, then the landlord may work out an "arrangement." The tenant signs a lease for $10,000 per annum, but is given $2,000 per annum in concession or free rent. This is done by separate letter so as not to be a part of the lease and subject to a bank's inspection. If the tenant signs a five-year lease, then the landlord will have a reasonable lease, a good mortgage, and an opportunity to sell at a fair price. Speaking generally, good taxpayers sell at about eight and one half times the gross rent. Therefore, a $10,000 rent roll will command a purchase price of approximately $85,000. A rent roll of $8,000 will only command a purchase price of $68,000. Consequently, the "arrangement" is worth an additional $17,000, less the $10,000 in concessions, or a net gain of $7,000 to the seller. Be wary and do not accept any lease at face value; set your own rental value. Comparables will be of great help to you.

Now, let us look at the other side of the situation. Many landlords "underrent" their property. This is not done because these gentlemen are charitable or because they are not knowledgeable. Buildings are underrented for many reasons, included among which are undercapitalization, temporary financial lulls, and a variety of other reasons. The underrented buildings, provided that the leases are not too long, provide an opportunity to purchase, change tenancy, or merely raise rents and then sell at a profit.

One of the other big problems that face the realty managing agent is poorly financed property. The poorly financed building can show a small return and yet be a good buy. As an example, let us assume that a $30,000 mortgage was placed 15 years ago at 6% interest and 2% amortization, constant. The payments would be $2,400 per annum. Fifteen years ago the mortgage was $30,000. Today the mortgage is amortized by almost 50%. The balance today is approximately $15,000. The trick in this case is to purchase the property, refinance and thereby reduce the cash investment, and create a greater yield. I strongly suggest that the possibility of renewing existing leases should always be investigated. With suitable leases, a property of this type can be purchased advantageously.

THREE BASIC SALES METHODS

Now we come to the meat of this chapter—the so-called "tax picture." Basically, there are three methods of sales that a seller has the option of choosing.

These methods are:

(a) Outright sale.
(b) Sale-leaseback.
(c) Leasehold.

In order to be able to advise a seller as to which method is most advantageous, there must be a basic understanding of each system. Each of these options will be explained briefly.

The outright sale is, of course, quite simple. The property is either sold for more or less than it was originally purchased, thereby showing a simple profit or loss.

The sale-leaseback technique is slightly more complicated. The property is sold for a specified amount of cash, usually over existing financing. The seller then takes back a long-term lease, guarantees a previously agreed upon return, and actually manages and runs the property. In the event of refinancing of the property, the owner and tenant usually share in the proceeds on a 50–50 basis.

The leasehold is another rather simple arrangement. Many commercial buildings are erected on leased land. The owner of the building does not own the land. The land is leased on a long-term lease at a specified rental. The rental is in most cases about 10% of the actual market value of the land. Upon the expiration of the lease, the building becomes the property of whomever you leased the land from. There are several ramifications of some importance in this type of transaction. Ordinarily, it is not permissible to finance the land, but it is possible that a portion of the fee may be financed. The generally accepted method is to permit mortgaging the fee up to a certain percentage or else place no limitations, provided that any financing must be institutional. By institutional, I mean either a bank or an insurance company is the lender.

I am going to take a hypothetical shopping center and show first the various ways that this center may be sold. Then I am going to show the advantages or disadvantages that each situation may offer. Each method will differ, but the return to the purchaser will be in all instances 10% on equity (invested cash).

HOW THE VARIOUS OPTIONS WORK

The following are the three proposed options available to the seller. There are others, but the following are those most generally in use.

Let us assume that a shopping center is purchased for $80,000 cash over a $20,000 mortgage at 6% interest and 2% amortization. Income and expenses are as follows:

Rent Roll		$40,000
Estimated Expenses		
Mortgage-Interest and Amortization	$16,000	
Taxes	9,000	
Maintenance, Repairs, Etc.	2,500	
Insurance	2,000	29,500
Net Return (Cash Flow)		$10,500

The owner of this shopping center decides to dispose of it. There are three general ways in which this may be done. The prices, of course, are purely hypothetical.

(A) *Outright Sale*—The seller decides to sell for $100,000 cash over the existing mortgage. This will show a $20,000 cash profit for the seller and approximately a 10% yearly profit to the purchaser.

(B) *Sale-Leaseback*—The seller decides to sell on a sale-leaseback arrangement, whereby he will give the purchaser a 10% return. The deal will work out as follows:

Rent Roll	$40,000
Expenses	29,500
Net	$10,500
Leasing Fee Guarantee	5,000
Seller's Remaining Balance	$5,500

Exploring the above example, the rent roll, of course, remains the same, as do the expenses. The net profit is $10,500. In this sale-leaseback arrangement, the purchaser has paid $50,000 over financing to buy this property. The seller then takes back a long-term lease and guarantees the purchaser a net income of $5,000 per annum. The purchaser, of course, has a 10% net deal. He has invested $50,000 over financing and will be receiving a $5,000 per annum net. In addition, the seller will manage and run the property. In the event that vacancies occur or expenses increase, the seller absorbs these increases because he has guaranteed the purchaser $5,000 per annum for the length of his lease.

How good is the guarantee on a sale-leaseback arrangement? Ordinarily, this guarantee is worthless. The seller takes a long-term lease and provides a guarantee, but it has been my personal experience that over 90% of the time, the seller places a worthless holding corporation on the lease. As long as the job shows money, he stays with it. If the job starts to show a loss, then he drops it. How can this type of situation be averted? The easiest system is probably the most difficult. Request the seller to go on the lease personally or place a financially good corporation on it. If unable to obtain either of these two options, then the third and to my mind, the best solution, is to pay less cash when purchasing and part of the price, in the form of a purchase money mortgage. The mortgage is then put up by the seller as security for the lease. If the seller decides to drop the lease, the mortgage then becomes fully paid and the purchaser, with less cash in the enterprise, can work with a smaller return if need be.

In the sale-leaseback arrangement, it is common practice to divide the proceeds of refinancing on a 50/50 basis between the purchaser and the seller.

(C) *Leasehold Arrangement*—The seller decides to lease the property for a period of 99 years. Income and expenses remain the same, except for the additional expense of $2,000 per annum leasehold rent. The leasehold rent changes the net figure as follows:

Gross Rent	$40,000
Expenses	29,500
	$10,500
Leasehold Rent	2,000
Net Profit (Cash Flow)	$ 8,500

On the basis of the above figures, the seller decides that the price for the leasehold is $85,000 cash over financing to show a 10% profit to the purchaser.

As I have shown, the seller, in most instances, has three possible sales options. The seller's decision as to his selection will be arrived at after he has determined which option is more advantageous, "taxwise." A careful study of each possible sales option will show that in each instance, the profit or return to the purchaser is 10% net after all expenses are paid.

I will outline the seller's tax position in each of the three proposed transactions.

(A) *Outright Sale*—The seller will obtain a profit of $20,000.

Selling Price	$100,000	(Over Financing)
Cash Paid on Purchase	80,000	(Over Financing)
Profit	$20,000	(Difference Between Buying and Selling Price)

(Depreciation and amortization are not being taken into consideration in this determination.)

If the property is held for more than six months, the sale will be treated as a long-term capital gain at a maximum tax rate of 25%.

(B) *Sale-Leaseback*—The seller will be selling property with a value of $100,000 for $50,000, upon assumption of the $20,000 mortgage by the purchaser, thus incurring a $30,000 loss on the sale (exclusive of depreciation and amortization). The property sold would probably be classified as that used in trade or business and the loss on the sale would be recognized as an ordinary loss which would be deducted from current income, the excess being subject to the net operating carry-back and carry-over provision of the Internal Revenue Code. This would mean that the income earned from operations in the year of the sale would be eliminated, and taxes paid in the prior three years could be recovered by carrying back this loss, the remaining loss being carried forward to the succeeding years. It is possible that the Internal Revenue Service would consider this transaction a sale of investment property, Under this determination the loss would be considered a capital loss, which would allow an individual to offset any capital gains against it, or if no capital gains are available, to offset ordinary income in any calendar year by a $1,000 of the capital loss until the entire loss is absorbed.

(C) *Leasehold*—The sale of the leasehold for $85,000 over financing, even though it is for a period of 99 years, which in some states is considered a sale of property, would be treated by the Internal Revenue as ordinary income. The result would be that in the year the $85,000 is received by the seller, the profit would be taxable in full as ordinary income.

I am sure that the initial question to be asked by the real estate agent is, "Which method is best?" The only practical answer is that all are good. This is subject to the individual seller's particular problem. Each seller has his own problems and it is the job of the managing agent to discuss these problems and arrive at the best possible sales option. There is a suitable option that will generally be of help to almost any seller.

COMMERCIAL LEASING BONANZAS

9

Commercial leasing is a fascinating business, one that still affords the small man an opportunity to create a bonanza. It is possible to achieve financial independence with just a little commercial leasing knowledge.

One method of hitting it big is to let the government do some of the work for you. The federal government has a law on its books that permits it, through the Small Business Administration, to guarantee rent payments by small businessmen. I will cover this in more depth and show how this law can be applied to aid both leasing agent and owner.

A small businessman now has the leasing strength of a major chain. Previously, the small businessman was excluded from large shopping centers because he did not have the magic AAA-1 credit rating. Lately, this situation has been substantially corrected.

RENT GUARANTEE POLICIES

Private insurance companies now issue "Rent Guarantee" policies. These policies are, when approved, guaranteed by the Small Business Administration. The procedure is for the tenant to first make application to the S.B.A. for approval. Both the prospective tenant and the location are checked by this organization. If approved, the applicant may then go to an insurance company and secure a policy.

Federal guarantees run from a minimum of five years to a maximum of 20 years. The premiums are based on a sliding scale, commencing at $6\frac{1}{2}\%$ of the total rent for the first five years and decreasing to 2.1% during the twentieth year. In addition the tenant must also post three months' rent in advance, which will be held in escrow. If, at the termination of the lease, the tenant is not in default, then the advance rent monies are returned plus 4% interest. In the event that the prospective tenant requires aid with the advance rent and/or insurance premium, the S.B.A. will consider making a partial loan.

As we progress in this chapter, I shall show you how the guaranteed lease may be of great importance and possibly create a bonanza for you.

WORK ON "EXPIRED BUILDINGS"

The trick in making money is to either raise the rent, mortgage, or both. The type property we require is one that I like to call an "expired building." I refer to a property having a mortgage that will shortly, or has already, expired, plus leases that have already run out or are almost due.

A great many owners hold property that they are afraid of. The only reason the property was purchased in the first place was because it probably had a long-term mortgage and the tenants had long-term leases. The fears of the owners are not unjustly warranted in the event that they maintain a status quo. As leases grow shorter and financing nears the due date, the market value of the building drops. Further, the lending institution will look for the return of the balloon (remaining balance) on the mortgage.

So, what makes this type property a potential bonanza? Just one word, knowledge. The true value of a taxpayer or shopping center can best be determined by mentally picturing the property as being completely vacant. Remove all tenants. Now decide what rental you could get if the building had to be rented immediately. The experienced managing agent will have a good idea of what prevailing rentals are. The novice may speak with adjacent storekeepers and neighborhood brokers; in this way, he can acquire information relative to neighborhood rental values.

In order to show how money can be made, I am going to create a hypothetical shopping center. Our building will be an average neighborhood shopping center containing a supermarket, drugstore, luncheonette, and dry cleaner, all tenants being individuals. To further illustrate what we have and what changes will be made, Exhibit 9-1 shows the listing for the property.

EXHIBIT 9-1. The Bonanza Formula.

LOCATION: Main Street, U.S.A.
DESCRIPTION: One-story, modern taxpayer with basements and

EXHIBIT 9-1 (Contd.)

individual gas heating units. On-premises parking for 60 cars.

BLDG. SIZE: 16,000' PLOT SIZE: 40,000'

FINANCING: First Mortgage: Present balance $55,200; originally $120,000. 6% interest—4.1% amortization. Cost of carrying, $12,000 per annum. Due in six months. Was placed 9½ years ago.

RENT ROLL: $30,000

ESTIMATED EXPENSES:

First Mortgage: I and A	$12,000	
Taxes	10,000	
Insurance	1,200	
Water/Sewer	250	
Repairs/Maintenance	1,400	$24,850

NET PROFIT: $ 5,150

SIZE	TENANCY	RENTAL	LEASE EXPIRES
100'×100'	Supermarket	$10,000	6 months
34'× 60'	Drug	7,000	6 months
33'× 60'	Luncheonette	7,000	6 months
33'× 60'	Cleaner	6,000	6 months

ANALYSIS OF EXHIBIT: Ordinarily a building of this type, a neighborhood taxpayer, will sell for a 12% return on equity. In other words, the property could be sold for approximately $42,899 cash over existing financing. Therefore, the total price for the property will be:

Present Mortgage Balance	$55,200
Cash	42,899
TOTAL PRICE	$98,099

HOW MUCH MONEY CAN BE MADE?

It should be noted that the property now brings a total price of $98,099 or about $21,901 less than the original mortgage. The property, even though fully rented, appears to have lost substantial value.

Rentals are, on a comparative basis, checked in the area and we find that comparative service stores are renting for $300 per front foot per annum and larger units, like our supermarket space, will bring $4 per square foot per annum. The job is now to secure new leases. The new leases will be at prevailing rents. If our survey of comparable rentals had shown that rentals were on the downgrade, then I would have avoided the property. Even if this property had been offered at a greater yield than market value, it would still have contained no interest for me. To make big money, it is essential that the property, rentwise, be on the upswing.

We now turn to the problem of securing adequate leases. First we secure a lease for the larger space, the supermarket. This space should be leased to a major tenant. In most cases an AAA-1 supermarket will be available, because markets are constantly on the lookout for locations. In this particular type situation, where the area has appreciated, the rentals will show an increase. However, the well-rated tenant will, because of lease security, insist upon paying less than the going rental market. We must have a chain supermarket for this type property because the chain has substantial drawing power. If we have found the individual markets are paying $4 per square foot per annum plus tax and maintenance stops, then we will sign with a chain market at 25% less or $3 per square foot. The individual tenancies will pay the going rate plus maintenance and tax stops.

Now we put the federal government to work through the Small Business Administration. As a condition of each individual tenancy, it is mandatory that they secure S.B.A. approval for lease guarantees, and then take out the necessary insurance company policies. With the three service stores guaranteed by the S.B.A. and the supermarket an AAA-1 chain, we can secure new, increased financing.

The entire property now becomes the equivalent of an AAA-1 property. We should, according to the existing mortgage market, secure a mortgage of about five times the gross rent. The terms will be approximately 8% interest and 3% amortization. I have raised the interest rate because after almost ten years it is reasonable to assume that interest rates will rise. The financing is superior to the previous financing because the tenancy is either stronger or guaranteed.

Our new setup will appear as follows:

FINANCING: First Mortgage: $300,000 at 8% interest and 3% amortization. Due 15 years.

RENT ROLL: $60,000

ESTIMATED EXPENSES:

First Mortgage: I and A	$33,000	
*Taxes (Allow Inc.)	12,000	
Insurance (Allow Inc.)	1,500	
Water/Sewer	250	
*Repairs/Maintenance	1,400	$48,150
NET RETURN	$11,850	

*These items stopped.

NOTE: An allowance is permitted for an increase during last year, prior to stops, on taxes and insurance.

Now let us examine the figures and determine exactly what we have. Well, first you must determine the price or market value of the property. The tenancy no longer involves individuals only. All leases are either government guaranteed or AAA-1. The price for this type of property, particularly where there are tax, repair, and maintenance stops, is 10% return on equity or $118,500 over and above financing. A breakdown is as follows:

Present Mortgage:	$300,000
Cash	$118,500
Total Price	$418,500
Old Value	$ 98,099
Total Value Increase	$320,401

I have used a hypothetical situation. An extreme situation it is true, but one that is constantly being repeated throughout the country. In this particular type situation, the owner would show almost a third of a million dollars profit and the managing agent would probably walk away with, including leasing and selling commissions, about $40–50,000. (Rates vary in different sectors.)

THE FABULOUS FRANCHISE SOURCE

10

The commercial store leasing broker of today may consider himself to be an extremely lucky individual. Since the termination of World War II, beginning around the end of 1946, a tremendous business was born—the business of franchising.

As a broker, I have never been concerned with the business or administration of any franchise. I have only had one concern and that is to secure locations to house the franchise operations.

My usual procedure is to write to the home offices of all franchise companies that I am aware of and request information relative to new locations. New companies are continually starting in the franchise business and many old-line chain firms are converting their operations to franchising. My best source for reaching the late starters in the franchise field is the business opportunity columns of the newspapers; the outstanding paper being *The New York Times*.

FIND OUT FRANCHISE REQUIREMENTS

The following (Exhibit 10-1) is a form that is sent to all franchise companies. With this form, a letter should be included, explaining that you are interested in the leasing of commercial space.

EXHIBIT 10-1. Franchise Questionnaire Form.

1. Company Name:
2. Address:
3. Type Area:

EXHIBIT 10-1 (Contd.)

4. Desired Rent:
5. Plot Size:
6. Do You Require a Building to Be Erected?   Size:
7. What Areas Are You Concerned With?
8. Length of Lease:
9. Amount of Security
10. Who Signs Lease:

Do You Prefer: _____ Shopping Centers
              _____ Office Space
              _____ Main Street
              _____ Drive-in

Remarks:

Date:

In this chapter, you will find a list of franchising firms. The list is incomplete but adequate enough for any office or individual to handle.* This list will get the reader off to a running start with hundreds of potential customers. The customer leads are given to you by the franchising firms. Try, as accurately as possible, to meet the required demands relative to locations. When writing, strive to send complete information. Do not be brief. The more information you send, the more interest you will arouse in your submission. I wish to again stress that accuracy in reporting a location is of prime importance. Never make the mistake of deliberately coloring the truth. If the location is weak, it should never have been submitted in the first place. If the location has one or two drawbacks, don't worry, because few locations are perfect.

SITE EVALUATION METHOD

In order to present, properly, a location for analysis to a firm doing franchising, it is mandatory that the agent have a working knowledge of the "site evaluation."

It must be noted at this time that in order to achieve success, a businessman must be situated at a prime selling location. The most experienced businessman featuring a tremendous product, has very little chance of success if his place of business is at a wrong location.

---

* As far as I know, this is the most detailed list of franchise firms seeking locations available.

You must determine what goes into making a right location. You can only arrive at a successful conclusion by realizing upon what foundation you are to base your evaluation. To this problem there is only one answer, the automobile. The car manufacturers are presently creating some 7 million cars per annum. The fantastic increase in cars during the last 60 years has grown from approximately 10,000 cars in 1900 to the millions now produced annually. During this period, there has been a constant changing in the buying habits of the public. The old-time main street locations have weakened, because they were centralized in order to be in close proximity to trolley cars, subways, buses, railroads, etc. The automobile has changed all of this. What were once important modes of transportation are now secondary means, and the stores around these transportation hubs have become second-class shopping areas. The automobile has, depending on traffic patterns, stretched the potential shopping draw to 15 and, in some areas, 20 miles.

Our initial consideration is what city is the location in or near? Quite frankly, cities under 10,000 population offer too limited a range. Always try to submit locations in or adjacent to towns having a 10,000 or better population. A letter to the local post office or chamber of commerce will aid you in getting the necessary population information. The franchise companies will advise you how large a population is required for their type of business. Check as to the number of similar businesses in this area; then divide the population number by the number of competitors. If you still have sufficient population, then the location has possibilities. Now we must determine what percentage of this population actually can, or will, pass this location. At this point, a traffic count is necessary.

A traffic count is a relatively easy method of determining potential gross business. However, a traffic count is slightly more involved than just counting cars. The following form (Exhibit 10-2) is used to evaluate a traffic count in a hypothetical situation.

EXHIBIT 10-2. Street and Traffic Information.

TIME	*Day (Wed.)*	*Day (Sat.)*	*Total*	*Average*
30 minutes, 10:30 AM	320	500	720	360
30 minutes, 3:00 PM	250	280	535	265
30 minutes, 8:00 PM	175	205	380	190
30 minutes, 10:00 PM	205	225	430	215
(Average) 2 hours daily count				1,030 cars
(Average) 1 hour daily count				515 cars
(Average) 12 hours daily count				6,180 cars

	Addition		*Subtraction Net*
Working Trip	−33%		−33%
Shopping Trip	+20%	+20%	

EXHIBIT 10-2 (Contd.)

Pleasure Trip	+40%	+40%	
3 Lanes	−15%		−15%
30–40 mph	+60%	+60%	
Over 40 mph	−40%		−40%
Service Road	None		
Stoplight	+20%	+20%	
		+140%	−88%
Factor	+52%	(+140%	−88%)

52% of 6,180 cars=3,213 cars potential
Purchasing percentage 10% or 321 cars
*Average sale $1.10 per car (Hamburger Drive-in)
Estimated gross $353.10 daily

---

* This varies with different types of businesses.

It is not practical to clock cars for 12 hours daily, so I use four representative hours during a weekday, usually a Wednesday. I then use four representative hours on a Saturday. As you will note in the form, I clock for 30 minutes during each representative period. I then average the weekday and the Saturday, break down the figures to a one-hour number, and multiply by 12. The 12 figure represents the number of hours the retail unit is open. If the unit will be open eight hours daily, then I would use the number 8.

Often, I determine the total number of cars that would pass in a 12-hour day. I then determine the number of potential cars that will stop.

The addition and subtraction part of the form is important in that it tends to give a determination of the potential of the traffic flow. The hours up to 10:30 generally included many working people. The average was 360 cars against a two-hour daily count of 1,030 cars or roughly 33%. We subtract because these people are not interested in purchasing at this time of day. The 3:00 PM group is a definite shopping group. The average here was 265 cars against a daily count of 1,030, or roughly 20%. Naturally, these shoppers go into the plus column. The pleasure group includes the 8:00 PM clocking and also the 10:00 PM clocking. The average was 405 cars as against a two-hour daily count of 1,030 cars, or roughly 40%. People out pleasure-driving are excellent retail prospects, and so this group is included in the plus section.

Cars traveling at about 40 mph are most likely to stop. Cars traveling over 40 mph are generally traveling too quickly to make up their minds about stopping. Let me give you an example. The location we are presently discussing has three lanes of traffic, with one lane being used as a speed lane and the other two lanes containing traffic moving along at a moderate rate of speed. Consequently, I deducted 40% for the speed lane which handles about 40% of the traffic. However, I am also obliged to add 60% for the balance of the traffic which moves along moderately.

If there should be a service road separating the location from the main highway, I generally reject the location, because by the time the retail unit is seen, the driver has passed any means he may have had to pull off the highway and on to the service road.

Stoplights are important in that they give the driver an opportunity to see the retail unit and also allow him time to decide if he wishes to stop.

Now I come to the conclusion. If the factor is negative, by that I mean where the subtraction is greater than the addition, then the location is a poor one and should not be submitted. If the factor is a plus, then we proceed further. In this particular location, under discussion, we subtracted the negative of 88% from the positive of 140% and arrived at plus 52%. Fifty-two per cent of the 12-hour total of 6,180 cars left 3,213 cars potential.

Now I must decide just how good the 3,213-car figure is for business. To arrive at a real meaning, we must come up with a "purchasing percentage."

In order to arrive at a "purchasing percentage," we go to a nearby competitor, take a traffic count, and also check the number of customers he serves during this period. We divide the number of cars in the traffic count by the number of customers and a "purchasing percentage" is arrived at.

Now, getting back to our form, the "purchasing percentage" in this case is 10%. Ten per cent of 3,213 cars will give us a 321 purchasing power. I was advised by the franchise company that their average sale is $1.10 per car. By multiplying, I arrived at an estimated daily gross of $353.10. The franchise company advised me that $253 was the amount needed to cover all expenses. Consequently, this retail unit has a potential of earning $100 net daily.

In the estimated expenses, 10% of gross is figured by the franchise company for rent. This is a six-day operation and the estimated weekly gross is $2,110 or $211 per week for rent. In order to justify the location, the rental submitted should be in the vicinity of $10,000 per annum or about $200 per week.

The active franchise firms are well known to commercial leasing brokers. Consequently, these firms receive hundreds of available locations from them. The great majority of these managing agents have little if any conception of what is required. However, the continual submission of poor and, in a great many cases, slipshod information or locations, does serve a purpose. The franchise people are quick to throw away any submission that is not properly backed up with essential information. In order to be sure that each and every submission receives the proper attention that it deserves, a "Location Form" should be used. The form is actually a checklist that supplies almost all available information. The form should be prepared in such a manner as to provide the franchise people with an opportunity to evaluate the location quickly, subject to inspection.

The list of franchise companies found in this book is a partial one. To gather a complete list would have been an almost impossible job. Consequently, I have tried to assemble those that I felt were most suited to the aims of the book.

The following pages will contain four important exhibits, Exhibits 10-3, 10-4, 10-5, and 10-6.

Exhibit 10-3 will be used constantly. This is a list of various types of franchise businesses. The different lines of business will aid you in determining the one most suited for a particular location.

Exhibit 10-4 will provide the names of companies. After deciding what line of business is best suited to a location, you may then pick out actual companies to be contacts.

Exhibits 10-5 and 10-6 are included for handy reference. Time is precious and the commercial store leasing broker must try to save as much as possible.

EXHIBIT 10-3. Types of Franchises Listed.

Code

1. Auto Supplies and Services
2. Bakery
3. Battery Reconditioning
4. Beauty Salon, Cosmetics
5. Candy
6. Car Wash
7. Chemicals
8. Clothing and Accessories
9. Construction
10. Consultants
11. Department Stores
12. Dry Cleaning, Laundry
13. Employment Agencies
14. Fabrics
15. Floor Covering
16. Fund Raising
17. Furniture

EXHIBIT 10-3. (Contd.)

18. Gifts and Cards
19. Hardware, Paint
20. Home Improvement
21. Home Service
22. Ice Cream
23. Kiosk
24. Model Racing Cars
25. Motor Lodges
26. Pet Shops
27. Protective Devices
28. Rentals
29. Restaurant, Drive-in, Take-out
30. Schools
31. Self-Defense
32. Shoes
33. Signs
34. Sports, Golf, Billiards
35. Supermarkets, Retail Food
36. Tools
37. Transmission, Mufflers, Brakes
38. Tuxedo Rental
39. Vacuum Systems
40. Variety
41. Waste Deposits
42. Water Conditioning and Softening

EXHIBIT 10-4. Index of Franchises by Type.

AUTO SUPPLIES AND SERVICES

    The Abel Corporation
    Aid Stores, Inc.
    Auto Driveway Company
    Coast-to-Coast Stores
    Oklahoma Tire and Supply and Economy Auto Stores
    Penn-Jersey Auto Stores, Inc.
    Pioneers. Inc.
    Rayco Mfg. Co.
    United Merchandising Corp.
    Western Auto Co.

EXHIBIT 10-4 (Contd.)

BAKERY
- Burney Bros., Inc.
- Holiday Bakers
- Lone Star Donut, Inc.
- Lucky Dozen Donuts, Inc.

BATTERY RECONDITIONING
- Electone Chemical Co.

BEAUTY SALON, COSMETICS
- Goubaud de Paris, Inc.
- Harper Method, Inc.
- Norman, Merle Cosmetics

CANDY
- Barton Candy
- Corn Cabin Co.
- Grace, Helen Candies
- Karmelkorn
- Loft's Candy

CAR WASH
- Council Mfg. Corp.
- Sherman Car Wash Equipt. Co.
- United Sales and Services

CHEMICALS
- International Building Maintenance Co.

CLOTHING AND ACCESSORIES
- Bond Stores, Inc.
- Gaylord's
- The Richmond Brothers Co.
- Stein's Stores, Inc.
- The Tie Rak

CONSULTANTS (Franchise)
- American Franchise Systems, Inc.
- Chain Locations of America, Inc.
- Marketing Management and Development Corp.
- Sales Research Corp.

DEPARTMENT STORES
- Sears, Roebuck & Co.
- United Dollar Stores, Inc.
- West Bros., De Ridder, La.

EXHIBIT 10-4 (Contd.)

DRY CLEANING, LAUNDRY

    All-State Laundry Equipt. Co.
    American Permal Inc.
    Avis Machinery Distributors, Inc.
    Bronx Pressing Machine Co., Inc.
    Capitol Varsity Cleaning Co.
    Cleanex Machinery Corp.
    Comet Cleaners
    Hampton Cleaners
    Johnny-on-the-Spot
    Kent Cleaners
    Martin Equipt. Sales
    N.Y. Valetone Sales Corp.
    One-Hour Valetone of America, Inc.
    Pilgrim Laundry Co.
    Prosperity Cleaning Stores
    Spotless Stores

EMPLOYMENT AGENCIES

    Availability, Inc.
    Bailey Employment System, Inc.
    International Personnel Service
    Manpower, Inc.
    Olstein's U.S.A., Inc.
    Western Girl, Inc.
    Western Man, Inc.

FLOOR COVERING

    Lester, Mary Fabrics

FURNITURE

    Biederman National Stores, Inc.

GIFTS AND CARDS

    Carey's Card Shops
    Fifth Avenue Cards, Inc.
    Happy Family
    Spencer Gifts Retail Stores, Inc.

HARDWARE, PAINT

    Carter, Mary Paint Co.
    Handyman America, Inc.
    Martin's Paint
    Morris Paint & Varnish Co.

HOME IMPROVEMENT

    Lusterrock International

EXHIBIT 10-4 (Contd.)

ICE CREAM
- Baskin Robbins
- Dairy Queen
- Dairy Sweet Co.
- Tastee Freez

MOTOR LODGES
- Congress International, Inc.
- Coopp's, Inc.
- Horne's
- Hyatt Chalet Motels, Inc.
- Imperial "400" National, Inc.
- Johnson, Howard Motor Lodges, Inc.
- Quality Courts Motels, Inc.
- Ramada Inns, Inc.

PROTECTIVE DEVICES
- Campus Industries

RENTALS
- A to Z Rental, Inc.
- A to Z Rentals, Inc.
- United Rent-Alls

RESTAURANT, DRIVE-IN, TAKE-OUT
- Arby's International
- A & W Root Beer Co.
- Beef's, Inc.
- Blimpie Corp. of America
- Burger Broil System, Inc.
- Burger Castle
- Burger Chef Systems, Inc.
- Burger King
- Burger Queen Systems, Inc.
- Chicken Delight, Inc.
- Chip's Franchise System, Inc.
- Chock Full O' Nuts Corp.
- The Cobbs Company, Inc.
- Cock-A-Doodle-Doo of America, Inc.
- Commissary Corp.
- Country Styled Donuts
- Dairy Isle
- Danny's Restaurants, Inc.
- Denny's Restaurants, Inc.
- Der Wienerschnitzel
- Dog-N-Suds, Inc.
- Dunkenburger Self-Service Restaurant

EXHIBIT 10-4 (Contd.)

Dunkin Donuts
Eastern Sizzler, Inc.
Franksville, Inc.
Freez-ette Corporation
French Cafes, Inc.
Frostop Corp.
Hardee's Food Systems, Inc.
Harry's Pizza
Henry's Drive-in, Inc.
Hilleary & Partners, Ltd.
International House of Pancakes
Jerry's Drive-in Restaurants
Jerry's Restaurants
Jolly Giant Systems
Kelly's System of New England, Inc.
Kenney's Franchise Corp.
King's Food Host U.S.A., Inc.
K–N Root Company
Kwik Kook. Inc.
Lane's Drive-Inns, Inc.
Little Pigs of America
Lum's
Maryland Fried Chicken, Inc.
Meyenberg Milk Products, Inc.
Mister Donut
Mister Softee
Mister Steak, Inc.
Mr. Swiss of America, Inc.
Mr. T's Pizza
Monterey House
Mugs-Up Root Beer, Inc.
National Cibo House Corp.
Orange Julius of America
Orange Winzit Corp.
The Original Pancake Houses
Pancake Cottage Drive-in Restaurant
Perkins' Pancake Houses, Inc.
Pizza Hut, Inc.
Pizza Inn, Inc.
Pizza King Franchises, Inc.
The Red Bar System, Inc.
Red Rams of America, Inc.
Sanders, Fred
Satellite Systems, Inc.
Shakey's, Inc.
The Shrimp Boats, Inc.
Steer Inn Systems, Inc.

EXHIBIT 10-4 (Contd.)

Stewart's Ice Cream Co., Inc.
Stewart's Root Beer, Inc.
Sveden House Developers, Inc.
Taco Bell
Uncle John's Restaurants, Inc.
Village Inn

SCHOOLS

Napoleon Hill Academy

SHOES

Felsway Shoe Corp.
Shoe Corporation of America
Shtofman Co.
The United States Shoe Corp.

SPORTS, GOLF, BILLIARDS

Mr. Golf, Inc.
Kramer, Sam Enterprises
Lads & Lassies Billiard Recreation Centers
Lomma Billiard Corp.
Mulloy, Gardner International Athletic Clubs
Palmer, Arnold Putting Course
Putt-Putt Golf Courses of America
Putt-R-Golf, Inc.

SUPERMARKETS, RETAIL FOOD

Convenient Food Mart, Inc.
Convenient Food Mart of Louisville, Inc.
Farm Stores International
Open Pantry Food Marts, Inc.
The Southland Corporation
U-Tote-M, Inc.

TOOLS

The Cornwell Quality Tools, Inc.

TRANSMISSIONS, MUFFLERS, BRAKES

Aamco Auto Transmissions
Midas, Inc.
Lee Myles Associates, Inc.
Nationwide Safti-Brake Centers

TUXEDO RENTAL

Randall's Formal Wear, Inc.

VACUUM SYSTEMS

Fornaire

EXHIBIT 10-4 (Contd.)

VARIETY
>Big Top Stores, Inc.
>City Products Corp.
>Southern Dollar Stores, Inc.

WASTE DEPOSITS
>Carey O'Madison Associates

WATER CONDITIONING AND SOFTENING
>Culligan, Inc.
>Rainsoft Water Conditioning Co.

EXHIBIT 10-5. Index of Franchises by Name.

Name	*State	†*Type*
Aamco Auto Transmissions	Pa.	37
Arby's International	O.	29
Bailey Employment System, Inc.	Conn.	13
Barton Candy	N.Y.	5
Baskin Robbins	Calif.	22
Beefy's, Inc.	Del.	29
Biederman National Stores, Inc.	Mo.	17
Big Top Stores, Inc.	N.Y.	40
Blimpie Corp. of America	N.J.	29
Bond Stores, Inc.	N.Y.	8
Bronx Pressing Machine Co.	N.Y.	12
Burger Broil System, Inc.	Ky.	29
Burger Castle	Fla.	29
Burger Chef Systems, Inc.	Ind.	29
Burger King	Fla.	29
Burger Queen Systems, Inc.	Fla.	29
Burney Bros., Inc.	Ill.	2
Campus Industries	N.Y.	27
Capitol Varsity Cleaning Co.	O.	12
Carey O'Madison Associates	Mich.	41
Carey's Card Shops	N.Y.	18
Chain Locations of America, Inc.	N.Y.	10
Chicken Delight, Inc.	Ill.	29

* Home office.
† Refer to "Type Franchise Listed" code number, Exhibit 10-3.

EXHIBIT 10-5 (Contd.)

Chip's Franchise System, Inc.	N.C.	29
Chock Full O' Nuts	N.Y.	29
City Products Corp.	Ill.	40
Cleanex Machinery Corp.	N.Y.	12
Coast-to-Coast Stores	Minn.	1
The Cobbs Co., Inc.	Fla.	29
Cock-A-Doodle-Doo of America, Inc.	Io.	29
Comet Cleaners	Fla.	12
Commissary Corp.	Ohio	29
Congress International, Inc.	Fla.	25
Convenient Food Mart, Inc.	Ill.	35
Convenient Food Mart of Louisville, Inc.	Ky.	35
Coopp's Inc.	Ariz.	25
Corn Cabin Co.	Calif.	5
Cornwell Quality Tools Co.	O.	36
Council Mfg. Co.	Ark.	6
Country Style Donuts	Va.	29
Culligan, Inc.	Ill.	42
Dairy Isle	O.	29
Dairy Queen	Texas	22
Dairy Sweet Co.	Io.	22
Danny's Restaurants, Inc.	Calif.	29
Denny's Restaurants, Inc.	Calif.	29
Der Wienerschnitzel	Calif.	29
Dog-N-Suds, Inc.	Ill.	29
Dunkenburger Self-Service Restaurant	Ind.	29
Dunkin Donuts	Mass.	29
Eastern Sizzlers	N.J.	29
Electone Chemical Co.	Ark.	3
Farm Stores International	Fla.	35
Felsway Shoe Corp.	N.Y.	32
Fifth Avenue Cards, Inc.	N.Y.	18
Forney Industries, Inc.	Colo.	39
Franksville, Inc.	Ill.	29
Freez-ette Corp.	Fla.	29
French Cafes, Inc.	Ill.	29

EXHIBIT 10-5 (Contd.)

Frostop Corp.	N.Y.	29
Fund Ways, Inc.	Wisc.	16
Gaylord's	N.Y.	8
Goubaud de Paris, Inc.	N.Y.	4
Grace, Helen Candies	Calif.	5
Hampton Cleaners	Mo.	12
Happy Family	Ill.	18
Hardee's Food Systems, Inc.	N.C.	29
Harper Method, Inc.	N.Y.	4
Harry's Pizza	Pa.	29
Henry's Drive-in, Inc.	Ill.	29
Hilleary & Partners, Ltd.	Mo.	29
Holiday Bakers	N.Y.	2
Horne's	Mich.	25
Imperial "400" National, Inc.	Calif.	25
International Building Maintenance Co.	Mich.	7
International House of Pancakes	Calif.	29
International Personnel Service	Mich.	13
Johnny-on-the-Spot	N.Y.	12
Johnson's, Howard Motor Lodges, Inc.	N.Y.	25
Jerry's Drive-in Restaurants	Ky.	29
Jerry's Restaurants	Ky.	29
Jolly Giant Systems	N.Y.	29
Kelly's System of New England, Inc	R.I.	29
Karmelkorn	Neb.	5
Kent Cleaners	N.Y.	12
King's Food Host U.S.A., Inc.	Neb.	29
Kiosk Corp. of America, Inc.	Calif.	23
K-N Root Beer Co.	Tex.	29
Kwik Kook, Inc.	Pa.	29
Lads & Lassies Billiard Recreation Centers	Pa. N.Y.	29 34
Lane's Drive-Inns, Inc.	Mo.	29
Lee Myles Associates, Inc.	N.Y.	37
Lester, Mary Fabrics	Wisc.	15
Little Pigs of America	Tenn.	29

EXHIBIT 10-5 (Contd.)

Loft's Candy	N.Y.	5
Lomma Billiard Corp.	Pa.	34
Lomma Golf Enterprises	Pa.	34
Lone Star Donut, Inc.	Tex.	2
Lucky Dozen Donuts, Inc.	N.M.	2
Lum's	Fla.	29
Lusterrock International	Tex.	20
Manpower, Inc.	Wisc.	13
Market Management and Dev. Corp.	Fla.	10
Martin Equipment Sales	O.	12
Martin's Paint	N.Y.	19
Mary Carter Paint Co.	Fla.	19
Maryland Fried Chicken, Inc.	Fla.	29
Meyenberg Milk Products, Inc.	Calif.	29
Midas, Inc.	Ill.	37
Mister Donut	Mass.	29
Mister Golf, Inc.	Mich.	34
Mister Softee	N.J.	29
Mister Steak, Inc.	Colo.	29
Mr. Swiss of America, Inc.	N.Y.	29
Mr. T's Pizza, Inc.	Fla.	29
The Monterey House	Tex.	29
Morris Paint & Varnish Co.	Neb.	19
Mugs-Up Root Beer Co., Inc.	Mo.	29
Mulloy, Gardner International Athletic Clubs	Fla.	34
Napoleon Hill Academy	S.C.	30
National Cibo House Corporation	Tenn.	29
N.Y. Valetone Sales Corp.	N.Y.	12
Norman, Merle Cosmetics	Calif.	4
Olstein's U.S.A., Inc.	N.Y.	13
Oklahoma Tire & Supply Co. and Economy Auto Stores	Okla.	1
One-Hour Valetone of America, Inc.	Fla.	12
Open Pantry Food Marts, Inc.	Ill.	35
Orange Julius of America	Calif.	29
Orange Winzit Corp.	Calif.	29

EXHIBIT 10-5 (Contd.)

The Original Pancake Houses	Ore.	29
Palmer, Arnold Putting Course	N.J.	34
Pancake Cottage Drive-in Restaurant	N.Y.	29
Penn-Jersey Auto Stores, Inc.	Pa.	1
Perkins' Pancake Houses, Inc.	O.	29
Pilgrim Laundry Co.	Tex.	12
Pioneers, Incorporated	Calif.	1
Pizza Hut, Inc.	Kan.	29
Pizza Inn, Inc.	Tex.	31
Pizza King Franchises, Inc.	Ind.	29
Prosperity Cleaners	N.Y.	12
Putt-Putt Golf Courses of America	N.C.	34
Putt-R-Golf, Inc.	O.	34
Quality Courts Motels, Inc.	Md.	25
Rayco Mfg. Co.	N.J.	1
Rainsoft Water Conditioning Co.	Ill.	42
Ramada Inns, Inc.	Ariz.	25
Randall's Formal Wear, Inc.	Colo.	38
The Red Barn System, Inc.	Fla.	29
Red Rams of America, Inc.	Colo.	29
The Richmond Bros. Co.	O.	8
Sanders, Fred	Mich.	29
Satellite Systems, Inc.	Ind.	29
Sears Roebuck & Co.	Pa.	11
Shakey's, Incorporated	Calif.	29
Sherman Car Wash Equipt. Co.	N.J.	6
Shoe Corp. of America	O.	32
The Shrimp Boats, Inc.	Ga.	29
Shtofman, Joseph Co.	Tex.	32
Southern Dollar Stores, Inc.	Ky.	40
The Southland Corporation	Tex.	35
Spencer Gifts Retail Stores, Inc.	N.J.	18
Spotless Stores	N.J.	12
Steer Inn Systems, Inc.	Pa.	29
Stein's Stores, Inc.	O.	8
Stewart's Ice Cream Co., Inc.	N.Y.	29
Stewart's Root Beer, Inc.	O.	29

EXHIBIT 10-5 (Contd.)

Sveden House Developers, Inc.	Fla.	29
Taco Bell	Calif.	29
Tastee Freez	Ill.	22
The Tie Rak	Mich.	8
Uncle John's Restaurants, Inc.	Calif.	29
United Dollar Stores, Inc.	Ark.	11
United Merchandising Corp.	Calif.	1
United Rent-Alls	Calif.	28
The United States Shoe Corp.	O.	32
U-Tote-M	Tex.	35
Village Inn	Ariz.	29
West Bros., De Ridder La.	La.	11
Western Auto Co.	Mo.	1
Western Girl/Western Men, Inc.	Calif.	13

Exhibit 10-6 that follows, gives the home office and refers to the franchise type by code number.

EXHIBIT 10-6. Index of Franchises by State.

*State		†Code
ARIZONA:	Coopp's, Inc.	25
	Ramada Inns, Inc.	25
	Village Inn	29
ARKANSAS:	Council Mfg. Co.	6
	Electone Chemical Co.	3
	United Dollar Stores, Inc.	11
CALIFORNIA:	A & W Root Beer Co.	29
	Astro Motels, Inc.	25
	Baskin Robbins	22
	Corn Cabin	5
	Denny's Restaurants, Inc.	29
	Der Wienerschnitzel	29
	Grace, Helen Candies	5

---

* Location of home office.
† Refer to Exhibit 10-3.

EXHIBIT 10-6 (Contd.)

	Imperial "400" National, Inc.	25
	International House of Pancakes	29
	Meyenberg Milk Products, Inc.	29
	Norman, Merle Cosmetics	4
	Orange Julius of America	29
	Orange Winzit Corp.	29
	Pioneers, Inc.	1
	Shakey's Inc.	29
	Taco Bell	29
	Uncle John's Restaurants, Inc.	29
	United Merchandising Corp.	1
	United Rent-Alls	28
	Universal Franchising, Inc.	10
	Western Girl, Inc./Western Men, Inc.	13
COLORADO:	A to Z Rentals, Inc.	28
	Mr. Steak, Inc.	29
	Randall's Formal Wear, Ltd.	38
	Red Rams of America, Inc.	29
CONNECTICUT:	Bailey Employment System, Inc.	13
DELAWARE:	Beefy's Inc.	29
FLORIDA:	Burger Castle	29
	Burger King	29
	Burger Queen Systems, Inc.	29
	The Cobbs Co., Inc.	29
	Comet Cleaners	12
	Congress International, Inc.	25
	Farm Stores International	35
	Freez-ette Corporation	29
	Handyman America, Inc.	19
	Kelly's Jet System Corp.	29
	Lum's	29
	Marketing Management and Dev. Corp.	10
	Mary Carter Paint Co.	19
	Maryland Fried Chicken, Inc.	29
	Mr. T's Pizza, Inc.	29
	Mulloy, Gardner International Athletic Clubs, Inc.	34

EXHIBIT 10-6 (Contd.)

	One-Hour Valetone of America, Inc.	12
	The Red Barn System, Inc.	29
	Sales Research Corp.	10
	Sveden House Developers	29
GEORGIA:	The Shrimp Boats, Inc.	29
ILLINOIS:	A to Z Rental, Inc.	28
	Auto Driveway Co.	1
	Availability, Inc.	13
	Burny Bros., Inc.	2
	Chicken Delight, Inc.	29
	City Products Corp.	40
	Corn Cabin Co.	5
	Convenient Food Mart, Inc.	35
	Culligan, Inc.	42
	Dog-N-Suds, Inc.	29
	Franksville, Inc.	29
	French Cafes, Inc.	29
	Happy Family	18
	Henry's Drive-in, Inc.	29
	Midas, Inc.	37
	Open Pantry Food Marts, Inc.	35
	Rainsoft Water Conditioning Co.	42
	Tastee Freez	22
IOWA:	Cock-A-Doodle-Doo of America, Inc.	29
	Dairy Sweet Co.	22
INDIANA:	Burger Chef Systems, Inc.	29
	Dunkenburger Self-Service Restaurant	29
	Pizza King Franchises, Inc.	29
	Satellite Systems, Inc.	29
KANSAS:	Pizza Hut, Inc.	29
KENTUCKY:	Convenient Food Mart of Louisville, Inc.	29
	Jerry's Drive-in Restaurants	29
	Southern Dollar Stores, Inc.	40
LOUISIANA:	West Bros., De Ridder, La.	11
MARYLAND:	Quality Courts Motels	25

EXHIBIT 10-6 (Contd.)

MASSACHUSETTS:	Dunkin Donuts	29
	Mister Donut	29
MICHIGAN:	American Franchise Systems, Inc.	10
	Carey O'Madison Associates	41
	Horne's	25
	International Bldg. Maintenance Co.	7
	International Personnel Service	13
	Mr. Golf, Inc.	34
	Sanders, Fred	29
	The Tie Rak	8
MINNESOTA:	Coast-to-Coast Stores	1
MISSOURI:	Biederman National Stores, Inc.	17
	Hampton Cleaners	12
	Hilleary & Partners, Ltd.	29
	Lane's Drive-Inns, Inc.	29
	Mugs-Up Root Beer	29
	Western Auto Co.	1
NEBRASKA:	Karmelkorn	5
	King's Food Host U.S.A., Inc.	29
	Morris Paint & Varnish Co.	19
NEW JERSEY:	Avis Machinery Distributors, Inc.	12
	Blimpie Corporation of America	29
	Eastern Sizzler, Inc.	29
	Imperial "400" National, Inc.	25
	Mister Softee	31
	Palmer, Arnold Putting Courses	34
	Rayco Mfg. Co.	1
	Sherman Car Wash Equipt. Co.	6
	Spencer Gifts Retail Stores, Inc.	18
	Spotless Stores	12
NEW MEXICO:	Lucky Dozen Donuts, Inc.	2
NEW YORK:	Aid Stores, Inc.	1
	All-State Laundry Equip. Corp.	12
	American Permac, Inc.	12
	Barton Candy Corp.	5
	Big Top Stores, Inc.	40

EXHIBIT 10-6 (Contd.)

Bond Stores, Incorporated	8
Bronx Pressing Machine Co., Inc.	12
Campus Industries	27
Carey's Card Shops	18
Chain Locations of America, Inc.	10
Chip's Franchise System, Inc.	29
Chock Full O' Nuts Corp.	29
Cleanex Machinery Corp.	12
Felsway Shoe Corp.	32
Fifth Avenue Cards, Inc.	18
Frostop Corp.	29
Gaylord's	8
Goubaud de Paris, Inc.	4
Hardee's Food Systems, Inc.	29
Harper Method, Inc.	4
Holiday Bakers	2
Jolly Giant Systems	29
Johnny-on-the-Spot	12
Johnson's, Howard Motor Lodges, Inc.	25
Kent Cleaners	12
Kramer, Sam Enterprises	34
Lads & Lassies Billiard Recreation Centers	34
Lee Myles Associates, Inc.	37
Loft's Candy	5
Martin's Paint	19
Mister Swiss	29
N.Y. Valetone Sales Corp.	12
Olstein's U.S.A., Inc.	13
Pancake Cottage Drive-in Restaurant	29
Prosperity Cleaners	12
Putt-Putt Golf Courses of America	34
Stewart's Ice Cream Co., Inc.	29

OHIO:

The Abel Corporation	1
Arby's International	29
Capitol Varsity Cleaning Co.	12

The Fabulous Franchise Source / 123

EXHIBIT 10-6 (Contd.)

	Commissary Corporation	29
	The Cornwell Quality Tools Co.	36
	Dairy Isle	29
	Martin Equipment Sales	12
	Perkins' Pancake Houses, Inc.	29
	Putt-R-Golf	34
	The Richmond Bros., Co.	8
	Stein's Stores, Inc.	8
	Stewart's Root Beer, Inc.	29
	The United States Shoe Corp.	32
OKLAHOMA:	Mr. Swiss of America, Inc.	29
	Oklahoma Tires & Supply and Economy Auto Stores	1
OREGON:	The Original Pancake Houses	29
PENNSYLVANIA:	Aamco Auto Transmissions, Inc.	37
	Harry's Pizza	29
	Kwik Kook, Inc.	29
	Lomma Billiard Corporation	34
	Lomma Enterprises, Inc.	34
	Mosconi, Willie Enterprises, Inc.	34
	Penn-Jersey Auto Stores, Inc.	1
	Sears, Roebuck & Co.	11
	Steer Inn Systems, Inc.	29
RHODE ISLAND:	Kelly's System of New England, Inc.	29
SOUTH CAROLINA:	Napoleon Hill Academy	30
TENNESSEE:	Burger Broil System	29
	Little Pigs of America	29
	National Cibo House Corporation	29
TEXAS:	Dairy Queen	22
	K-N Root Beer Co.	29
	Lone Star Donut, Inc.	2
	Lusterrock International	20
	The Monterey House	29
	Pilgrim Laundry Co.	12
	Pizza Inn, Inc.	29
	Shtofman, Joseph Co.	32
	The Southland Corporation	35

EXHIBIT 10-6 (Contd.)

	U-Tote-M, Inc.	35
VIRGINIA:	Country Style Donuts	29
	Kenney's Franchise Corporation	31
WISCONSIN:	Lester, Mary Fabrics	15
	Manpower, Inc.	13

FRANCHISING LOCATION AND LEASING INFORMATION

11

The format used in Exhibit 11-1, following, is to convey leasing information. This will require some explanation. The first line is self explanatory; it contains the firm's name and address. The balance of the information is as follows:

LEASE— Period of tenant's obligation. When I state "long term," I mean ten to 20 years.

TYPE LOCATION— There are the following types:
(A) Main Street
(B) Shopping Center
(C) Free Standing
(D) Heavy Walking Traffic
(E) Heavy Auto Traffic
Each of the firms will require either one of the preceding or a combination.

REALTY OFFICER— This is the individual to whom you will submit your offerings. This is also the man who can best advise you relative to his company's requirements or changes in requirements.

SPECIAL BUILDING—This of course refers to free-standing units. Many firms have their own plans and specifications.

FRANCHISE— This is the number of units already operating.

COST— The cost of the special building is important in that it will determine the tenant's rent.

TOTAL UNITS— Number of operating units, including both company and franchise units.

STORE SIZE— This is the size of either the store or special building.

TYPE—   This is the type of business. Refer to "type franchise listed" code number in preceding chapter.

RENTAL—   Some firms have a firm policy; others will pay the going rate; some will pay a percentage of gross business. The explanations are as close as possible to the company's thinking.

PLOT—   This comes into play only when a free-standing unit is required, and designates the size of same.

It should be understood that in addition to submitting the leasing information you will have to include a shopping center survey, as covered in the previous chapter. Try not to be too lengthy. If your report is too long, it may conceal vital facts that should stand out. The happy medium is to attempt to be both brief and effective. Also, if the location is poor, do not submit the site.

EXHIBIT 11-1. Franchising Location and Leasing Information.*

The Abel Corporation, Columbus 19, Ohio

Lease: 10 years
Type Location: Middle to high traffic
Rental: Open, subject to vehicular exposure
Realty Officer: Robin A. Schmidt
Total Units: 180   Type: 1

Aid Stores, Inc., 34–36 65th St., Woodside, New York

Lease: 5 years plus option
Type Location: Main street or shopping center
Rental: Depends on projected gross
Realty Officer: Allen Koller
Company Units: 40   Franchise: 7
Special Building: No   Cost: $17,000
Bldg. or Store Size: 2,100′   Type: 1

All-State Laundry Equipt. Corp., 1 Pond Field Rd., Bronxville, New York

Lease: Long term
Type Location: Average income—well populated
Rental: $2,400 to $4,800 per annum
Realty Officer: Att: real estate dept.
Special Building: No   Type: 12

---

* Note: For "type" listed as a number, see Exhibit 10-3.

EXHIBIT 11-1 (Contd.)

Amco Auto Transmissions, 651 Allendale Rd., King of Prussia, Pennsylvania

    Lease: Long term
    Type Location: Main street, drive-in
    Rental: Comparative
    Realty Officer: Att: real estate dept.
    Special Building: No   Type: 37
    Bldg. or Store Size: 4–8,000′

American Franchise Systems, Inc., 184–15 W. 8 Mile Rd., Detroit, Michigan

    Lease: All types
    Type Location: Sectors of country
    Rental: Franchise consultants
    Type: 10

American Permac, Inc., 1 Commercial Ave., Garden City, New York

    Lease: 5 to 10 years
    Type Location: Shopping center or drive-in
    Rental: Open
    Realty Officer: E. Beekman or H. Kleinman
    New York Units: 400   National Units: 7,000
    Special Building: No   Cost: Varies
    Bldg. or Store Size: 750′ up   Type: 12

Arby's International, 17 Colonial Dr., Youngstown, Ohio

    Lease: 15 years plus, 2- to 5-year options
    Type Location: Heavy artery near shopping center
    Rental: Varies with location
    Realty Officer: LeRoy B. Raffel
    Company Units: 6   Franchise: 75
    Special Building: Yes   Cost: $70,000
    Plot Size: 3,500′   Type: 29

A to Z Rentals, Inc., 4185 Wadsworth Blvd., Wheat Ridge, Colorado

    Lease: 5 years plus 5-year option
    Type Location: Heavy traffic—retail
    Rental: $2 sq. ft. maximum per annum
    Realty Officer: Glen Mercer
    Units: Over 100
    Bldg. or Store Size: 2,000′ bldg.; 6,000′ land
    Type: 28

EXHIBIT 11-1 (Contd.)

A to Z Rentals, Inc., 201 N. Wells St., Chicago, Illinois
    Lease: 10 years plus 2- to 5-year options
    Type Location: Middle income—suburban
    Rental: $500/month vs. 7% gross
    Realty Officer: W. F. Goss
    Units: 130 in 39 states
    Special Building: Yes   Cost: $8–$10/sq. ft.
    Bldg. or Store Size: 3,000'   Type: 28
    Plot: 80' × 150'

Auto Driveway Company, 343 S. Dearborn St., Chicago, Illinois
    Lease: 5 to 10 years
    Type Location: Main street office
    Rental: $1,200 per year
    Realty Officer: Att: real estate dept.
    Type: 1

Availability, Inc., 125 N. Church St., Rockford, Illinois
    Lease: Variable
    Type Location: Main street; heavy population base
    Rental: Open
    Realty Officer: Att: real estate dept.
    Type: 13

Avis Machinery Distributors, Kenilworth, New Jersey
    Lease: 10 years plus 5-year option
    Type Location: Shopping center or free standing
    Rental: $4/sq. ft. per annum
    Realty Officer: Alan R. Liederman
    Company Units: None   Franchise: 40
    Special Building: No   Plot: 100' × 100'
    Bldg. or Store Size: 12–1,500'   Type: 12

A & W Root Beer Co., 922 Broadway, Santa Monica, California
    Lease: Long term
    Type Location: Heavy traffic drive-in; shopping centers
    Rental: Variable
    Realty Officer: Julian J. Iorio
    Franchise Units: 2,400   Plot: 22,000'
    Special Building: Yes   Cost: $40–100,000
    Bldg. or Store Size: 20' × 60' and up   Type: 29

Franchising Location and Leasing Information / 129

EXHIBIT 11-1 (Contd.)

Bailey Employment System, Inc., 3 Colony St., Meriden, Connecticut
    Lease: Varies
    Type Location: Commercial office space
    Rental: Open
    Realty Officer: Att: real estate dept.
    Type: 13

Barton Candy Corp., 80 DeKalb Ave., Brooklyn, New York
    Lease: 5–10 years
    Type Location: Heavy foot traffic
    Rental: Variable. Minimum vs. %
    Realty Officer: Albert Firstman
    Total Units: 2,550   Special Building: No
    Bldg. or Store Size: 13′ × 60′   Type: 5

Baskin Robbins, 1119 South Victory St., Burbank, California
    Lease: 10 years or longer
    Type Location: Residential backing
    Rental: $2.50 to $3.50 per sq. ft. per annum
    Realty Officer: Att: real estate dept.
    Total Units: 1,000 stores in 16 states
    Special Building: Sometimes   Cost: $2,000
    Bldg. or Store Size: 1,000′   Type: 22

Beefy's Inc., 108 W. Ninth St., Wilmington, Delaware
    Lease: 20 years
    Type Location: Highway or downtown
    Rental: $19–22,000
    Realty Officer: Daniel M. Gellan
    Company Units: 4   Franchise: Opening many
    Special Building: Yes   Cost: $75,000
    Bldg. or Store Size: 40′ × 70′   Type: 29
    Plot: 125′ × 150′

Biederman National Stores, Inc., 801 Franklin Ave., St. Louis, Missouri (American Stores)
    Lease: 20 years
    Type Location: Roadside
    Rental: 8–9% of land and building cost
    Realty Officer: P. Schaefer
    Company Units: 115   Franchise: Planned

EXHIBIT 11-1 (Contd.)

Special Building: Yes Cost: $10/sq. ft.
Bldg. or Store Size: 50,000' Type: 17

Big-Top Stores, Inc., 177 Westmoreland Ave., White Plains, New York
Lease: Long term
Type Location: Suburban, shopping center
Rental: $2 to $3/sq. ft. per annum
Realty Officer: Att: real estate dept.
Bldg. or Store Size: 3,000' Type: 40

Blimpie Corp. of America, 26 Journal Sq., Jersey City, New Jersey
Lease: 10–15 years Size: 1–2,000'
Type Location: Prime "in town" shopping Units: 73
Rental: Determined by projected gross
Realty Officer: David L. Siegal
Type: 29

Bond Stores, Inc., Fifth Ave. and 35th St., New York, N.Y.
Lease: 15–20 years
Type Location: Shopping areas or centers
Rental: 4% of gross
Realty Officer: Laurence L. Shapiro
Company Units: 150 Franchise: 13
Special Building: Yes, interior
Bldg. or Store Size: 12–15,000' Type: 8

Bronx Pressing Machine Co., Inc., 1101 E. Tremont Ave., New York, N.Y.
Lease: 10 years plus
Type Location: Main streets
Rental: $6,000/year
Realty Officer: Att: real estate dept.
Special Building: No Type: 12
Bldg. or Store Size: 1,500'

Burger Broil System, Inc., 3935 Gallatin Rd., Nashville, Tennessee
Lease: Long term
Type Location: 2,500 population in 2-mile area
Rental: $600 to $750/mo. including improvements
Realty Officer: Att: real estate dept.
Special Building: Yes Cost: $35,000
 Type: 29

Franchising Location and Leasing Information / 131

EXHIBIT 11-1 (Contd.)

Burger Castle, 1035 N. 125th St., North Miami, Florida
- Lease: 15 years
- Type Location: Heavy traffic; leading corner
- Rental: 10% of value of land and building
- Realty Officer: R. D. Webb
- Company Units: 1
- Franchise: 11
- Special Building: Yes
- Cost: $45,000
- Plot Size: 150′ × 160′
- Type: 29

Burger Chef Systems, Inc., 1348 W. 16th St., Indianapolis, Indiana
- Lease: 15 years plus 2- to 5-year options
- Type Location: Roadside; top commercial
- Rental: 8% on land, 12% on bldg. vs. 5% gross
- Realty Officer: James C. Frey
- Company Units: 15
- Franchise: 700
- Special Building: Yes
- Cost: $55,000
- Plot Size: 150′ × 150′
- Type: 29

Burger King, 3051 Coral Way, Miami, Florida
- Lease: 10 to 20 years
- Type Location: Prime corner locations
- Rental: Minimum vs. 6% of sales
- Realty Officer: James Trotter
- Company Units: 12
- Franchise: Not available
- Special Building: Yes
- Cost: $70–85,000
- Plot Size: 150′ × 150′
- Type: 29

Burger Queen Systems, Inc., Drawer 4254, Florence Villa St., Winter Haven, Florida
- Lease: Long term
- Type Location: Heavy auto traffic drive-in
- Rental: $7,500 per annum
- Realty Officer: Att: real estate dept.
- Plot Size: 150′ × 150′
- Type: 29
- Bldg. or Store Size: 2,000′

Burny Bros., Inc., 4600 Chicago Ave., Chicago, Illinois
- Lease: 10 years plus 5-year option
- Type Location: High traffic
- Rental: $10,000 vs. 4% per annum
- Realty Officer: Fred F. Ecker

EXHIBIT 11-1 (Contd.)

Company Units: 35 Franchise: 105
Bldg. or Store Size: 20′ × 75′ Type: 2

Campus Industries, 25–35 Main N., Portville, New York
    Lease: Open
    Type Location: Small office or store
    Rental: Nominal
    Realty Officer: Att: real estate dept.
    Special Building: No Type: 27

Capitol Varsity Cleaning Co., Oxford, Ohio
    Lease: 5–10 years with option
    Type Location: Shopping center
    Rental: $400/mo. vs. 7%
    Realty Officer: Robert Friedman
    Company Units: 19 Franchise: 107
    Special Building: No Type: 12
    Bldg. or Store Size: 20′ × 60′

Carey O'Madison Associates, Box 328, Bloomfeld Hills, Michigan
    Lease: Will negotiate
    Type Location: Main street or shopping center
    Rental: Moderate
    Realty Officer: Real estate dept.
    Bldg. or Store Size: Small Type: 41

Carey's Card Shops, Wrightstown, New Jersey
    Lease: 5 years plus 5-year option
    Type Location: Shopping center
    Rental: $2.50 to $3.50/sq. ft. per annum
    Realty Officer: C. J. Hughes
    Company Units: 2 Franchise: 3
    Special Building: No Type: 18
    Bldg. or Store Size: 1,000′–2,000′

Chain Locations of America, Inc., 430 Nepperhan Ave., Yonkers, New York
    All types of situations
    Franchise consultants
    Type: 10

EXHIBIT 11-1 (Contd.)

Chicken Delight, Chicken Delight Bldg., Rock Island, Illinois

    Lease: Long term
    Type Location: Shopping centers, drive-ins
    Rental: $200 to $275/month
    Realty Officer: Att: real estate dept.
    Special Building: No   Type: 29
    Bldg. or Store Size: 20' × 50'

Chip's Franchise System, Inc., P.O. Drawer 1620, Rocky Mount, North Carolina

    Lease: Long term
    Type Location: Drive-in
    Rental: $500 to $1,500/month
    Realty Officer: Att: real estate dept.
    Special Building: Yes   Cost: $50,000
    Plot Size: 2,200'   Type: 29

Chock Full O' Nuts Corp., 425 Lexington Ave., New York, N.Y.

    Lease: 30 years
    Type Location: Office building; dense shopping areas
    Rental: Varies
    Realty Officer: Att: real estate dept.
    Total Units: 41   Type: 29

City Products Corp., Box 5938, Chicago, Illinois

    Lease: Long term
    Type Location: Shopping centers; no drive-in
    Rental: 5% of gross
    Realty Officer: Att: real estate dept.
    Special Building: Yes   Cost: Varies
                                                          Type: 40

Cleanex Machinery Corp., 433 E. 148th Street, Bronx, New York

    Lease: 10 to 20 years
    Type Location: Drive-in with parking
    Rental: Varies depending on location
    Realty Officer: Att: real estate dept.
    Special Building: Yes   Cost: Varies
    Bldg. or Store Size: 3,000'   Type: 12

EXHIBIT 11-1 (Contd.)

Coast-to-Coast Stores, 7500 Excelsior Blvd., Minneapolis, Minnesota
    Lease: 5 years plus 5-year option or 15 years
    Type Location: Downtown or shopping center
    Rental: Depending on area
    Realty Officer: R. A. Pert
    Company Units: 0   Franchise: 1,080
                                    Type: 1

The Cobbs Company, Inc., Cobbs Bldg., Miami, Florida
    Lease: 15 years plus 2- to 5-year option
    Type Location: Highway—interstate
    Rental: $8 to $12,000 per annum
    Realty Officer: William Thomas
    Company Units: 20   Franchise: Not available
    Special Building: Yes   Cost: $65,000
    Bldg. or Store Size: 200′ × 200′   Type: 29

Cock-A-Doodle-Doo of America, Inc., 1250 Robin Lane N.E., Cedar Rapids, Iowa
    Lease: 10 to 15 years plus options
    Type Location: Near corner with traffic signal
    Rental: $6,000/year vs. 5% of gross
    Realty Officer: E. P. Eustice, Jr.
    Company Units: 1   Franchise: 4
    Special Building: Yes   Cost: $60,000
    Plot Size: 125′ × 150′   Type: 29

Comet Cleaners, P.O. Box 2305, W. Palm Beach, Florida
    Lease: 5–10 years
    Type Location: Convenient access; heavy traffic
    Rental: $335/mo.
    Realty Officer: Att: real estate dept.
    Company Units: 20   Franchise: 5
    Special Building: No   Cost: $25,000
    Bldg. or Store Size: 1,500′   Type: 12
    Plot Size: 2,500 sq. ft.

Commissary Corporation, 345 N. Market St., Wooster, Ohio
    Lease: 10 plus two 5-year options
    Type Location: Good commercial with residential backing
    Rental: Negotiable

EXHIBIT 11-1 (Contd.)

Realty Officer: Ron Baus
Company Units: None   Franchise: 200
Special Building: Yes   Cost: $45,000
Bldg. or Store Size: 2,000′   Type: 29
Plot Size: 15,000′

Congress International, Inc.. 7880 Biscayne Blvd., Miami, Florida

Lease: Long term
Type Location: Resort or highway location
Rental: Open
Realty Officer: Att: real estate dept.
Bldg. or Store Size: 50 units   Type: 25

Convenient Food Mart, Inc., John Hancock Center, 875 N. Michigan Ave. Chicago, Illinois

Lease: Long term   Plot: 100′ × 130′
Type Location: Urban and suburban shopping centers
Rental: $8,000 net, net
Realty Officer: Att: real estate dept.
Special Building: Yes   Cost: $40,000
Bldg. or Store Size: 3,000′   Type: 35

Convenient Food Mart of Louisville, Inc., 981 53rd St., Louisville, Kentucky

Lease: 15 years, with 2- to 5-year options
Type Location: Free-standing or "strip" centers
Rental: $8,000 net, net
Realty Officer: B. F. Miller
Company Units: 10   Franchise: 127
Special Building: Yes   Cost: $40,000
Plot Size: 12,000′   Type: 35
Bldg. or Store Size: 3,000′

Coopps, Inc., 3802 East Hazellwood St., Phoenix, Arizona

Lease: 7 to 10 years
Type Location: Shopping center, highway
Rental: Variable
Realty Officer: William J. Lord
Company Units: 3   Franchise: 1
Special Building: Hotel   Bldg. Size: 20–50,000′
Plot Size: 215 acres   Type: 25

EXHIBIT 11-1 (Contd.)

Corn Cabin Co., 1901 S. Broadway, Santa Maria, California
    Lease: Varies
    Type Location: Main street; shopping centers
    Rental: Moderate
    Realty Officer: Att: real estate dept.
    Bldg. or Store Size: 10′ × 35′   Type: 5

Cornwell Quality Tools Co., Mogadore, Ohio
    Lease: Varies
    Type Location: Drive-in
    Rental: $2,400 to $3,600 per year
    Realty Officer: Att: real estate dept.
    Special Building: No   Type: 36
    Bldg. or Store Size: 2,500′ to 10,000′

Council Mfg. Corp., 420 N. Second St., Fort Smith, Arkansas
    Lease: Long term
    Type Location: Retail on traveled street
    Rental: $100 to $300 per month
    Realty Officer: Att: real estate dept.
    Special Building: No   Type: 6
    Bldg. or Store Size: 24′ × 88′
    Plot Size: 100′ × 140′

Country Style Donuts, 406 E. Broad St., Richmond, Virginia
    Lease: Long term
    Type Location: Main street and drive-ins
    Rental: $300 to $1,100 per month
    Realty Officer: Mrs. Diane Barbuto
    Special Building: Sometimes   Cost: $40,000 to $50,000
    Bldg. or Store Size: 1,200′ to 2,700′
         Type: 29

Dari-Delite, 437 S. Hill St., Los Angeles, California
    Lease: 15 years
    Type Location: Drive-in, residential and commercial
    Rental: $450 to $550/mo.
    Realty Officer: Att: real estate dept.
    Special Building: Yes   Cost: $30,000
    Bldg. or Store Size: 28′ × 40′   Type: 22

Franchising Location and Leasing Information / 137

EXHIBIT 11-1 (Contd.)

Dairy Isle, 345 N. Market St., Wooster, Ohio
- Lease: 10 years plus 4- to 5-year options   Plot: 15,000′
- Type Location: Near shopping plazas, schools
- Rental: 10–12% of total cost
- Realty Officer: Att: Real estate officer
- Total Units: 130   Type: 29

Dairy Queen, 1412 Texas St., Bryan, Texas
- Lease: 15 years
- Type Location: Heavy auto traffic
- Rental: 6% of gross
- Realty Officer: Att: real estate dept.
- Total Units: 3,200   Type: 22
- Special Building: Yes   Cost: Varies

Dairy Sweet Co., 610 Des Moines St., Ankeny, Iowa
- Lease: Long term
- Type Location: Good population backing
- Rental: Depends on estimated gross
- Realty Officer: Att: real estate dept.
- Total Units: 300   Type: 22

Denny's Restaurants, Inc. 142–56 E. Firestone Blvd., La Mirada, California
- Lease: 20 years or purchase
- Type Location: Heavily populated
- Rental: 8–10% on land; 10–12% on bldg.
- Realty Officer: John W. Landis
- Total Units: 85   Type: 29

Denny's Restaurants, Inc., 142–56 E. Firestone Blvd., La Mirada, California
- Lease: 20 years
- Type Location: Downtown or U.S. highways
- Rental: 5% of gross
- Realty Officer: Att: real estate dept.
- Total Units: 100   Type: 29

Der Wienerschnitzel, 1047 W. Carson St., Torrance, California
- Lease: 15 with 2- to 5-year option
- Type Location: Highly traveled corners

EXHIBIT 11-1 (Contd.)

Rental: $500 to $1,000 per month
Realty Officer: James E. Rice
Company Units: 48   Franchise: 162
Special Building: Yes   Cost: $42,500
Plot Size: 125′ × 125′   Type: 29

Dog-N-Suds, Inc., 748 Arlington Heights, Illinois

Lease: 15 years   Plot: 100′ × 150′
Type Location: Drive-in
Rental: 12% on bldg., 8% on land
Realty Officer: Fred D. Coffman
Total Units: Over 500   Type: 29
Special Building: Yes   Cost: $30–45,000

Dunkenburger Self-Service Restaurant, 4680 E. Melton Rd., Gary, Indiana

Lease: 15 years
Type Location: Residential and highway
Rental: $9,000/year
Realty Officer: L. Cowan
                           Plot Size: 15′ × 100′
Special Building: Yes   Cost: $45,000
Bldg. or Store Size: 38′ × 38′   Type: 29

Dunkin Donuts, 440 Hancock St., Quincy, Massachusetts

Lease: 20 years
Type Location: Top commercial locations   Plot: 10,000′
Rental: Varies; about $9,500 net
Realty Officer: David Segal
Total Units: 580   Type: 29
Special Building: Yes, 1,500′   Cost: Varies

Eastern Sizzler, Inc., 200 Route 17, Lodi, New Jersey

Lease: 21 years
Type Location: High volume, residential
Rental: $14,000/year, no percentage
Realty Officer: Walter Hertz
Company Units: None   Franchise: 195
Special Building: Yes   Cost: $70,000
Plot Size: 25,000′   Type: 29

EXHIBIT 11-1 (Contd.)

Electone Chemical Co., 722 W. Broadway, N. Little Rock, Arkansas
    Lease: Open
    Type Location: Cities of 25,000 and larger
    Rental: $100/month
    Realty Officer: Att: real estate dept.
    Special Building: No   Type: 3

Farm Stores International, Center Suite, Du Pong Plaza, Miami, Florida
    Lease: 15 years plus 2- to 5-year options
    Type Location: Dense population
    Rental: $6,500–$7,000/year; no percentage
    Realty Officer: Melvin S. Rosenberg
    Company Units: 127   Franchise: 24
    Special Building: Yes   Cost: $20,000
        Type: 35

Felways Corp., 994 Riverview Dr., Totowa, New Jersey
    Lease: 20 years with options
    Type Location: Shopping center or free standing
    Rental: $2.50/sq. ft. vs. 4% per annum
    Realty Officer: M. J. Ruddy
    Company Units: 90   Franchise: 0
    Special Building: Yes   Cost: $75,000
    Free-Standing Plot: 30,000'   Type: 32
    Store Size: 7–10,000'

Fifth Avenue Cards, Inc., 18 W. 34th St., New York, N.Y.
    Lease: 20 years
    Type Location: 100% urban and shopping centers
    Rental: Varies
    Realty Officer: Mr. Cohen
    Company Units: 13   Franchise: 6
    Special Building: No   Type: 18
    Bldg. or Store Size: 4–5,000'

Forney Industries, Inc., Box 563, Fort Collins, Colorado
    Lease: Open
    Type Location: Main street locations
    Rental: $50 to $100
    Realty Officer: Att: real estate dept.
    Bldg. or Store Size: 40' × 40'   Type: 39

EXHIBIT 11-1 (Contd.)

Franksville, Inc., 2550 W. Peterson Ave., Chicago, Illinois
    Lease: 10 years plus 2- to 5-year options
    Type Location: Major routes
    Rental: 8% on fair valuation
    Realty Officer: Andres Mora
    Total Units: 14   Type: 29

Freez-ette Corp., 24 Madonna Blvd. Tierra Verde, Florida
    Lease: Min. 10 years
    Type Location: Walking or auto traffic
    Rental: 6–8% gross; 10–12% cost
    Realty Officer: James B. Jerles
    Company Units: 4   Franchise: 114
    Special Building: Yes   Cost: $40,000
    Bldg. or Store Size: 40' × 70'   Type: 29
    Plot Size: 130' × 150'

French Cafes, Inc., Rahdhurst Center, Mt. Prospect, Illinois
    Lease: 20 years
    Type Location: Enclosed mall shopping center
    Rental: $6/sq. ft. vs. 6% per annum
    Realty Officer: D. C. Linn
    Total Units: 11   Type: 29

Frostop Corp., 645 First Ave., New York, N.Y.
    Lease: Long term
    Type Location: Good traffic; drive-in
    Rental: Depends on area
    Realty Officer: Att: real estate dept.
    Special Building: Yes   Cost: $25–50,000
    Bldg. or Store Size: 15' × 20', 20' × 30', 25' × 40', varies
    Plot: 20,000'   Type: 29

Gaylord's, 306 W. 37th St., New York, N.Y.
    Lease: 20 years
    Type Location: Commercially developed suburbs
    Rental: Flexible
    Realty Officer: Harry Cohen
    Company Units: 17   Franchise: 2
    Special Building: Yes   Cost: $600,000
    Bldg. or Store Size: 80,000'   Type: 8
    Size Plot: 6 to 10 acres

Franchising Location and Leasing Information / 141

EXHIBIT 11-1 (Contd.)

Goubaud de Paris, Inc., 580 Fifth Ave., New York, N.Y.
- Lease: Varies
- Type Location: Main streets and shopping centers
- Rental: According to location
- Realty Officer: Att: real estate dept.
- Special Building: No   Type: 4
- Bldg. or Store Size: 12' × 50'

Grace, Helen Candies, 3303 Century Blvd., Lynwood, California
- Lease: 10–20 years
- Type Location: Regional centers
- Rental: 6–8%
- Realty Officer: Gary R. Grace
- Total Units: 18
- Special Building: No   Type: 5
- Bldg. or Store Size: 1,500'

Hampton Cleaners, 4233 Hampton Blvd., St. Louis, Missouri
- Lease: 5 years
- Type Location: Shopping centers
- Rental: 10% of gross per annum
- Realty Officer: M. Averbuch
- Company Units: 35   Franchise: 15
- Special Building: No   Type: 12
- Bldg. or Store Size: 1,000'

Happy Family, 611 N. Sacramento St., Chicago, Illinois
- Lease: 5 years
- Type Location: Regional centers
- Rental: $350/month
- Realty Officer: Edwin S. Burt
- Total Units: 78   Type: 18
- Special Building: No

Hardee's Food Systems, Inc., Rocky Mt., North Carolina
- Lease: 10–15 years with options
- Type Location: Prime corner, main artery
- Rental: 10–12% of cost vs. 5% of sales
- Realty Officer: Charles R. Granger
- Company Units: 110   Franchise: 175
- Special Building: Yes   Cost: $125,000

EXHIBIT 11-1 (Contd.)

Bldg. or Store Size: 3,600'   Type: 29
Plot: ½ acre

Harper Method, Inc., 1233 Main St., Rochester, New York
  Lease: Open
  Type Location: Main street or shopping center
  Rental: $3,600/year
  Realty Officer: Att: real estate dept.
  Special Building: No   Type: 4
  Bldg. or Store Size: 20' × 50'

Harry's Pizza, 311 Warren St., Johnston, Pennsylvania
  Lease: 5 years
  Type Location: Heavy residential
  Rental: Open
  Realty Officer: Att: real estate dept.
  Company Units: 18   Franchise: 2
  Special Building: No   Type: 29

Henry's Drive-in, Inc., 1 E. Wacker Dr., Chicago, Illinois
  Lease: 20 years
  Type Location: Corner; high population
  Rental: Going price
  Realty Officer: J. F. Dunn
  Total Units: 140   Plot: 125' × 125'
  Special Building: Yes   Cost: Varies
  Type: 29

Hilleary & Partners, Ltd., 11715 Administration Dr., St. Louis, Missouri
  Lease: 20 years
  Type Location: Shopping center
  Rental: Negotiable individually
  Realty Officer: Nancy McKown
  Company Units: 9   Franchise: 5
  Special Building: Yes   Cost: $170,000
  Bldg. or Store Size: 10,000'   Type: 29
  Plot: 40,000'

Holiday Bakers, 332 N. Main St., Freeport, New York
  Lease: Open

EXHIBIT 11-1 (Contd.)

Type Location: Main street
Rental: $6–800/month
Realty Officer: Mr. Wexler
Special Building: No   Type: 2
Bldg. or Store Size: 20' × 50'

Horne's, 2301 W. Lafayette Blvd., Detroit, Michigan

Lease: 20-year leaseback
Type Location: Within motor lodge area
Rental: Minimum vs. 2% over $300,000
Realty Officer: F. B. Drostein
Special Building: Yes   Cost: Varies
                               Type: 25

Imperial "400" National, Inc., 460 Sylvan St., Englewood Cliffs, New Jersey

Lease: Long term
Type Location: Main street and drive-in
Rental: $600 to $1,200/month
Realty Officer: Att: real estate dept.
Special Building: Yes   Cost: Variable
                               Type: 25

International Bldg. Maintenance, Blissfield, Michigan

Lease: Open
Type Location: Shopping centers
Rental: $100/month
Realty Officer: Att: real estate dept.
Special Building: No   Type: 7
Bldg. or Store Size: 30' × 50'

International House of Pancakes, 6837 Lankersheim Blvd., North Hollywood, California

Lease: 15 years plus 2- to 5-year option
Type Location: High income; high density
Rental: $15,000 vs. 5% per annum
Realty Officer: David Rappaport
Total Units: 200   Cost: $90,000
Special Building: Yes   Type: 29
Plot Size: 15,000'

EXHIBIT 11-1 (Contd.)

International Personnel Service, 17544 W. McNichols St., Detroit, Michigan

    Lease: Open
    Type Location: Main street
    Rental: $3.75 to $4.75/sq. ft. per annum
    Realty Officer: J. Heritage
    Special Building: No   Type: 13

Jerry's Restaurants, 1949 Nicholasville Rd., Lexington, Kentucky

    Lease: 15 years with options
    Type Location: U.S. route in city suburbs
    Rental: 10% of cost of land and building
    Realty Officer: Desha N. Sanders, Jr.
    Company Units: 62   Franchise: 54
    Special Building: Yes   Cost: $100,000
    Bldg. or Store Size: 4,000'   Type: 29
    Plot Size: 45,000'

Johnny-on-the-Spot, 830 Central Ave., Scarsdale, New York

    Lease: 21 years
    Type Location: Drive-in or shopping center
    Rental: $2.50/sq. ft. vs. 10% of gross
    Realty Officer: Morris Friedman
    Total Units: 43   Cost: Variable
    Special Building: Yes   Type: 12

Johnson, Howard Motor Lodges, Inc., 45 Rockefeller Plaza, New York, N.Y.

    Lease: Open
    Type Location: All types
    Rental: Variable
    Realty Officer: Att: real estate dept.
    Total Units: 750 restaurants, 250 motor lodges
    Special Building: Yes   Cost: Variable
                                           Type: 25

Jolly Giant Systems, 791 Central Ave., Scarsdale, New York

    Lease: 21 years
    Type Location: Near shopping center and residential
    Rental: $10,000 annually
    Realty Officer: Frederick V. Krak
    Total Units: 14   Type: 29

EXHIBIT 11-1 (Contd.)

Karmelkorn, Norfolk, Nebraska

    Lease: 5 years
    Type Location: Main street and shopping centers
    Rental: 18% of gross
    Realty Officer: E. W. Fleming
    Total Units: 20   Type: 5
    Special Building: No

Kelly's System of New England, 600 Taunton Ave., E. Providence, Rhode Island

    Lease: 10 years or will buy
    Type Location: Heavy commercial
    Rental: $12,000 per annum
    Realty Officer: Att: real estate dept.
    Company Units: 20
    Special Building: Yes; 2,800'   Cost: $85,000
    Plot Size: 30,000'   Type: 29

Kenney's Franchise Corp., 3032 Frontier Rd., N.W., Roanoke, Virginia

    Lease: 10 years with 5-year option
    Type Location: Main arteries
    Rental: $750/month vs. 11–12%
    Realty Officer: William Kenney
    Company Units: 25   Franchise: 4
    Special Building: Yes   Cost: $60,000
    Bldg. or Store Size: 49' × 52'   Type: 31
    Plot Size: 200' × 150'

Kent Cleaners, 17–45 Clintonville St., Whitestone, New York

    Lease: 5–10 years
    Type Location: Shopping centers; main streets
    Rental: $450/month vs. 9%, maximum
    Realty Officer: Michael Onaredo
    Total Units: 125   Type: 12
    Special Building: No
    Bldg. or Store Size: 15' × 60'

King's Food Host, U.S.A., Inc., 4701 O St., Lincoln, Nebraska

    Lease: 20 years
    Type Location: "Where the family meets"
    Rental: $1,800/month vs. 5%

EXHIBIT 11-1 (Contd.)

Realty Officer: James H. Kerrey
Company Units: 33 Franchise: 11
Special Building: Yes Cost: $80,000
Bldg. or Store Size: 60′ × 90′ Type: 29
Plot Size: 20–45,000′

K–N Root Beer Company, 1620 S. Green St., Longview, Texas

Lease: 10 years plus 5-year option
Type Location: Slow traffic and good buying area
Rental: Ground lease; $150 per month
Realty Officer: L. W. Knutson
Company Units: 9 Franchise: 52
Special Building: Yes Cost: $9–15,000
Plot Size: 110′ × 140′ Type: 29

Kramer, Sam Enterprises, 2222 Broadway, New York, N.Y.

Lease: 10–15 years
Type Location: Main street and shopping centers
Rental: $8,000 to $50,000/year
Realty Officer: Att: real estate dept.
Bldg. or Store Size: 5–15,000′ Type: 34

Kwik Kook, Inc., R.D. #1, P.O. Box 311, Coatesville, Pennsylvania

Lease: 15 years
Type Location: Shopping centers
Rental: $150 to $350/month
Realty Officer: Att: real estate dept.
Plot Size: 6-car parking
Special Building: No
Bldg. or Store Size: 6–1,200′ Type: 29

Lads & Lassies Billiard Recreation Centers, 391 Coleridge Rd., Rockville Center, New York

Lease: 10 years
Type Location: Active commercial
Rental: $2/sq. ft.
Realty Officer: Att: real estate dept.
Special Building: No
Bldg. or Store Size: 3–4,000′ Type: 34

EXHIBIT 11-1 (Contd.)

Lane's Drive-Inns, Inc., Kirksville, Missouri
- Lease: 10 years plus 5-year option
- Type Location: Corner location in downtown area
- Rental: Minimum vs. 5%
- Realty Officer: Del H. Wheeler
- Company Units: 0   Franchise: 45
- Special Building: Yes   Cost: $23,000
- Plot Size: 120' × 120'   Type: 29

Lee Myles Associates, Corp., 59-24 Maurice Ave., Maspeth, New York
- Lease: 15 years
- Type Location: Good auto traffic, service station
- Rental: $500–$850/month
- Realty Officer: c/o franchise director
- Total Units: 53
- Special Building: Sometimes   Cost: Varies
                                 Type: 37

Lester, Mary Fabrics, 325 N. Milwaukee St., Milwaukee, Wisconsin
- Lease: 5–10 years
- Type Location: Regional shopping center
- Rental: $10–$13,000 vs. 5%
- Realty Officer: Att: real estate dept.
- Company Units: 34   Franchise: 3
- Bldg. or Store Size: 4–4,500' Type: 15

Little Pigs of America, 100 N. Main Bldg., Memphis, Tennessee
- Lease: 10–15 years
- Type Location: Heavy traffic drive-ins
- Rental: $500–600/month
- Realty Officer: Att: real estate dept.
- Plot Size: 150' × 150'
- Special Building: Sometimes   Cost: $32,500
- Bldg. or Store Size: 30' × 50'   Type: 29

Loft's Candy, 38-38 Ninth St., L.I.C., New York
- Lease: 10 years
- Type Location: Shopping centers
- Rental: Variable, depends on estimates
- Realty Officer: Sydney Margolis
- Special Building: No
- Bldg. or Store Size: 12' × 60'   Type: 5

EXHIBIT 11-1 (Contd.)

Lomma Billiard Corp., 305 Cherry St., Scranton, Pennsylvania
  Lease: 10–15 years
  Type Location: Main street
  Realty Officer: Att: real estate dept.
  Special Building: No   Type: 34
  Bldg. or Store Size: 6,000′   Rental: Open

Lomma Enterprises, Inc., 305 Cherry St., Scranton, Pennsylvania
  Lease: 10–15 years
  Type Location: Main street and shopping centers
  Rental: $200 to $1,000 per month
  Realty Officer: Att: real estate dept.
  Plot Size: 10,000′   Type: 34
  Special Building: No   Franchise: 745
  Bldg. or Store Size: 2,000′; indoor or outdoor

Lone Star Donut, Inc., 1727 N. Beckley St., Dallas, Texas
  Lease: 5 years
  Type Location: Corner, main street
  Rental: Depends on location
  Realty Officer: Fred Height
  Company Units: 8   Franchise: 6
  Special Building: No   Type: 2
  Bldg. or Store Size: 25′ × 40′

Lucky Dozen Donuts, Inc., 1513 Menaul N.E., Albuquerque, New Mexico
  Lease: 15 years
  Type Location: Shopping centers
  Rental: 6% of estimated gross
  Realty Officer: Sam Pachanian
  Company Units: 1   Franchise: 4
  Bldg. or Store Size: 40′ × 85′   Type: 2

Lum's, 1959 71st St., Miami Beach, Florida
  Lease: 15 years
  Type Location: Good commercial traffic
  Rental: 6% of gross
  Realty Officer: Jay Leshaw
  Company Units: 4   Franchise: 60
  Special Building: Yes   Cost: $55,000
  Plot Size: 20,000′   Type: 29

Franchising Location and Leasing Information / 149

EXHIBIT 11-1 (Contd.)

Lusterrock International, 4203 Richmond Ave., E. Houston, Texas
- Lease: Variable
- Type Location: Shopping center, for display purposes
- Rental: Open
- Realty Officer: Att: real estate dept.
- Bldg. or Store Size: 50′ × 100′   Type: 20

Manpower, Inc., 820 N. Planilinton Ave., Milwaukee, Wisconsin
- Lease: Varies
- Type Location: Store or office space on first floor
- Rental: $275 to $350/month
- Realty Officer: Att: real estate dept.
- Bldg. or Store Size: 40′ × 100′   Type: 13

Marketing Management and Development Corp., Home Federal Tower, Hollywood, Florida
- Lease: 15 years plus options
- Type Location: Prime; high traffic count
- Rental: 10% on cost of land and building
- Realty Officer: Joseph Battaglia
- Total Units: 80   Cost: $50,000
- Special Building: Yes   Type: 10
- Plot Size: 30,000′

Martin Equipment Sales, 5000 Section Ave., Cincinnati, Ohio
- Lease: 10–15 years
- Type Location: Drive-ins
- Rental: Approximately $300 to $500/month
- Realty Officer: M. Devanney
- Bldg. or Store Size: 2,500′   Type: 12

Martin's Paint, 155-22 Jamaica Ave., Jamaica, New York
- Lease: 10–15 years
- Type Location: Main street or shopping center
- Rental: Variable depending on location
- Realty Officer: Att: Real estate dept.
- Company Units: 200   Franchise: 25
- Special Building: No   Type: 19
- Bldg. or Store Size: 5,000′

EXHIBIT 11-1 (Contd.)

Mary Carter Paint Co., Gunn Highway and Henderson Rd., Tampa, Florida

    Lease: Open
    Type Location: Free standing; high traffic; stores
    Rental: Approximately $200/month
    Realty Officer: William Lohue
    Total Units: 1,100   Type: 19
    Special Building: No

Maryland Fried Chicken, Inc., P.O. Box 452, Winter Park, Florida

    Lease: 15–20 years
    Type Location: High volume; free standing
    Rental: Generally 5% of gross
    Realty Officer: Duane C. Doherty
    Total Units: 18   Type: 29

Meyenberg Milk Products, Inc., Box 817, Industrial Ave., Ripon, California

    Lease: 15 years
    Type Location: Heavy auto traffic
    Rental: $600 to $700/month
    Realty Officer: C. H. Tiemeier
    Company Units: 3   Franchise: 232
    Special Building: Yes   Cost: $75,000
    Bldg. or Store Size: 3,000   Type: 29
    Plot Size: 14,000'

Midas, Inc., 4101 W. 42nd Place, Chicago, Illinois

    Lease: 15–20 years   Plot: 15,000'
    Type Location: Main street and drive-ins
    Rental: $12,000 to $18,000 per year
    Realty Officer: Att: real estate dept.
    Special Building: Yes   Cost: $60,000
    Bldg. or Store Size: 43' × 93'   Type: 37

Mister Donut, 89 Providence Highway, Westwood, Massachusetts

    Lease: 20 years with 2- to 10-year options
    Type Location: Suburban with shopping
    Rental: Negotiated
    Realty Officer: Donald S. King
    Total Units: 200   Type: 29

EXHIBIT 11-1 (Contd.)

Mr. Golf, Inc., 2250 South Dort Highway, Flint, Michigan

Lease: Open	
Type Location: Minimum 15,000 traffic flow	
Rental: $2,400 to $3,600/year	
Realty Officer: Att: real estate dept.	
Special Building: Yes	Plot Size: 150′ × 300′
Bldg. or Store Size: 20′ × 15′	Cost: $5/sq. ft.
	Type: 34

Mister Softee, 901 E. Clements Bridge Rd., Runnemede, New Jersey

Lease: 10 years plus 2- to 5-year options	
Type Location: High traffic count	
Rental: Depends on estimated gross	
Realty Officer: Dave Heim	
Company Units: 10	Franchise: 12
Special Building: Yes	Cost: $40–60,000
Bldg. or Store Size: 21′ × 40′	Type: 31
30′ × 45′	
40′ × 70′	

Mr. Steak, Inc., P.O. Box 5805 T.A., Denver, Colorado

Lease: 15 years plus 2- to 5-year options	
Type Location: Shopping center or free standing	
Rental: 5% of projected gross	
Realty Officer: Thomas P. Scifo	
Total Units: 40	Type: 29

Mr. Swiss of America, Inc., 14 Maiden Lane, New York, N.Y.

Lease: 10–15 years	
Type Location: Easy access, residential area	
Rental: Open	
Realty Officer: W. R. Thompson	
Company Units: 3	Franchise: 60
Special Building: Yes	Cost: $19,000
Plot Size: 100′ × 120′	Type: 29

Mr. T's Pizza, Inc., 1105 Navy Blvd., Pensacola, Florida
(c/o Tony's Pizza)

Lease: 10–15 years
Type Location: Main streets, 30,000 population

EXHIBIT 11-1 (Contd.)

Rental: $450 to $550 per month
Realty Officer: Att: real estate dept.
Plot Size: 125′ × 150′
Special Building: Yes
Cost: $25,000
Bldg. or Store Size: 44′ × 54′
Type: 29

Monterey House, 3310 S. Richey St., Houston, Texas

Lease: 20 years
Plot: 30,000′
Type Location: Main street, $7–10,000 income group, free standing
Rental: 12–13% of investment by lessor
Realty Officer: Att: real estate dept. Units: 56
Special Building: Yes
Cost: $65,000
Bldg. or Store Size: 2,700′
Type: 29

Morris Paint and Varnish Co., 27th and Douglas Sts., Omaha, Nebraska

Lease: 5–10 years
Type Location: Free standing
Rental: 5%
Realty Officer: A. Sophir
Company Units: 52
Franchise: 120
Special Building: No
Type: 19
Bldg. or Store Size: 3,000′

Mugs-Up Root Beer Co., Inc., 6235 Raytown Rd., Kansas City, Missouri

Lease: 10–15 years
Type Location: Drive-in locations
Rental: $100 to $400/month
Realty Officer: Att: real estate dept.
Special Building: Yes
Cost: $20,000
Plot Size: 150′ × 150′
Type: 29

Mulloy, Gardner, International Athletic Clubs, 9627 S. Dixie Highway, Miami, Florida

Lease: 5 years plus 5-year option
Type Location: Middle class; high density
Rental: 10–12 ½% of gross
Realty Officer: L. J. Bennet, Jr.
Total Units: 3
Type: 34

EXHIBIT 11-1 (Contd.)

Napoleon Hill Academy, P.O. Box 1721, Columbus, South Carolina
    Lease: 5–10 years
    Type Location: Drive-in, classrooms, office
    Rental: $100 to $250/month
    Realty Officer: Sidney N. Bremer
    Special Building: No   Type: 30

National Cibo House Corp., 700 N. Main Bldg., Memphis, Tennessee
    Lease: 10 years
    Type Location: Shopping centers; free standing
    Rental: $4,800/year maximum
    Realty Officer: Att: real estate dept.
    Plot Size: 100′ × 100′
    Special Building: Yes   Cost: $25,000
    Bldg. or Store Size: 1,200′   Type: 29

N.Y. Valetone Sales Corp., 133 E. Jericho Turnpike, Mineola, New York
    Lease: 10–15 years
    Type Location: Residential; shopping center
    Rental: $250/month, and up
    Realty Officer: Att: real estate dept.
    Special Building: No
    Bldg. or Store Size: 16′ × 70′ and up   Type: 12

Norman, Merle Cosmetics, 9130 Bellance Ave., Los Angeles, California
    Lease: 10 years
    Type Location: Regional or community shopping center
    Rental: $350/month vs. 6%
    Realty Officer: Jim Jertson
    Total Units: 2,500
    Special Building: No
    Bldg. or Store Size: 400′–800′   Type: 4

Oklahoma Tire & Supply, 6901 E. Pine St., Tulsa, Oklahoma
    Lease: 12 years
    Type Location: 100% downtown or shopping centers
    Rental: Negotiable rent vs. 3%
    Realty Officer: Paul Marks
    Company Units: 157   Franchise: 330
    Special Building: Yes   Cost: $85,000
    Bldg. or Store Size: 10,000′   Type: 1

EXHIBIT 11-1 (Contd.)

Olstein's U.S.A., Inc., 152 W. 42nd St., New York, N.Y.
    Lease: Moderate term
    Type Location: Main street office location
    Rental: $100–$150/month
    Realty Officer: Att: real estate dept.
    Special Building: No   Type: 13
    Bldg. or Store Size: 400'–600'

Open Pantry Food Marts, Inc., 75 E. Wacker Dr., Chicago, Illinois
    Lease: 15 years and 2- to 5-year options
    Type Location: Heavily populated
    Rental: $6,000/year or 2% of sales per annum
    Realty Officer: Harry M. Pollay
    Company Units: 0   Franchise: 192
    Special Building: Yes   Cost: $30,000
    Bldg. or Store Size: 2,500   Type: 35
    Plot Size: 50' × 125' minimum

Orange Julius of America, 6464 W. Sunset Blvd., Los Angeles, California
    Lease: Long term
    Type Location: Main street locations and regional centers
    Rental: $350 to $750/month vs. 8% of gross
    Realty Officer: Dean Miller
    Special Building: Yes   Plot Size: 60' × 100'
    Bldg. or Store Size: 20' × 40'   Cost: $25–50,000
         Type: 29

Orange Winzit Corp., 8601 Wilshire Blvd., Beverly Hills, California
    Lease: 10 years
    Type Location: Shopping centers and main streets
    Rental: $150 to $500/month
    Realty Officer: Albert A. Galston
    Total Units: 20   Plot Size: 50' × 100'
    Special Building: Sometimes   Cost: Varies
    Bldg. or Store Size: 750'   Type: 29

The Original Pancake Houses, 8601 S.W. Barbor Blvd., Portland, Oregon
    Lease: 15 years
    Type Location: Heavy auto traffic
    Rental: Minimum vs. 6% gross

EXHIBIT 11-1 (Contd.)

Realty Officer: Att: real estate dept.
Special Building: Yes   Plot Size: 100′ × 100′
Bldg. or Store Size: 2,500′ × 3,600′
                               Cost: $30,000
                               Type: 29

Palmer, Arnold Putting Course, 239 N. Missouri Ave., Atlantic City, New Jersey

Lease: Long term
Type Location: Shopping centers or drive-ins
Rental: Depending on area
Realty Officer: Att: real estate dept.
Bldg. or Store Size: 3,000′   Type: 44

Pancake Cottage Drive-in Restaurant, Box 371, Smithtown, New York

Lease: 10 years, plus 10-year option
Type Location: Highway near shopping centers
Rental: $12,000/year vs. 7%
Realty Officer: Morton Fluhr
Company Units: None   Franchise: 3
Special Building: Yes   Cost: $45,000
Bldg. or Store Size: 1,800′   Type: 29
Plot Size: 125′ × 125′

Penn-Jersey Auto Stores, Inc., 6951 State Road, Philadelphia, Pennsylvania

Lease: 10 years or 5 years plus 5-year option
Type Location: Highway near major shopping centers
Rental: $2/sq. ft. plus 4% over $150,000 gross
Realty Officer: J. L. Rounds
Company Units: 34   Franchise: 74
Special Building: No   Cost: $40,000
Bldg. or Store Size: 30′ × 100′ Type: 1
Plot Size: 9,000′

Perkins' Pancake Houses, Inc., 15076 Pearl Rd., Strongville, Ohio

Lease: 15 years
Type Location: High traffic; good income area, suburbs
Rental: $1,000–$1,800 per month
Realty Officer: R. Geer and H. W. Kochs, Jr.
Company Units: 16   Franchise: 90
Special Building: Yes   *Cost: $100,000

EXHIBIT 11-1 (Contd.)

Plot Size: 20–35,000′   Type: 29
*4 different types

Pilgrim Laundry Co., 1522 Isabella St., Houston, Texas
- Lease: 15–20 years
- Type Location: Strip center
- Rental: 6% of gross
- Realty Officer: Att: real estate dept.
- Company Units: 70   Franchise: 70
- Special Building: No
- Bldg. or Store Size: 1–5,000′   Type: 12

Pioneers, Inc., 1310 Echo Park Ave., Los Angeles, California
- Lease: Open
- Type Location: Office area
- Rental: Low
- Realty Officer: Att: real estate dept.
- Special Building: No
- Bldg. or Store Size: Small   Type: 1

Pizza Hut, Inc., 4328 E. Kellogg St., Wichita, Kansas
- Lease: 15 years with options
- Type Location: Suburban, free standing
- Rental: $600–700/month
- Realty Officer: John Songer
- Company Units: 300+   Franchise: 400+
- Special Building: Yes; 1,800′   Cost: $50,000
- Plot Size: 12–15,000′   Type: 29

Pizza Inn, Inc., 2930 Stemmons Freeway, Dallas, Texas
- Lease: 10 years
- Type Location: Free standing
- Rental: $1,200/month vs. 8% of gross
- Realty Officer: John Tenery
- Company Units: 200   Franchise: 21
- Special Building: No
- Bldg. or Store Size: 30′ × 60′   Type: 29

Pizza King Franchises, Inc., 1181 S. Bypass 52, Lafayette, Indiana
- Lease: 5 years plus 5-year option
- Type Location: Residential with heavy traffic

EXHIBIT 11-1 (Contd.)

Rental: Will negotiate
Realty Officer: Donald E. Schutz
Type: 29

Prosperity Cleaning Stores, 48–12 25th Ave., Long Island City, New York

Lease: 5–10 years
Type Location: Shopping centers or main streets
Rental: $450/month vs. 8% maximum
Realty Officer: John Pardi
Special Building: No
Bldg. or Store Size: 12' × 70'   Type: 12

Puppy Palace, 355 Letitia St., Philadelphia, Pennsylvania

Lease: 5-year lease plus 5-year option
Type Location: Regional shopping centers
Rental: $4/sq. ft. vs. 4% over $200,000
Realty Officer: Att: real estate dept.
Company Units: 5   Franchise: 45
Type: 26

Putt-Putt Golf Courses of America, P.O. Box 5237, Fayeteville, North Carolina

Lease: Open
Type Location: Center of nighttime activity
Rental: 10% of gross
Realty Officer: Att: real estate dept.
Special Building: No   Cost: Varies
Plot Size: 70,000'   Type: 34

Putt-R-Golf, Inc., 3914 W. Market St., Akron, Ohio

Lease: Variable
Type Location: Drive-in locations
Rental: Open; will negotiate
Realty Officer: Att: real estate dept.
Special Building: Yes   Cost: $22,000
Plot Size: 40,000'   Type: 34

Quality Courts Motels, Inc., 11161 New Hampshire Ave., Silver Springs, Maryland

Lease: 20 years
Type Location: Interstate ramp close to business area

EXHIBIT 11-1 (Contd.)

Rental: $800 per room per year or 25% of gross
Realty Officer: J. R. Barron
Total Units: 500 Cost: Varies
Special Building: Yes Type: 25

Rainsoft Water Conditioning Co., 1950 E. Estes Ave., Elk Grove Village, Illinois

Lease: Open
Type Location: Main street office with storage
Rental: $100 per month
Realty Officer: Att: real estate dept.
Special Building: No
Bldg. or Store Size: 800' Type: 42

Ramada Inns, Inc., P.O. Box 590, Phoenix, Arizona

Lease: 99 years with subordination
Type Location: Highway sites
Rental: 6% of land value
Realty Officer: D. M. Henward
Company Units: 32 Franchise: 83
Special Building: Yes Cost: Variable
  Type: 25

Randall's Formal Wear, Inc., 5138 W. 38th St., Denver, Colorado

Lease: 5 years with options
Type Location: Corner sites
Rental: $375/month vs. 6%
Realty Officer: C. E. Fuller
Company Units: 10 Franchise: 8
Special Building: No
Bldg. or Store Size: 2,000' Type: 38

Rayco Mfg. Co., E. 221 State Highway St., Paramus, New Jersey

Lease: 15 years plus options
Type Location: Shopping centers and drive-ins
Rental: $800–$1,200/month
Realty Officer: Gerald Graff
Total Units: 160 Plot: 20,000'
Special Building: Sometimes Cost: $60,000
Bldg. or Store Size: 4–6,000' Type: 1

EXHIBIT 11-1 (Contd.)

The Red Barn System, Inc., Suite 500, 2701 E. Sunrise Blvd., Fort Lauderdale, Florida

Lease: 15 years plus 205-year option	
Type Location: High population density; main street	
Rental: Normally $1,000 per month	
Realty Officer: Willard C. Eichenberger	
Total Units: 287	Plot: 22,500'
Special Building: Yes	Cost: $90,000
Bldg. or Store Size: 2,400'	Type: 29

Red Rams of America, Inc., 6045 W. Alameda St., Denver, Colorado

Lease: 10 years plus options	
Type Location: College town or resort city	
Rental: Varies	
Realty Officer: W. R. Seaberg	
Company Units: 1	Franchise: 9
Special Building: No	Plot: Ample parking
Bldg. or Store Size: 3–4,000'	Type: 29

The Richman Bros. Co., 1600 E. 55th St., Cleveland, Ohio

Lease: 10 years	
Type Location: Major regional shopping centers	
Rental: Varies by 4%	
Realty Officer: William F. Kennedy	
Company Units: 287	Franchise: 16
Special Building: No	
Bldg. or Store Size: 4,200'	Type: 8

Sales Research Corp., Center Suite, Dupont Plaza Center, Miami, Florida

Franchise consultants	
Many types in different areas	
	Type: 10

Sanders, Fred, 100 Oakman Blvd., Detroit, Michigan

Lease: 15 to 20 years	
Type Location: Large center or mall type	
Rental: $15,000 minimum vs. 4% of gross	
Realty Officer: Roland J. Barrette	
Company Units: 56	Franchise: 127
Special Building: Yes	Cost: $75,000
Bldg. or Store Size: 25' × 150'	Type: 29

EXHIBIT 11-1 (Contd.)

Satellite Systems, Inc., 3720 Washington Blvd., Indianapolis, Indiana
- Lease: 5 years with 3- to 5-year options
- Type Location: Dense population plus transient
- Rental: $600 per month vs. 6%
- Realty Officer: William Matthysse
- Company Units: 0
- Franchise: 25
- Special Building: *Yes
- Cost: $45,000
- Plot Size: 150' × 150'
- Type: 29
- *Manufacture their own building that can be moved

Sears, Roebuck & Co., 4640 Roosevelt Blvd., Philadelphia, Pennsylvania
- Lease: Varies from 3 years up
- Type Location: Shopping centers
- Rental: Variable
- Realty Officer: H. G. Hillard
- Company Units: 801 retail
- Franchise: 250 agencies
- Special Building: Yes
- Cost: Varies
- Type: 11

Shakey's, Inc., 887 Mitten Rd., Burlingame, California
- Lease: Long term
- Type Location: Suburban drive-in
- Rental: $800–$1,200 per month
- Realty Officer: Att: real estate dept.
- Special Building: Yes
- Plot: ½ acre
- Bldg. or Store Size: 60' × 80'
- Cost: $60,000
- Type: 29

Sherman Car Wash Equipment Co., 600 W. Broad St., Palmyra, New Jersey
- Lease: Long term (3rd party)
- Type Location: Drive-in near shopping center
- Rental: Open
- Realty Officer: Att: Real estate officer
- Special Building: Yes
- Cost: Varies $35–$75,000
- Plot Size: 75' × 150'
- Type: 6

Shoe Corporation of America, 35 N. 4th St., Columbus, Ohio
- Lease: 10–20 years
- Type Location: *Regional shopping centers
- Rental: Subject to negotiation

EXHIBIT 11-1 (Contd.)

Realty Officer: C. Philip Christie
Total Units: 898
Special Building: No   Type: 32
Bldg. or Store Size: 3,600′
*175,000′ to 200,000′ centers

The Shrimp Boats, Inc., 3078 Vineville Ave., Macon, Georgia

Lease: 10 years
Type Location: Shopping centers and drive-ins
Rental: Open
Realty Officer: Att: real estate dept.
Plot Size: 100′ × 100′   Type: 29

Shtofman, Joseph, Co., 1905 W. Bow St., Tyler, Texas

Lease: 5 years
Type Location: Downtown-intense only, shopping centers
Rental: Open to negotiation
Realty Officer: J. Shtofman
Company Units: 20   Franchise: 7
Special Building: No   Type: 32
Bldg. or Store Size: 2,500′–3,500′

Southern Dollar Stores, Inc., P.O. Drawer L, Richmond, Kentucky

Lease: 1–5 years with options
*Type Location: Traffic locations
Rental: 3% of expected volume
Realty Officer: Reuben N. Rozen
Company Units: 28   Franchise: 6
Special Building: No   Type: 40
Bldg. or Store Size: 5–10,000′
* No locations over 150 miles from Richmond, Kentucky

The Southland Corporation, 2828 N. Haskell Ave., Dallas, Texas

Lease: 15 years
Type Location: Residential neighborhood corner
Rental: Minimum against 1½%
Realty Officer: Robert D. Whitted
Company Units: 2,440   Franchise: 470
Special Building: Yes   Cost: $30,000
Bldg. or Store Size: 80′ × 120′   Type: 35

EXHIBIT 11-1 (Contd.)

Spencer Gifts Retail Stores, Inc., P.O. Box 500X, Atlantic City, New Jersey

    Lease: Long term
    Type Location: Regional and enclosed malls
    Rental: Open
    Realty Officer: Richard Z. Shur
    Total Units: 120
    Special Building: No   Type: 18
    Bldg. or Store Size: 2–2,400'

Spotless Stores, 317 9th Ave., Paterson, New Jersey

    Lease: 5–10 years
    Type Location: Shopping centers and main streets
    Rental: Maximum of $450/month vs. 8%
    Realty Officer: I. Denberg
    Total Units: 200   Type: 12
    Special Building: No
    Bldg. or Store Size: 12' × 80'

Steer Inn Systems, Inc., Benson East, Jenkintown, Pennsylvania

    Lease: Long term
    Type Location: Drive-ins; highway frontage
    Rental: $8–11,000/year
    Realty Officer: Att: real estate dept.
    Store Size: 16,000'   Cost: $45,000
    Special Building: Perferable   Type: 29
    Plot Size: 25,000'

Stein's Stores, Inc., 1600 E. 55th St., Cleveland, Ohio

    Lease: 10 years
    Type Location: Major regional centers
    Rental: Varies with location vs. 4%
    Realty Officer: William F. Kennedy
    Company Units: 281   Franchise: 16
    Special Building: No   Type: 8
    Plot Size: 4–5,000'

Stewart's Ice Cream Co., Inc., Saratoga Springs, New York

    Lease: 10 years
    Type Location: Free standing or shopping center corner
    Rental: $450/month

Franchising Location and Leasing Information / 163

EXHIBIT 11-1 (Contd.)

Realty Officer: Charles S. Dake
Company Units: 42   Franchise: 6
Special Building: No   Type: 29
Plot Size: 100' × 100'

Stewart's Root Beer, Inc., 60 Ashland Rd., Mansfield, Ohio

Lease: 10–15 years
Type Location: Main street locations
Rental: Varies
Realty Officer: J. Stewart
                          Plot Size: 200' × 200'
Special Building: Yes   Cost: $10,500
Bldg. or Store Size: 28' × 30'   Type: 29

Sveden House Developers, Inc., 5445 N. Federal H'way, Fort Lauderdale, Florida

Lease: 10 years with 2- to 5-year options
Type Location: Close to shopping center
Rental: $20,000/year
Realty Officer: Gordon L. Roberts
Company Units: 7   Franchise: 39
Special Building: Yes   Cost: $100,000
Bldg. or Store Size: 8,000'   Type: 29
Plot: 45,000'

Taco Bell, 2424 Moreton St., Torrance, California

Lease: 20 years
Type Location: Busy corner, free standing
Rental: Varies
Realty Officer: Richard Jazwin
Company Units: 55   Franchise: 365
Special Building: Yes   Cost: $45,000
Plot Size: 10,000'   Type: 29

Tastee Freez, 1200 N. Homan Ave., Chicago, Illinois

Lease: 10 years with 5-year option
Type Location: Dense traffic
Rental: $300/month vs. 5%
Realty Officer: Bernard L. Spira
Total Units: 1,500   Cost: Varies
Special Building: Yes   Type: 22
Bldg. or Store Size: 10–15,000'

EXHIBIT 11-1 (Contd.)

The Tie Rak, 19158 James Couzens Dr., Detroit, Michigan

    Lease: 10 years
    Type Location: High traffic area
    Rental: $7/sq. ft. vs. 7% per annum
    Realty Officer: Sam Dryman
    Company Units: 20   Franchise: 1
    Special Building: No   Type: 8
    Bldg. or Store Size: 15′ × 50′

Uncle John's Restaurants, Inc., 500 S. Main St., Orange, California (c/o Evirofood, Inc.)

    Lease: 20 years
    Type Location: Major boulevard near motel
    Rental: Negotiable
    Realty Officer: Paul Hultman
    Plot Size: 30,000′   Cost: $60–70,000
    Special Building: Yes   Type: 29

United Dollar Stores, Inc., Highway 54 West, Dumas, Arkansas

    Lease: 5–10 years
    Type Location: Shopping center or downtown
    Rental: 3% sales
    Realty Officer: Don Rash
    Company Units: 148   Franchise: 73
    Special Building: No
    Bldg. or Store Size: 5–15,000′   Type: 11

United Merchandising Corp., 5740 Lankersheim St., N. Hollywood, California

    Lease: 10 years plus options
    Type Location: Free standing; traffic
    Rental: Open. No per cent take
    Realty Officer: H. A. Liff
    Company Units: 10   Franchise: 5
    Special Building: Shell   Plot: 10,000′
    Bldg. or Store Size: 5,000′   Type: 1

United Rent-Alls, 10131 National Blvd., Los Angeles, California

    Lease: Open
    Type Location: Main streets with parking

EXHIBIT 11-1 (Contd.)

Rental: $200/month
Realty Officer: Att: real estate dept.
Special Building: No Type: 28
Bldg. or Store Size: 2-4,000'

The United States Shoe Corp., 1658 Herald Ave., Cincinnati, Ohio
Lease: 10-20 years
Type Location: Shopping centers or strip centers
Rental: $5 to $6/sq. ft. vs. 6%
Realty Officer: Stanley Becker
Company Units: 50 Type: 32
Bldg. or Store Size: 1,500'-3,000'

Universal Franchising, Inc., 8300 Santa Monica Blvd., Los Angeles, California
Franchise consultants
Many types in different areas

U-Tote-M, Inc., 5300 W. Loops, Houston, Texas
Lease: 15 years
Type Location: Dense residential
Rental: $350/month
Realty Officer: LeRoy Melabe
Company Units: 300 Franchise: 100
Special Building: No Plot: 100' × 125'
Bldg. or Store Size: 40' × 60' Type: 35

Village Inn, 413 N. Winfield Scott Pl., Scottsdale, Arizona
Lease: 20 years
Type Location: New residential areas, 100,000 population
Rental: $1,200/month
Realty Officer: Stanley E. Short
Total Units: 25 Type: 29

West Bros., De Ridder La., P.O. Box 569, De Ridder, Louisiana
Lease: 12 years
Type Location: Area shopping center
Rental: $1/sq. ft. vs. 2%
Realty Officer: E. D. Brandt, Jr.
Company Units: 32 Franchise: 10
Special Building: No Plot: 8 acres
Bldg. or Store Size: 35,000' Type: 11

EXHIBIT 11-1 (Contd.)

Western Auto Co., 2107 Grand Ave., Kansas City, Missouri
- Lease: 10 years
- Type Location: Shopping center
- Rental: Variable
- Realty Officer: T. V. Richeson
- Company Units: 400   Type: 1

Western Girl Inc./Western Men, Inc., 55 New Montgomery St., San Francisco, California
- Lease: Moderate
- Type Location: Office, street front locations
- Rental: $100 to $500/month
- Realty Officer: Att: real estate dept.
- Total Units: Over 100   Type: 13
- Special Building: No
- Bldg. or Store Size: Small

Because of the fantastic growth of the franchise field, it is impossible to include all of the firms seeking locations. Exhibit 11-2 contains additional firms that may be contacted. It will be necessary to secure from each firm's real estate department the same information contained in Exhibit 11-1.

EXHIBIT 11-2. Additional Franchise Sources to Be Contacted.

Allcoin Equipment Corp., 364 Livingston St., Brooklyn, New York.
All-Pro Chicken, 2945 Banksville Rd., Pittsburgh, Pennsylvania.
American Girl Service, 300 Madison Ave., New York, N.Y.
Angelo's Pizza, 811 Jefferson St., Cincinnati, Ohio.
A.P. Cleaning Center Sales, 5050 Section Ave., Cincinnati, Ohio.
Astrodine Systems, Inc., 300 W. 55th St., New York, N.Y.
Bart Starr's Huddle, 425 S. 20th St., Birmingham, Alabama.
Bath Fair, 814 W. 77½ St., Minneapolis, Minnesota.
Beltone Electronics Corp., 4201 W. Victoria St., Chicago, Illinois.
Betty Brite Associates, P.O. Box 501, Detroit, Michigan.
Big Brake, 330 W. Olympic Blvd., Los Angeles, California.
Bo Michaels' Chick "N" Treat, 1 South West St., Mt. Vernon, New York.
Bonanza International, 6116 N. Central Expressway, Dallas, Texas.
Bread Basket Corps., Penthouse A, 1001 International Bldg., Atlanta, Georgia.

EXHIBIT 11-2 (Contd.)

Bride Showcase International, Inc., 635 Madison Ave., New York, N.Y.
Buck Forty-Nine, 734 S. Carrollton Ave., New Orleans, Louisiana.
Carrol's Systems, 710 Kirkpatrick St., Syracuse, New York.
Carvel, 480 Nepperhan Ave., Yonkers, New York.
Char-Steak Hours, Inc., 1000 16th St. N. W., Washington, D.C.
Chicken Champ International, 151 E. 55th St., New York, N.Y.
Chicken Holiday, Route 18 and Tiles Lane, E. Brunswick, New York.
The Chicken Hut Systems, Inc., P.O. Drawer W, Fayetteville, Arkansas.
The Chicken Patch, 925 Livonia Ave., Brooklyn, New York.
Chicken Out, 645 First Ave., New York, N.Y.
Continental Art Galleries, 221 N. La Salle St., Suite 331F, Chicago, Illinois.
Copper Kenny, 6837 Lankersheim Blvd., N. Hollywood, California.
Cotter & Co., 2740 Clipbourn Ave., Chicago, Illinois.
Dairy Fresh Stores, c/o Genie Associates, 170 Old Country Rd., Hicksville, New York.
Davis Point Co., 1311 Iron St. N., Kansas City, Missouri.
Dean Floor Covering, 6 Eastmans Rd., Parsippany, New Jersey.
Delco Transmissions, 250 Fulton St., Brooklyn, New York.
Docktor Pet Centers, Caroline and Charter Rds., Philadelphia, Pennsylvania.
Dorothy Adams, Paints, P.O. Box 128, E. Brunswick, New Jersey.
The Downtowner Corp., 202 Union Ave., Memphis, Tennessee.
Dyna-Tune Corp., 16514 So. Vermont Ave., Gardena, California.
Dyne-Quick Division, 1020 S. McComas St., Wichita, Kansas.
Edie Adams Cut and Curl, c/o Franchises International, Inc., 285 Central Ave., White Plains, New York.
Firestone Tire and Rubber Co., Akron, Ohio.
Floating Henryburger Systems, Inc., 410 N. West St., Wichita, Kansas.
Franchise Analysts and Consultants, Inc., 930 S. La Brea Ave., Los Angeles, California.
Franchise Mart., Ltd., Centennial Plaza, St. Cloud, Minnesota.
Frederick's of Hollywood, 6608 Hollywood Blvd., Hollywood, California.
Fugazy Travel Bureau, 13–07 43rd Ave., Long Island City, New York, N.Y.
Gamble-Skogmo, Inc., 15 N. 8th St., Minneapolis, Minnesota, Att: Franchise Dept.
G.F.A. Industries, Inc., 111 W. 57th St., New York, N.Y.
Golf Players, Inc., 5952-A Brainerd Rd., Chattanooga, Tennessee.

EXHIBIT 11-2 (Contd.)

Goodway Copy Centers, 11401 Roosevelt Blvd., Philadelphia, Pennsylvania.
Happy Charley Restaurants, Inc., 27691 Euclid Ave., Euclid, Ohio.
Hardee's, P.O. Box 1619, Rocky Mount, North Carolina.
Hiah's of Baltimore, Inc., 2630 Sisson St., Baltimore, Maryland.
Honey Fried Chicken Corp., 409 Blossom St., Columbia, South Carolina.
Holiday Inns of America, 3736 Lamar Ave., Memphis, Tennessee.
Honey Fried Chicken Corp., 7334 Sumter Highway, Columbia, South Carolina.
Hot Bagel Shops, 3601 N.W. 50th St., Miami, Florida.
House of Fabrics (Gambles), 5400 Antioch Dr., Merriman, Kansas.
Howdy Beefburger Drive-ins, 440 Hancock St., Quincy, Massachusetts.
Humble Oil & Refining Co., Hutchinson River Parkway, Pelham, New York.
Hungry Lion, 7300 Biscayne Blvd., Miami, Florida.
Ice Cream Parlor Franchise, Inc., 1188 Main St., Bridgeport, Connecticut.
Inn America, Inc., 14922 Dix, Southgate, Michigan.
Jahn's, 921 E. New York Ave., Brooklyn, New York.
Jerry Lewis Cinemas, 505 Park Ave., New York, N.Y.
Jolly Troll, 444 E. Main St., Decatur, Illinois.
King George Ltd., 2750 Linden Blvd., Brooklyn, New York.
Koretizing, Inc., 457 Howard St., Buffalo, New York.
Kostick, Grant & Associates, 151 E. 55th St., New York, N.Y.
LaBeef International, Inc., 3520 W. Browane Blvd., Suite 217, Fort Lauderdale, Florida.
Lafayette Radio & Electronics, P.O. Box 10, Syosset, Long Island, New York.
Little King International, Inc., 1703 Main St., Vancouver, Washington.
Love's Enterprises, 14265 Oxnard St., Van Nuys, California.
Major Brands Food Corp., 25 Mercer St., New York, N.Y.
Manpower, 820 N. Dlankinton St., Milwaukee, Wisconsin.
McDonald's Hamburgers, 221 N. LaSalle St., Chicago, Illinois.
McManus, James H., Ice Cream Shoppes, 246 Arlington St., Quincy, Massachusetts.
Michelle International, Inc., 122 N. Tejon St., Colorado Springs, Colorado.
Mr. Fish & Chips, 4242 Campus Drive, Newport Beach, California.
Mr. Quick, Inc., 3760 41st St., Moline, Illinois.
Modular Cinemas of America, Inc., P.O. Box 1737, Atlanta, Georgia.

EXHIBIT 11-2 (Contd.)

Moo's Ice Cream Stores, 3001 MacDonald Ave., Richmond, California.
Murray, Arthur, 11 E. 43rd St., New York, N.Y.
National Mercantile Clearing House Sales Corp., 633 N.E. 125th St., Miami, Florida.
Nickerson Farms, Rt. 3, Eldon, Missouri.
Pail O'Chicken, 1996 E. St., San Bernardino, California.
Paint-A-Rama, Inc., 301 City Line Ave., Bala Cynwyd, Pennsylvania.
Pancake Man of America, 100 N. Main Bldg., Memphis, Tennessee.
Panchito's, Inc., 261 S. Mission Dr., San Gabriel, California.
Paraphernalia, 316 State St., Hackensack, New Jersey.
Pasquale Foods, Inc., 1025 Township St., Cincinnati, Ohio.
Petite Sophisticates, 6372 Hollywood Blvd., Los Angeles, California.
Pizza-on-Call, 48th St. and Indiana St., Oak Grove, Kentucky.
Radio Shack Corp., 730 Commonwealth Ave., Boston Massachusetts.
Rasco 5-10-25¢ Stores, 1840 N. Soto St., Los Angeles, California.
Red Wing Shoe Co., Inc., 113–129 Main St., Redwing, Minnesota.
Restaurant Trends Research, Box 353, Rangerly Lakes, Maine.
Robo Wash, 2 E Gregory St., Kansas City, Missouri.
R.S. Concessions, Deal Rd., Oakhurst, New Jersey.
Rudominer, David & Associates, 316 State St., Hackensack, New Jersey.
Saddleback Inns, 1655 E. 1st St., Santa Ana, California.
Sandy's Franchise, Inc., 838 Burlington Ave., Kewanee, Illinois.
Saxon's, Inc., 35 Broadmeadows Blvd., Columbus, Ohio.
Schertle Galleries, Inc., 9380 Baltimore National Pike, Ellicott City, Maryland.
Seltz Franchise Developments, 30 E. 42nd St., New York, N.Y.
Sema Wig Creations, Inc., 1267 W. Broadway, Hewlett, New York.
7 Steers Restaurants, 691 Peachtree St. N.E., Atlanta, Georgia.
Sheraton Inns, Inc., 470 Atlantic Ave., Boston, Massachusetts.
Sherry, Louis, Inc., P.O. Box E, Garden City, New York.
Siesta Sleep Shops, Inc., 221 Parkingway, Quincy, Massachusetts.
Simon-Sez Hamburgers System, 151 E. 55th St., New York, N.Y.
60-Minute Systems, Inc., 1401 Hibiscus Blvd., Melbourne, Florida.
Sizzlcbörd, c/o Mutual Franchise Corp., 33 Highland Ave., Needham Heights, Massachusetts.
Sno-Cap Root Beer Co., 7603 Forsythe Blvd., Clayton, Missouri.
Speedy Copy Centers, 845 N. Broadway, Santa Ana, California.

EXHIBIT 11-2 (Contd.)

Spudnuts, Inc., 450 W. 17th South, Salt Lake City, Utah.
Star-Ways Petroleum, Inc., 2101 14th St., Boulder, Colorado.
Status Marketing Corp., 124 E. 38th St., New York, N.Y.
Stuckey's, Inc., McRae Rd., Eastman, Georgia.
Sunnydale Franchise System, Inc., 400 Stanley Ave., Brooklyn, New York.
Taco Tio International, 4625 E. 2nd St., Long Beach, California.
Tad's Steak Houses, c/o Alexander Aronoff, 299 Madison Ave., New York, N.Y.
Tandy Leather Co., 100 Foch St., Fort Worth, Texas.
Tasty Dog, Inc., 605 Mony Building, Atlanta, Georgia.
3 Kings Steakery, 717 Merchant St., Emporia, Kansas.
Tic Tok Markets, 2588 Newport Blvd., Costa Mesa, California.
Tobacco Village, Inc., 1 Tobacco Village Rd., Cherry Hill Industrial Park, New Jersey.
Torch House Enterprises, Inc., 8743 Cooper Road, Alexandria, Virginia.
Trader Eng Hibachi Steak Houses, Inc., 300 W. Peachtree St. NW, Atlanta, Georgia.
Trini's Restaurants, Inc., Noel Page Bldg., Dallas, Texas.
Twin-Kiss, Inc., 135 N. State St., Ephrata, Pennsylvania.
Valley Forge Products, 151 E. 55th St., New York, N.Y.
Vicon Instrument Co., P.O. Box 1676, Colorado Springs, Colorado.
The Waffle House Franchise Co., 1827 Columbia Dr., Decatur, Georgia.
Wetson's Drive-in Restaurants, 30 E. Sunrise Highway, Valley Stream, New York.
What A Burger Drive-ins, P.O. Box 6742, Corpus Christi, Texas.
White Stores, Inc., 3910 Call Field Rd., Wichita Falls, Texas.
Whopper Restaurants, Inc., 7120 W. Roosevelt Rd., Oak Park, Illinois.
Wigwam Wiener International, 457 S. Robertson Blvd., Beverly Hills, California.
Wil Wright's, 8252 Santa Monica Blvd., Los Angeles, California.
Winchell's Donut House, 3200 Valhalla Dr., Burbank, California.
World of Fabrics, 1375 N. Broadway, Walnut Creek, California.
Zuider Zee, c/o Bill Martin, P.O. Box 9044, Fort Worth, Texas.

CHAIN STORES AND THEIR AVAILABILITY

12

Chain stores are similar to franchise stores, only more so. To carry out this thought, I must explain more fully. The franchise real estate director will check one of your submissions, and if he approves the location the franchise firm will then attempt to secure an operator. The chain has an advantage in that it does not have to secure an operator, but takes the store itself.

For the past two decades, the chain stores of this country have been involved in a tremendous expansion program. There has been a great influx of commercial building during the past 20 years. This mass creation of commercial building has served to provide an outlet for the expanding chains.

I have, in the following pages, set up a brief outline of a great many chain-store needs. The list is not complete, but it is comprised of a group of chains which are seeking new outlets. This group is more than ample to meet the needs of almost any store leasing broker.

HOW TO SUBMIT CHAIN LOCATIONS

When submitting your location to a chain, I would recommend the illustration in this chapter, "Store Location Report," be followed. (See Exhibit 12-1.) Starting at the top, the date of course is your date of submission. The next line should, after "Att.," contain the name of the real estate officer. Under "Location" write the address and also show by means of a diagram where the property is located. "Checked" should contain the date you last examined the property. "Basement" should be full, part, or none. "Type of Storefront" is best shown with a snapshot. "Competition" may be shown by listing businesses of the same type in the immediate area. "Type of Neighborhood" should be broken down to high, low, or middle income and also as to shopping center, main street, drive-in, factory, residential, or any combination that may exist. "Approximate Income" is the earning power per adult. An educated guess should get you close enough. If you have difficulty, I would suggest that you check as to apartment rents in the area. The monthly rental is generally close to the family's weekly take-home pay. If the area has only one-family homes, check mortgages. Estimate insurance, heat, and mortgage payments. The total will be close to the family's weekly take-home pay. Mortgages may be checked in the hall of records or general advice may be available at the local banks. "Approximate Support" is the immediate population. These figures are available from the post office or utility companies. "Future Planning" may be determined by visiting the town hall or municipal building and requesting this information. "Remarks" should contain reasons you feel will convince the client that the location is suitable for his type of operation. Be brief but accurate.

EXHIBIT 12-1. Store Location Report.

Date:

STORE LOCATION REPORT

Location: *Att:*

Town:

Checked: *Basement:* *Lease:*

Rent: *Size:* *Heat:*

Type of Storefront:

Competition:

Type of Neighborhood:

Approximate Income: *Approximate Support:*

EXHIBIT 12-1 (Contd.)

Future Planning:

Remarks:

                    Submitted by:
                    Company:
                    Address:

Exhibit 12-2 is a good list to keep handy. You may not always be able to recall the type of business needed for a vacant location. This list will help. It will also advise you as to the types of businesses included in this book.

EXHIBIT 12-2. Types of Chain Businesses Listed.

Amusement	Floor Covering
Appliances	Furniture
Auto Supply, Tires, Rentals	Haberdashery
Bakery	Hardware
Beauty Shops	Hobby
Bookshops	Hosiery
Business Aids	Jewelry
Cameras	Maternity
Candies	Paint
Cigar Stores	Restaurant
Clothing	Shoes
Department Stores	Sporting Goods
Discount	Supermarkets, Meat Stores,
Drug	Groceries, Dairy
Dry Cleaning	Variety
Employment Agency	
Fabric	

In order to simplify your looking up a particular company in a particular business, Exhibit 12-3 has been provided.

EXHIBIT 12-3. Index of Chains by Type.

Appliances: Savemart, Inc.
Auto Supply: Brewer, J.W. Tire Co.
                  Coast-to-Coast Stores
                  Friend, Inc.
                  Green Motor Parts

EXHIBIT 12-3 (Contd.)

Auto Supply: Joe the Motorist's Friend, Inc.
Kaufman & Chernick, Inc.
Lucky Auto Supply
Mashburn, Jack, Inc.
Merchants, Inc.
Miller Auto Supplies
Moore's
National Auto
Nationwide Safti-Brake Centers
Oklahoma Tire & Supply Co.
Rayco Mfg. Co.
Western Auto Supply Co.
Zippy Car Rentals, Inc.

Bakery: Eagle Baking Co.
Ebinger Baking Co.
Liberty Bakeries at Springfield, Inc.
Marilonis Pastry Shop
New York Bakery, Inc.

Beauty Shops: Goubaud de Paris, Inc.
Regis Beauty Salons, Inc.

Bookshops: Honolulu Bookshops
Walden Book Co.

Business Aids: Staff, Business & Data Aid, Inc.

Cameras: Wolfe's Camera Shop
Zercher Photo, Inc.

Candy: Dairy Gold, Inc.
Fernwood Candy & Ice Cream
Mae, Fannie, Candy Shops, Inc.
Puritan Confectionery Co. Inc.
Ricelli Candies, Inc.

Cigar Stores: Capitol Cigar Stores Co.

Clothing: Alden's, Inc. of Boston
Arnold's, Inc.
Bailey's of Boston, Inc.
Beard & Gableman, Inc.
Becker's in the Loop
Beno's Inc.
Buttrey Stores
Carol-Ann Shoppes, Inc.
Colony Shops
Crane's-Mayo's Clothes
Eleanor Shops, Inc.
Fremacs
Harris, Paul, Stores, Inc.
House of Nine
Howard Stores Corp.
Kennedy's, Inc.

Chain Stores and Their Availability / 175

EXHIBIT 12-3 (Contd.)

Clothing:
Kenwin Shops, Inc.
King Clothing Co., Inc.
Sigmond Kohn
Lanz of California, Inc.
Lerner Shops
Libson Shops, Inc.
Larkin's, C.H. Clothing Store
Lory's Fashion Shop
Lynn's Discount Centers, Inc.
Mae-Moon Associates, Inc.
Mangnin, Joseph Co.
Maurice's Apparel, Inc.
Mode O' Day Company
Modern Women
Mo-Ray Frocks
Moss Clothing Store
National Shirt Stores
Neumode Hosiery
Nobby Knit Shops
Ormond Shops, Inc.
Paris Style
Peck & Peck
Petric Stores Corp.
Princess Shops, Inc.
Rainbow Shops
Remar's
Richman Bros. Co.
Rich's
Roe, E.P. Stores
Rogers Clothiers
Roos Atkins
Rosen, George, & Sons
Sally Shops of California, Inc.
Sekulow Bros. Inc.
7–11 Fashions, Inc.
Silver Brand Clothes, Inc.
Smith's Clothiers of California
Stevens
Vogue Shops
Ward & Ward, Inc.
Webster Clothes, Inc.
Whitney Stores, Inc.

Dept. Stores:
Ayres, L.S. and Co.
Bargain Town U.S.A., Inc.
Beall, W.F. Corp.
Campbell Stores
Dixie Stores, Inc.

EXHIBIT 12-3 (Contd.)

Dept. Stores:
Fisher Bros. Dry Goods Co.
Giant Tiger Stores, Inc.
Glik's Dept. Stores
Grant, W.T.
Habich & Habich
Harris, Joseph R. Co.
Interstate Dept. Stores
Jack's Dept. Store
Kohn, Sigmond & Sons
Kuhn Brothers
Levine's, Inc.
Mays, J.W., Inc.
McDonald, J.M. Co.
Modern Women
National Stores Co.
Pearl's Warehouse
Peebles, W.S. & Co., Inc.
Perlis, I. & Sons
Quisenberry's
Raylass Dept. Store
Rechter Bros. Clothing Co.
Reny, R.H., Inc.
Royal's, Inc.
Sample
Sharpe's Dept. Stores
Sinkin, N.
Spartan Dept. Stores
Spurgeon Mercantile Co.
Weiner's Stores, Inc.
West & Co., of L. A., Inc.
Willner, M. Co., Inc.

Discount:
Bargain City
Claber Distributing Co.
Community Discount Centers
Trend Stores, Inc.
Unimart
Washington Distributors, Inc.
Yankee Distributors, Inc.

Drugstores:
Bertis Drug, Inc.
Carwood Drug Co.
Casner's Drug Co.
Colonial Drug Co., Inc.
Craft's Drugstores
Davis, Nellie, Pharmacy
Eckerd Drugs of Fla., Inc.
Elite Laundry & Dry Cleaning Co.
Enloe Drug Co.

Chain Stores and Their Availability / 177

EXHIBIT 12-3 (Contd.)

Drugstores:
Erickson Pharmacy
Fountain Cut-Rate Stores
General Discount Centers
Gray Drugstores, Inc.
Guy's Drugstores
Haag Drug Co.
Hook Drugs, Inc.
Katz & Bestihoff, Inc.
Katz Drug Co.
Key Drugs, Inc.
La Verdiere's Super Drugstores
Lane Drugstores, Inc.
Lane, Harry J. Perfume, Inc.
Lewis Drugstores
McBride's Drugs, Inc.
People's Drugstores, Inc.
Revco Drugstores Inc.
Risch Drugstores
Rite Aid
Snyder's Drugstores, Inc.
Stineway—Ford Hopkins Co.
Thrifty Drugstores
Weatherwax's Inc.
White Drug
Widman, L.F., Inc.

Dry Cleaning:
Allen Stores, Inc.
Economy Cleaners
Johnny-on-the-Spot
Kent Cleaners
La Rose Cleaners
Prosperity Cleaners
Spotless Stores
Stacey, J.T. & Co., Inc.
Sun Ray Cleaners, Inc.
Swift Service Stores
Tuchman Cleaners
Utopia Cleaners & Dyers, Inc.
Whiteway Cleaners
Whiteway Laundry, Inc.

Employment Agency: Snelling & Snelling Co.

Fabrics:
Cleveland Fabric Shops, Inc.
Fabric Tree
Giltex Corp., for Gilberg's Fabrics
Home Trading Co., Inc.
House of Fabrics
Mill End Shops, Inc.
Olan Mills, Inc.

EXHIBIT 12-3 (Contd.)

Fabrics:	Piedmont Fabrics of Charlotte, Inc.
Floor Covering:	Lewis & Lewis
Furniture:	Bearden Furniture Co., Inc.
	Ginn, M.S. & Co.
	Homestead House, Inc.
	Maxwell Bros., Inc.
	Rhodes, Inc.
	Richman Bros. Co.
	Siesta Sleep Shop
	Stark, F.M. & Co.
	Walterborf Furniture
Haberdashery:	National Shoe Co., Ltd.
Hardware:	Bubuchon, W.E.
	Gilbert of Watertown
	King Hardware Co.
	Moore's Super Stores
Hobby:	Hobby Center, Inc.
Hosiery:	Parkland Hosiery Co., Inc.
	Royal Crown Hosiery Co., Inc.
Jewelry:	Friedman Jewelers, Inc.
	Gordon Jewelry Corp.
	Jewel Boy Stores Corp.
	Kay Jewelry Store
	Marks Bros. Jewelers, Inc.
	Weisfield's, Inc.
Maternity:	Motherhood Maternity Shops
Paint and Hardware:	Aubuchon, W.E.
	Boise Cascade Corp.
	Builder's Emporium
	Gilbert of Watertown
	Grossman, L. and Sons, Inc.
	King Hardware Co.
	Kohler-McCluster Paint Co.
	Majestic Paint Centers, Inc.
	Martin's Paint Co.
	Metropolitan Paint Stores, Inc.
	Moore's Super Stores
	Savitt Bros., Inc.
	Seaman Store Co.
	Stambaugh-Thompson Co.
Restaurant:	Balbaum, William J. Co.
	Blue Boar Cafeteria
	Burg-a-Cue
	Burger Chef Systems, Inc.
	Carousel Snack Bars, Inc.
	Chock Full O' Nuts
	Clark's Restaurant Enterprises, Inc.

EXHIBIT 12-3 (Contd.)

Restaurant:
Country Style Donuts
Daly Drive-in Management Co.
Dee's, Inc.
Friendly, Inc. Cream Corp.
Frisch's Restaurants, Inc.
General Cinema Corp.
Greyhound Food Mgmt. Corp.
H & N Restaurants, Inc.
Hector's, Inc.
Hyde Park Restaurant, Inc.
Jack's Hamburgers, Inc.
Marriott Hot Shoppes
Mister Donut
Minyard's Food Stores
Newport Creamery, Inc.
Onman House Corp.
Peters Family Holdings
Pixley & Ehlers
Pope's Cafeterias, Inc.
The Red Barn System, Inc.
Restaurant Associates, Inc.
Schensul's Cafeterias, Inc.
Sidney's, Inc.
Sno-White Co., Inc.
South Carolina Drive-ins, Inc.
Thompson, John R. Co.
Union News Co.
Vallins, Addie Co.
Village Inn Pancake House, Inc.
Waldorf System, Inc.
Waid's Restaurant
Wyatt Cafeterias, Inc.

Shoe Stores:
Allied Shoe Co.
Austin Shoe Stores
Bata Shoe Co., Inc.
Bowman Shoe Co.
Butler's Shoe Corp.
Childs, H. & Co., Inc.
Cannon Shoe Co.
Endicott Johnson Corp.
Epko Shoes, Inc.
Family Booteries
Frank's Shoes, Inc.
Gallenkamp Stores Co.
   (Shoe Corporations of America)
Genesco
Harrison's Shoe Stores

EXHIBIT 12-3 (Contd.)

Shoe Stores:
Kenmore Boot Shop
Kinney Shoe Corp.
Kirby's Shoe Stores
Knapp Shoes
Kostel Corp.
Leeds Shoes, Inc.
Levine, Samuel M.
National Shoe Co., Ltd.
Ostrov, Louis Shoe Co.
Perry's Shoes
Pix Shoes
Raff's Shoes
Rollnick Shoe Co.
Schugart Shoes
Self-Service Shoe Stores, Inc.
Shelbro, Inc.
Simon, I. Co., Inc.
Sibley's Shoes
Taggurt Shoes, Inc.
Thrift Shoe Shops
Thrift Shoes, Inc.
Triangle Shoe Co.
Uncle Sam's Shoe Stores
United Shoe Stores of La., Inc.
Vogue Shoes, Inc.
Volume Shoe Corp.
Weiner Shoes, Inc.
Weiss and Neuman
Wilkerson Shoe Co.

Sporting Goods:
Andrews, Stanley Sporting Goods
Broward Sport Shops
Sport & Fischer
Triangle Stores

Supermarkets:
Albertson's, Inc.
Alpha-Beta Acme Markets, Inc.
Arden Farms Co.
Be-Lo Markets
Bernstein Bros.
Better Foods, Inc.
Big Apple Supermarkets, Inc.
Big Bear Supermarkets
Big "C" Stores
Big Chief Markets, Inc.
Boysen's Supermarkets, Inc.
Brigham's, Inc.
Buy Ryte Supermarkets
Carr's Food Center, Inc.

EXHIBIT 12-3 (Contd.)

Supermarkets:
Central Markets, Inc.
Chase's Minit Markets
Colonial Stores
Cumberland Farms Dairy, Inc.
Dan's Supreme Supermarkets
Delchamp's Food Stores
Dixieland Food Stores, Inc.
Eagle Midwestern Region (Locky Stores, Inc.)
Echol's Majik Markets
Ellner & Pike
Fedco Foods Corp.
Federal Market Co., Inc. (Meat)
Fisher Food, Inc.
Food Fair Stores, Inc.
Food Giant Markets, Inc.
Food Mart
Giant Food, Inc.
Glen-Joe Inc. (Meat)
Green Hills Supermarkets
Gristede Bros., Inc.
Hickory Farms, Inc.
Hillman's, Inc.
Home Stores, Inc.
Hy-Vee Food Stores
In & Out Corp.
Jewel Food Stores
Kash N' Karry
Kimberling's
Kohl's Food Stores
Liberal Market, Inc.
Li'l General Stores
Malone & Hyde, Inc.
March Supermarkets
Mayfair Markets
Minyard's Food Stores
Pickett's Food Stores
Publix Supermarkets, Inc.
Puckett's Food Stores
Quality Markets, Inc.
Raley's Supermarkets
Red Owl Stores, Inc.
Reeves, Peter Markets
Reynolds, F.T. Co.
Rice Food Markets
Safeway Stores, Inc.
Save Way Food Markets, Inc.

EXHIBIT 12-3 (Contd.)

Supermarkets:
Shinner, E.G. Co., Inc. (Meat)
Smith Food King
Spies' Markets
Stop & Shop, Inc. (California)
Stop & Shop, Inc. (Massachusetts)
Supermarkets General Corp.
Weigel's, Inc. (Dairy)
Weingarten, J., Inc.
Weis Markets, Inc.

Variety:
Banner Bros. Co., Inc.
Barnet-Levy Co.
Belvedere's 5 & 10 Stores
Berlin-Spillane Stores
Cornet Stores
D & C Stores, Inc.
Devenport, J.L., & Co.
88¢ Stores, Inc.
Fishman, M.H. Co., Inc.
Gilbert 5-10-25¢ Stores, Inc.
Haffner's 5¢ to $1 Stores, Inc.
Harvey's
Hornsby's 5¢ to $1 Stores, Inc.
John's Bargain Stores
Johnson's 5-10¢ to $1 Stores, Inc.
King, M.H. Co.
Kuhn Brothers
Mack's 5, 10, 25¢ Stores, Inc.
Martini Co., Inc.
Moses, M.E. Co.
Nahas Dept. Stores
National 5 & 10 to $3 Stores, Inc.
Nichols, S.E. Co.
Nichols 5¢ to $1, Inc.
Silco Cut-Price Stores, Inc.
Sprouse-Reitz Co., Inc.
Super Stores, Inc.
T., G. & Y. Stores Co.
Variety Wholesalers, Inc.
Williams 5 & 10¢ Stores, Inc.

The chains in Exhibit 12-4 have been listed by states, because of bookkeeping. This is a handy reference and a great time-saver.

EXHIBIT 12-4. Index of Chains by State.

STATE*

Alabama: Bargain Town U.S.A. Inc.   Dept. Store

EXHIBIT 12-4 (Contd.)

	Delchamp's Food Stores	Supermarket
	Dixieland Food Stores, Inc.	Supermarket
	Jack's Hamburgers, Inc.	Restaurant
	Super Stores, Inc.	Variety
	Utopia Cleaners & Dyers	Dry Cleaning
Alaska:	Bertis Drug, Inc.	Drug
	Carr's Food Center, Inc.	Supermarket
Arizona:	Eagle Baking Co., Inc.	Bakery
	Martin Co., Inc.	Variety
Arkansas:	In & Out Corp.	Supermarket
	Seaman Store Co.	Paint & Hardware
California:	Alpha-Beta Acme Markets, Inc.	Supermarket
	Andrews, Stanley Sporting Goods	Sporting Goods
	Arden Farms Co.	Supermarket
	Beno's, Inc.	Clothing
	Better Foods Inc.	Supermarket
	Big Bear Supermarkets	Supermarket
	Builder's Emporium	Hardware-Paint
	Carwood Drug Co.	Drug
	Casner's Drug Co.	Drug
	Cornet Stores	Variety
	Economy Cleaners	Dry Cleaning
	Food Giant Markets, Inc.	Supermarket
	Gilbert 5, 10, 25¢ Stores, Inc.	Variety
	Glen-Joe, Inc.	Retail Meat
	Green Motor Parts	Automotive
	Guy's Drugstores	Drug
	House of Fabrics	Fabrics
	House of Nine	Clothing
	Kirby's Shoe Stores	Shoes
	Lanz of California, Inc.	Clothing
	Lewis & Lewis	Floor Covering
	Lucky Auto Supply	Auto Supply
	Magnin, Joseph Co.	Clothing
	Mayfair Markets	Supermarkets
	Mode O' Day Co.	Clothing
	Modern Women	Clothing
	Motherhood Maternity Shops	Clothing
	Nahas Dept. Store	Clothing
	National Stores Co.	Dept. Store
	Nobby Knit Shops	Clothing
	Raley's Supermarkets	Supermarket
	Remar's	Clothing
	Rich's	Clothing

---

* Home Office.

EXHIBIT 12-4 (Contd.)

California:	Roos Atkins	Clothing
	Safeway Stores	Supermarket
	Sally Shops of Calif., Inc	Clothing
	Smith's Clothiers of California	Clothing
	Snow-White Co., Inc.	Restaurant
	Stop N' Shop, Inc.	Supermarket
	U.N. Mart	Discount
Colorado:	Homestead House, Inc.	Furniture
	Howell's	Clothing
	Kohler-McLister Paint Co.	Paint-Hardware
	Mill End Shops	Fabrics
	Rollnick Shoe Co.	Shoe
	Stark, F. M. & Co.	Furniture
	Village Inn Pancake House	Restaurant
Connecticut:	Walden Book Co.	Books
Delaware:	National 5 & 10 –$3 Stores	Variety
Florida:	Belvedere 5 & 10 Stores	Variety
	Broward Sport Shops	Sporting Goods
	Colony Shops	Clothing
	Eckerd Drugs of Fla., Inc.	Drug
	Fremac's	Clothing
	Giltex Corp. for Gilberg's Fabrics	Fabric
	Kash N' Karry	Supermarket
	Lane, Harry J. Perfume, Inc.	Drug
	Leeds Shoes, Inc.	Shoes
	Li'l General Stores, Inc.	Supermarket
	Lory's Fashion Shop	Clothing
	Moss Clothing Store	Clothing
	New York Laundry	Dry Cleaner
	Pix Shoes	Shoes
	Red Barn System, Inc.	Restaurant
	Publix Supermarkets, Inc.	Supermarket
	Royal's Inc.	Shoes
	Self-Service Shoe Stores, Inc.	Shoes
	The Vogue Shops	Clothing
Georgia:	Butler's Shoe Corp.	Shoe
	Colonial Stores	Supermarket
	Echol's Majik Mkts.	Supermarket
	Enloe Drug Co., Inc.	Drug
	Friedman's Jewelers, Inc.	Jewelry
	Glik's Dept. Stores	Dept. Store
	King Hardware Co.	Hardware
	Maxwell Brothers, Inc.	Furniture
	Perlis, I. & Sons	Dept. Store
	Rhodes, Inc.	Furniture

EXHIBIT 12-4 (Contd.)

Hawaii:	Honolulu Bookshops	Books
Idaho:	Albertson's, Inc.	Supermarket
	Boise Cascade Corp.	Paint-Hardware
	King, M.H.	Variety
Illinois:	Becker's in the Loop	Clothing
	Bowman Shoe Co.	Shoes
	Capitol Cigar Stores Co.	Cigars
	Community Discount Centers	Discount
	Eagle Midwestern Region (Lucky Stores, Inc.)	Supermarket
	Erlich's Thrift Drugs, Inc.	Drug
	Fannie May Candy Shops	Candy
	Frank's Shoes, Inc.	Shoes
	Glik's Dept. Stores	Dept. Store
	Hector's, Inc.	Restaurant
	Hillman's, Inc.	Supermarket
	Home Trading Co.	Fabrics
	Hornsby 5¢ to $1 Stores	Variety
	Jewel Food Stores	Supermarket
	Kostel Corp.	Shoes
	McBride's Drugs, Inc	Drug
	Neumode Hosiery Co.	Clothing
	Pixley & Ehlers	Restaurant
	Schucart Shoes	Shoes
	Shinner, E.G. Co., Inc.	Meat & Frozen Foods
	Spurgeon Mercantile Co.	Dept. Store
	Stineway-Ford Hopkins Co.	Drug
	Sun-Ray Cleaners, Inc.	Dry Cleaning
	Thompson, John R. Co.	Restaurant
Indiana:	Ayres, L.S. and Co.	Dept. Store
	Burger Chef Systems, Inc.	Restaurant
	Colonial Drug Co., Inc.	Drug
	Danner Bros. Co., Inc.	Variety
	Haag Drug Co.	Drug
	Haffner's 5¢ to $1 Stores, Inc.	Variety
	Harris, Paul Stores, Inc.	Clothing
	Harvey's	Variety
	Hook Drugs, Inc.	Drug
	March Supermarkets, Inc.	Supermarket
	Paris Style	Clothing
	Tuchman Cleaners	Dry Cleaning
Iowa:	Arnold's, Inc.	Clothing
	Hy-Vee Food Stores, Inc.	Supermarket
Kansas:	National Shoe Co.	Shoes
	Trend Stores, Inc.	Discount
	Volume Shoe Corp.	Shoes
	Wolfe's Camera Shop	Cameras

EXHIBIT 12-4 (Contd.)

Kentucky:	Blue Boar Cafeteria	Restaurant
	Zercher Photo, Inc.	Cameras
Louisiana:	Beall, W.F.	Dept. Store
	Dixie Stores	Dept. Store
	Katz & Besthoff, Inc.	Drug
	Mashburn, Jack, Inc.	Auto Supply
	United Shoes Stores of L.A., Inc.	Shoes
	Weiner Shoes, Inc.	Shoes
	West & Co. of L.A., Inc.	Dept. Store
Maine:	Reny, R.H., Inc.	Dept. Store
	Laverdiere's Super Drugstores	Drug
Maryland:	Bata Shoe Co., Inc.	Shoe
	Cannon Shoe Co.	Shoes
	Giant Food, Inc.	Supermarket
	Princess Shops, Inc.	Clothing
	Sekulow Bros., Inc.	Clothing
	Webster Clothes	Clothing
Massachusetts:	Alden's, Inc., of Boston	Clothing
	Allied Shoe Co.	Shoes
	Bailey's of Boston	Clothing
	Brigham's, Inc.	Supermarket
	Bubuchon, W.E.	Hardware and Paint
	Cumberland Farms Dairy	Supermarket
	Dennis Shoe Co.	Shoes
	Friendly Ice Cream Corp.	Restaurant
	General Cinema Corp.	Restaurant
	L. Grossman Sons, Inc.	Paint and Hardware
	Kennedy's, Inc.	Clothing
	Knapp Shoes	Shoes
	Lane Drugstores, Inc.	Drug
	Liberty Bakeries at Springfield, Inc.	Bakery
	Mister Donut	Restaurant
	Siesta Sleep Shop	Furniture
	Sport & Fischer	Sporting Goods
	Stop & Shop	Supermarket
Michigan:	D & C Stores, Inc.	Variety
	Daly Drive-in Management Co.	Restaurant
	Greyhound Food Management Corp.	Restaurant
	H & N Restaurants, Inc.	Restaurant
	Davis, Nellie Pharmacy	Drug
	Ricelli Candies, Inc.	Candy
	Schensul's Cafeterias, Inc.	Restaurant
	Sibely's Shoes	Shoe
	Weatherwax's, Inc.	Drug

EXHIBIT 12-4 (Contd.)

Michigan:	Yankee Distributors, Inc.	Discount
Minnesota:	Buttrey Stores, Inc.	Clothing
	Carousel Snack Bars, Inc.	Restaurant
	Coast-to-Coast Stores	Auto Supply
	Maurice's Apparel, Inc.	Clothing
	Red Owl Stores, Inc.	Supermarket
	Regis Beauty Salons, Inc.	Beauty
	Savitt Bros., Inc.	Paint and Hardware
	Snyder's Drugstores, Inc.	Drug
	Whiteway Cleaners	Dry Cleaner
Missouri:	Beard & Gabelman, Inc.	Clothing
	Green Hills Supermarket, Inc.	Supermarket
	Katz Drug Co.	Drug
	Libson Shops, Inc.	Clothing
	Pope's Cafeterias, Inc.	Restaurant
	Rechter Bros. Clothing Co.	Clothing
	Waid's Restaurant	Restaurant
	Weiss & Neuman Shoe Co.	Shoes
	Western Auto Supply Co.	Auto Supply
	Wilkerson Shoe Co.	Shoes
Montana:	Reynolds, F.T. Co.	Supermarket
Nebraska:	McDonald, J.M.	Dept. Store
Nevada:	7-11 Fashions, Inc.	Clothing
New Hampshire:	Chase's Minit Markets	Supermarket
	Puritan Confectionery Co., Inc.	Candy
New Jersey:	Levine, Samuel L.	Shoes
	Rayco Mfg. Co., Inc.	Automotive
	Rogers Clothes	Clothing
	Stevens	Clothing
	Supermarkets General Corp.	Supermarket
	Spotless Stores	Dry Cleaners
	Uncle Sam's Shoe Stores	Shoes
New York:	Bernstein Bros.	Supermarket
	Big Apple Supermarkets, Inc.	Supermarket
	Burg-a-Cue	Restaurant
	Carol Ann Shoppes, Inc.	Clothing
	Central Markets, Inc.	Supermarket
	Chock Full O' Nuts	Restaurant
	Crane's-Mayo's Clothes	Clothing
	Dan Supreme Supermarkets, Inc.	Supermarket
	Eleanor Shops, Inc.	Clothing
	Ellner & Pike	Supermarket
	Endicott Johnson Corp.	Shoes
	Fabric Tree	Fabrics
	Fedco Foods Corp.	Supermarket
	Federal Market Co., Inc.	Meat

EXHIBIT 12-4 (Contd.)

New York:	Giant Food, Inc.	Supermarket
	Ginn, M.S. Co.	Furniture
	Harris, Joseph Co.	Dept. Store
	Kay Jewelry Stores, Inc.	Jewelry
	Key Drug Co.	Drugs
	Kinney Shoe Corp.	Shoes
	Lerner Shops	Clothing
	Lory's Fashion Shops	Clothing
	Lynn's Discount Centers, Inc.	Clothing
	Mae-Moon Assoc., Inc.	Clothing
	Mays, J.W., Inc.	Dept. Store
	Mo-Ray Frocks	Clothing
	National Shirt Shops	Clothing
	Nichols, S.E. Co.	Variety
	Ormond Shops, Inc.	Clothing
	Park Lane Hosiery Co., Inc.	Hosiery
	Perl's Dept. Stores, Inc.	Dept. Store
	Peck & Peck	Clothing
	Perry's Shoes	Shoes
	Petric Stores Corp.	Clothing
	Prosperity Cleaners	Dry Cleaner
	Quality Markets, Inc.	Supermarket
	Rainbow Shops	Clothing
	Raylass Dept. Store	Dept. Store
	Reeves, Peter Markets, Inc.	Supermarket
	Restaurant Associates, Inc.	Restaurant
	The Sample	Clothing
	Savemart, Inc.	Appliances
	Save Way Food Markets, Inc.	Supermarkets
	Shelbro, Inc.	Shoes
	Simon, I. Co., Inc.	Shoes
	Spartan Dept. Stores	Dept. Store
	Staff, Business & Data Aid, Inc.	Business Aids
	Triangle Stores	Sporting Goods
	Vallins, Addie, Inc.	Restaurant
	Union News Co.	Restaurant
	Waldorf System, Inc.	Restaurant
	Whitney Stores, Inc.	Clothing
	Zippy Car Rentals	Auto Rentals
North Carolina:	Jewel Box Stores Corp.	Jewelry
	Larkin's, C.H.	Clothing
	Lowe's Companies, Inc.	Paint Hardware
	Mack's 5, 10, 25¢ Stores, Inc.	Variety
	Piedmont Fabrics of Charlotte, Inc.	Fabrics

EXHIBIT 12-4 (Contd.)

North	Pope's	Variety
Carolina:	Williams 5 & 10¢ Stores, Inc.	Variety
North		
Dakota:	White Drug	Drug
Ohio:	Allen Stores, Inc.	Dry Cleaner
	Balaun, W.J. Co.	Restaurant
	Bargain City Stores	Discount
	Claber Distributing Co.	Discount
	Cleveland Fabric Shops Co.	Fabrics
	Epko Shoes, Inc.	Shoes
	Fisher Foods, Inc.	Supermarket
	Frisch's Restaurants, Inc.	Restaurant
	Gallenkamp Stores, Inc. (Shoe Corporations of America)	Shoes
	Giant Tiger Stores, Inc.	Dept. Store
	Gray Drugstores, Inc.	Drug
	Hickory Farms of Ohio, Inc.	Supermarket (Meat and Cheese)
	Hobby Center, Inc.	Hobby Shops
	Liberal Market, Inc.	Supermarket
	Majestic Paint Centers, Inc.	Paint Store
	Moore's	Auto Supply
	New York Bakery, Inc.	Bakery
	Nichol's 5¢ to $1, Inc.	Variety
	Richman Brothers Co.	Clothing and Furniture
	Ostrov, Louis Shoe Co.	Shoes
	Revco Drugstores, Inc.	Drug
	Risch Drugstores	Drug
	Roe, E.P. Stores, Inc.	Clothing
	Stambough-Thompson Co.	Paint and Hardware
	Swift Service Stores	Dry Cleaner
	Taggart Shoes, Inc.	Shoes
	Washington Distributors	Discount
Oklahoma:	Kimberling's	Supermarket
	Mariloni's Pastry Shop	Bakery
	Oklahoma Tire & Supply Co.	Auto Supply
	Pickett's Food Stores	Supermarket
	Sharpe's Dept. Stores	Dept. Store
	T., G. & Y. Stores Co.	Variety
Oregon:	Big "C" Stores (Bazar, Inc.)	Supermarket
	The 88¢ Stores	Dept. Store
	Quisenberry's	Dept. Store
	Sprouse-Reitz Co., Inc.	Variety
	Stacey, J.T. & Co., Inc.	Dry Cleaning
Pennsyl-	Berlin Spillane Stores	Variety
vania:	Big Chief Markets, Inc.	Supermarket
	Childs, H. & Co., Inc.	Shoes

EXHIBIT 12-4 (Contd.)

Pennsylvania:	Fisher Bros. Dry Goods, Co.	Dept. Store
	Food Fair Stores, Inc.	Supermarket
	Friend, Inc.	Auto Supply
	Joe, The Motorist's Friend, Inc.	Auto Supply
	Rite Aid Centers	Discount
	Miller Auto Supplies	Auto Supply
	Silco Cut-Price Stores, Inc.	Variety
	Snelling & Snelling	Employment Agency
	Thrift Shoe Store	Shoes
	Triangle Shoe Co.	Shoes
	Waltersdorf Furniture	Furniture
	Ward and Ward, Inc.	Clothing
	Weis Markets, Inc.	Supermarket
	Widman, L.F., Inc.	Drug
Rhode Island:	Kaufman & Chernick, Inc.	Auto Supplies
	Newport Creamery, Inc.	Restaurant
South Carolina:	Craft's Drugstores	Drug
	Gilbert of Watertown	Paint-Hardware
	Jack's Dept. Store	Dept. Store
	South Carolina Drive-ins, Inc.	Restaurant
South Dakota:	Gilbert of Watertown	Hardware
	Habicht & Habicht	Dept. Store
	Lewis Drugs	Drug
	Spies' Markets	Supermarket
Tennessee:	Barnet-Levy Co.	Variety
	Buy Ryte Supermarkets	Supermarket
	Dairy Gold, Inc.	Candy
	Family Booteries	Shoes
	Genesco	Shoes
	Harrison's Shoe Stores	Shoes
	Homes Stores, Inc.	Supermarket
	Kuhn's Big K Stores Corp.	Variety
	Malone & Hyde, Inc.	Supermarket
	Olan Mills, Inc.	Fabric
	Onman House Corp.	Restaurant
	Weigel's, Inc.	Dairy
Texas:	Austin Shoe Stores	Shoes
	Bearden Furniture Co., Inc.	Furniture
	Boysen's Supermarkets	Supermarkets
	Devenport, J.L. & Co.	Variety
	Food Mart	Supermarket
	Gordon Jewelry Corp.	Jewelry
	La Rose Cleaners	Dry Cleaner
	Levine's, Inc.	Dept. Store
	Minyard's Food Stores	Grocery
	Moses, M.E. Co.	Variety

EXHIBIT 12-4 (Contd.)

Texas:	Rice Food Markets	Supermarket
	Sinkin, N.	Dept. Store
	Vogue Shoes, Inc.	Shoes
	Weiner Shoe Co.	Shoes
	Weiner's Stores, Inc.	Dept. Store
	Weingarten, Inc.	Supermarket
	Willner Co., Inc.	Dept. Store
	Wyatt Cafeterias, Inc.	Restaurant
Utah:	Brewer, J.W.	Auto Access. & Tire
	Dee's Inc.	Restaurant
	Erickson Pharmacy	Drug
	Fernwood Candy & Ice Cream	Candy
	Smith Food King	Supermarket
Virginia:	Be-Lo Markets	Supermarket
	Fountain Cut-Rate Stores	Drug
	General Discount Centers	Drug
	Johnson's 5–10¢ to $1 Stores, Inc.	Variety
	Merchants, Inc.	Auto Supply
	Moore's Super Stores	Hardwares and Paint
	Peebler, W.S. & Co., Inc.	Dept. Store
	Peters Family Holdings	Restaurant
	Sidney's, Inc.	Restaurant
	Whiteway Cleaners	Dry Cleaner
	White Way Laundry	Dry Cleaner
Washington:	Clark's Restaurant, Enterprises Inc.	Restaurant
	Pay 'n Save Drug	Drug
	Raff's Shoes	Shoes
	Thrifty Drugstores	Drug
	Weisfield's	Jewelry
	Willner, M. Co., Inc.	Dept. Store
Washington D.C.:	Harris, Joseph R. Co.	Dept. Store
	Marriott Hot Shoppes	Restaurant
	Metropolitan Paint Stores, Inc.	Paint and Hardware
	People's Drugstores, Inc.	Drug
West Virginia:	Country Style Donuts	Restaurant
	Fountain Cut-Rate Stores	Drug
	Kohn, Sigmond	Dept. Store
	National Auto	Automotive
	Rosen, George & Sons	Clothing
	Silver Brand Clothes, Inc.	Clothing
Wisconsin:	Campbell Stores	Dept. Store
	Kohl's Food Stores	Supermarket
	Royal Crown Hosiery Co., Inc.	Hosiery

CHAIN STORES—LOCATION AND LEASING INFORMATION

13

In the pages that follow, I have supplied the necessary information to get you started with chain store submissions. I have given you the name of the company, address, type of business, and most of the real estate officers.

The balance of the information gives you an outline of individual chain requirements. Make sure that your submission coincides with the respective requirements of the particular chain you are interested in. Also, be careful not to submit a location that is too close to an existing location.

EXHIBIT 13-1. Leasing Formula.

THE ABLE CORP. (AUTO ACCESSORIES)
Columbus 19,
Ohio

    BASIC LEASE PERIOD: 10 years
    TYPE LOCATION PREFERRED: Middle to high traffic, good vehicle exposure
    REAL ESTATE OFFICER: Robin A. Schmidt
    UNITS PRESENTLY OPERATED: 180
    RENTAL: Open

ALBERTSON'S, INC. (SUPERMARKET)
1610 State Street
Boise, Idaho

    BASIC LEASE PERIOD: 20 years
    TYPE LOCATION PREFERRED: Suburban shopping center
    REAL ESTATE OFFICER: D. Bills

EXHIBIT 13-1 (Contd.)

UNITS PRESENTLY OPERATED: 139
RENTAL: $1.50/square foot or 1 to 1½% of gross

ALDEN'S, INC. OF BOSTON (CLOTHING)
1040 Commonwealth St.
Boston 15, Massachusetts

BASIC LEASE PERIOD: 10 years
TYPE LOCATION PREFERRED: 100% main street or shopping center
REAL ESTATE OFFICER: D. E. Price
UNITS PRESENTLY OPERATED: 13
RENTAL: Open

ARDEN FARMS CO. (SUPERMARKET)
Post Office Box 2256
Terminal Annex
Los Angeles, California

BASIC LEASE PERIOD: 20 years
TYPE LOCATION PREFERRED: Shopping center
REAL ESTATE OFFICER: Allan S. Tingley
UNITS PRESENTLY OPERATED: 230
RENTAL: No maximum or fixed rental; 1½% of gross

ALLEN STORES, INC. (DRY CLEANERS)
60 Willard Street
Akron, Ohio

BASIC LEASE PERIOD: 5 years
TYPE LOCATION PREFERRED: Shopping center
REAL ESTATE OFFICER: Arnold C. Cohn
UNITS PRESENTLY OPERATED: 50
RENTAL: $250 and 8%

ALLIED SHOE CO. AND DENNIS SHOE CO. (SHOE)
179 Lincoln Street
Boston, Massachusetts

BASIC LEASE PERIOD: 3 to 5 years
TYPE LOCATION PREFERRED: Department stores ($5 to $15 shoe retailers)
REAL ESTATE OFFICER: Allied Shoe Co.
Herman J. Haskell
Dennis Shoe Co.
Dennis F. Maguire

EXHIBIT 13-1 (Contd.)

UNITS PRESENTLY OPERATED: 35
RENTAL: Varies

ARNOLDS, INC. (CLOTHING)
217 Second Street
Davenport, Iowa

    BASIC LEASE PERIOD: 10 years plus option
    TYPE LOCATION PREFERRED: Downtown—perhaps good shopping center
    REAL ESTATE OFFICER: Bernard C. Goldberg
    UNITS PRESENTLY OPERATED: 10
    RENTAL: $20,000 maximum, plus percentage

W.E. AUBUCHON (HARDWARE)
29 Rollstone Street
Fitchburg, Massachusetts

    BASIC LEASE PERIOD: 10 years with options
    TYPE LOCATION PREFERRED: Shopping center
    REAL ESTATE OFFICER: M. Marcus Morah
    UNITS PRESENTLY OPERATED: 97
    RENTAL: Fixed rent only. $1.25/sq. ft. with maintenance and taxes

WM. J. BALAUN CO. (RESTAURANT)
596 South Main Street
Akron, Ohio

    BASIC LEASE PERIOD: 25 years
    TYPE LOCATION PREFERRED: Good downtown and suburban
    REAL ESTATE OFFICER: John L. Balaun
    UNITS PRESENTLY OPERATED: 12
    RENTAL: Depends on property and location.

BARGAIN CITY STORES (DISCOUNT)
1225 Indiana Avenue
Toledo, Ohio

    BASIC LEASE PERIOD: 15 years
    TYPE LOCATION PREFERRED: Highway on edge of city
    REAL ESTATE OFFICER: H. R. Swolsky
    UNITS PRESENTLY OPERATED: 10
    RENTAL: $1.25 per square foot

EXHIBIT 13-1 (Contd.)

BARNETT-LEAVEY CO. (VARIETY)
Fourth and Gayoso
Memphis, Tennessee

    BASIC LEASE PERIOD: 5 years with renewal option

    TYPE LOCATION PREFERRED: Main business section
    REAL ESTATE OFFICER: Stanley I. Barnett
    UNITS PRESENTLY OPERATED: 20

BATA SHOE CO., INC. RETAIL DIVISION (SHOE)
66–67 Moravail Road
Baltimore, Maryland

    BASIC LEASE PERIOD: 10 to 20 years
    TYPE LOCATION PREFERRED: Regional shopping centers
    REAL ESTATE OFFICER: Steve Herman
    UNITS PRESENTLY OPERATED: 46
    RENTAL: 5%; rent varies

W.F. BEALL CORP. (DEPT. STORE)
1200 Captain Shreve Drive
Shreveport, Louisiana

    BASIC LEASE PERIOD: 10 years
    TYPE LOCATION PREFERRED: Downtown or suburban shopping center
    REAL ESTATE OFFICER: R. C. Ladyman
    UNITS PRESENTLY OPERATED: 23
    RENTAL: Varies

BEARD & GABELMAN, INC. (CLOTHING)
26–10–A Grand Avenue
Kansas City 8, Missouri

    BASIC LEASE PERIOD: 2-3, 5 years plus option
    TYPE LOCATION PREFERRED: Downtown large city and small towns
    REAL ESTATE OFFICER: Fred. B. Gabelman
    UNITS PRESENTLY OPERATED: 24
    RENTAL: Varies on base—5%

BEARDEN FURNITURE CO., INC. (FURNITURE)
Post Office Box 281
Jacksonville, Texas

    BASIC LEASE PERIOD: 10 years
    TYPE LOCATION PREFERRED: Free standing adjacent to shopping center
    REAL ESTATE OFFICER: J. D. Bearden

EXHIBIT 13-1 (Contd.)

UNITS PRESENTLY OPERATED: 8
RENTAL: $1.50/square foot against 4% gross sales.

BECKER'S IN THE LOOP (CLOTHING)
201 West Jackson Street
Chicago 6, Illinois

BASIC LEASE PERIOD: 10 years
TYPE LOCATION PREFERRED: Chicago Loop only
REAL ESTATE OFFICER: Leonard D. Becker
UNITS PRESENTLY OPERATED: 5
RENTAL: Open

BELVEDERE 5 & 10 STORES (VARIETY)
111 North Congress Avenue
Lake Worth, Florida

BASIC LEASE PERIOD: Open
TYPE LOCATION PREFERRED: Open
REAL ESTATE OFFICER: Att: real estate dept.
UNITS PRESENTLY OPERATED: 11
RENTAL: Open

BENO'S, INC. (CLOTHING)
1500 Santee Street
Los Angeles, California

BASIC LEASE PERIOD: 10 years
TYPE LOCATION PREFERRED: Open–California only
REAL ESTATE OFFICER: Max Salter
UNITS PRESENTLY OPERATED: 18
RENTAL: $1,000 to $1,500/mo.

BERLIN-SPILLANE STORES (VARIETY)
565 Chain Street
Norristown, Pennsylvania

BASIC LEASE PERIOD: 10 years with option
TYPE LOCATION PREFERRED: Open
REAL ESTATE OFFICER: Robert Berlin
UNITS PRESENTLY OPERATED: 10
RENTAL: Open

BERTIS DRUG, INC. (DRUG)
Box 880
Anchorage, Alaska

BASIC LEASE PERIOD: 5 years—5-year option to renew

EXHIBIT 13-1 (Contd.)

TYPE LOCATION PREFERRED:	Shopping center or downtown mall
REAL ESTATE OFFICER:	Post Office Box 880
UNITS PRESENTLY OPERATED:	3
RENTAL:	Open, depends on location

BETTER FOODS, INC. (SUPERMARKET)
6801 E. Washington Street
City of Commerce, California

BASIC LEASE PERIOD:	20–25 years
TYPE LOCATION PREFERRED:	Residential
REAL ESTATE OFFICER:	L. Cirni
UNITS PRESENTLY OPERATED:	10
RENTAL:	1½ over $1,000,000 annually

BIG BEAR SUPERMARKETS (SUPERMARKET)
5075 Federal Building
San Diego, California

BASIC LEASE PERIOD:	20 years
TYPE LOCATION PREFERRED:	Shopping Center
REAL ESTATE OFFICER:	John C. Mabee
UNITS PRESENTLY OPERATED:	15
RENTAL:	$2,000 a month (average)

BIG "C" STORES, INC. (BAZAR, INC.) (SUPERMARKET)
1845 South, East Third Avenue
Portland, Oregon

BASIC LEASE PERIOD:	15–25 years
TYPE LOCATION PREFERRED:	Shopping center—dept. store (solo or shopping center)
REAL ESTATE OFFICER:	W. C. Tirplott
UNITS PRESENTLY OPERATED:	14 supermarkets; 3 discount dept. stores
RENTAL:	8% net net—no percentage

BIG CHIEF MARKETS, INC. (SUPERMARKET)
52–54 North Main Street
Carbondale, Pennsylvania

BASIC LEASE PERIOD:	10 years
TYPE LOCATION PREFERRED:	Supermarket—parking
REAL ESTATE OFFICER:	Frank W. Gaydesh
UNITS PRESENTLY OPERATED:	5
RENTAL:	Variable

Chain Stores—Location and Leasing Information / 199

EXHIBIT 13-1 (Contd.)

BLUE BOAR CAFETERIAS, INC. (RESTAURANT)
Louisville 2, Kentucky

    BASIC LEASE PERIOD: 20 years
    TYPE LOCATION PREFERRED: Suburban shopping center, free standing
    REAL ESTATE OFFICER: L. E. Johnson, Jr.
    UNITS PRESENTLY OPERATED: 15
    RENTAL: 5% of gross sales vs. base

BOISE CASCADE CORP. (HARDWARE)
Post Office box 200
Boise, Idaho

    BASIC LEASE PERIOD: 20 years—many on railroad leases
    TYPE LOCATION PREFERRED: Accessible (contractor yards); traffic volume (retail yards)
    REAL ESTATE OFFICER: Dale C. Hatfield
    UNITS PRESENTLY OPERATED: 104
    RENTAL: Variable

BOYSEN'S SUPERMARKETS, INC. (SUPERMARKET)
Post Office Drawer 432
Yoakum, Texas

    BASIC LEASE PERIOD: 5–10 years; 5-year option
    TYPE LOCATION PREFERRED: With parking areas
    REAL ESTATE OFFICER: B. C. Boysen, Sr.
    UNITS PRESENTLY OPERATED: 7
    RENTAL: 1% to $1\frac{1}{4}$% of sales

BURG-A-CUE (RESTAURANT)
540 Third Avenue
New York 16, N.Y.

    BASIC LEASE PERIOD: 15 years
    TYPE LOCATION PREFERRED: High traffic; residential or commercial
    REAL ESTATE OFFICER: Gerald S. Rothenberg
    UNITS PRESENTLY OPERATED: 6
    RENTAL: Varies

BURGER CHEF SYSTEMS, INC. (RESTAURANT)
1350 Stadium Drive
Indianapolis 7, Indiana

    BASIC LEASE PERIOD: 10 years plus options
    TYPE LOCATION PREFERRED: Prime—commercial
    REAL ESTATE OFFICER: R. E. Wildman

EXHIBIT 13-1 (Contd.)

UNITS PRESENTLY OPERATED: 360
RENTAL: About 8% ground, 12% improvements, 5% gross sales

BUTLER'S SHOE CORP. (SHOES)
Post Office Box 4023
Atlanta 2, Georgia

BASIC LEASE PERIOD: Varies
TYPE LOCATION PREFERRED: Shopping centers; 100% downtown locations
REAL ESTATE OFFICER: Clarence Feuer, Vice-President
UNITS PRESENTLY OPERATED: 241
RENTAL: Varies

BUTTREY STORES, INC. (CLOTHING)
Box 3186 Traffic Station
Minneapolis 3, Minnesota

BASIC LEASE PERIOD: 15–20 years
TYPE LOCATION PREFERRED: Regional shopping center
REAL ESTATE OFFICER: Harry E. Buttry
UNITS PRESENTLY OPERATED: 24
RENTAL: $2 per square foot vs. 4½%

BUY RYT SUPERMARKETS (SUPERMARKET)
2029 Dodson Road
Chattanooga, Tennessee

BASIC LEASE PERIOD: 10 years
TYPE LOCATION PREFERRED: Good service store areas
REAL ESTATE OFFICER: Joseph N. Johnson
UNITS PRESENTLY OPERATED: 3
RENTAL: 1% of gross

CAMPBELL STORES (APPLIANCES)
Post Office Box 259
Appleton, Wisconsin

BASIC LEASE PERIOD: 1 to 5 years
TYPE LOCATION PREFERRED: Center of town
REAL ESTATE OFFICER: Care of real estate department
UNITS PRESENTLY OPERATED: 10
RENTAL: Own several buildings; prefer not to go over 3% gross.

EXHIBIT 13-1 (Contd.)

CAPITOL CIGAR STORES CO. (CIGARS)
11060 South Michigan Ave.
Chicago, Illinois

    BASIC LEASE PERIOD: 5 years
    TYPE LOCATION PREFERRED: Corner with foot traffic
    REAL ESTATE OFFICER: M. Ganer
    UNITS PRESENTLY OPERATED: 5
    RENTAL: Varies

CAROL-ANN SHOPPES, INC. (WOMEN'S WEAR)
55 S. Denton Avenue
New Hyde Park, New York

    BASIC LEASE PERIOD: 10 years
    TYPE LOCATION PREFERRED: 100% hub
    REAL ESTATE OFFICER: Harry Brown
    UNITS PRESENTLY OPERATED: 25
    RENTAL: Will pay going rate

CARWOOD DRUG CO. (DRUG)
4234 Woodruff Avenue
Lakewood, California

    BASIC LEASE PERIOD: 15 years
    TYPE LOCATION PREFERRED: Shopping center
    REAL ESTATE OFFICER: L. Niemerow
    UNITS PRESENTLY OPERATED: 6
    RENTAL: Open

CASNER'S DRUG CO. (DRUG)
Post Office Box 1028
Fresno, California

    BASIC LEASE PERIOD: 10 years plus 10-year option
    TYPE LOCATION PREFERRED: Shopping center suburb
    REAL ESTATE OFFICER: Jack J. Casner
    UNITS PRESENTLY OPERATED: 4
    RENTAL: 2% maximum

H. CHILDS & CO., INC. (SHOES)
1205 Madison Avenue
Pittsburgh, Pennsylvania

    BASIC LEASE PERIOD: 5 years
    TYPE LOCATION PREFERRED: Shopping center
    REAL ESTATE OFFICER: C. L. Tuttle
    UNITS PRESENTLY OPERATED: 71
    RENTAL: 5% maximum rent

EXHIBIT 13-1 (Contd.)

CHOCK FULL O' NUTS (RESTAURANT)
425 Lexington Avenue
New York, N.Y.

- BASIC LEASE PERIOD: 30 years
- TYPE LOCATION PREFERRED: Office-building area—dense shopping areas
- REAL ESTATE OFFICER: Lester Feldson, Vice-President
- UNITS PRESENTLY OPERATED: 41
- RENTAL: Varies

CLABER DISTRIBUTING CO. (DISCOUNT)
21800 Emery Road
Cleveland, Ohio

- BASIC LEASE PERIOD: 15 years plus 4- to 5-year options
- TYPE LOCATION PREFERRED: Built-up residential section
- REAL ESTATE OFFICER: John E. Wade
- UNITS PRESENTLY OPERATED: 7
- RENTAL: Varies

CLARK'S RESTAURANT ENTERPRISES: (RESTAURANT)
1319 Dexter Avenue North
Seattle, Washington

- BASIC LEASE PERIOD: 10 years
- TYPE LOCATION PREFERRED: Suburban
- REAL ESTATE OFFICER: Walter F. Clark
- UNITS PRESENTLY OPERATED: 16
- RENTAL: $1,500/month maximum

CLEVELAND FABRIC SHOPS, INC. (FABRICS)
11 Rockside Drive
Bedford, Ohio

- BASIC LEASE PERIOD: 5-year period; 5-year option
- TYPE LOCATION PREFERRED: Downtown location or neighborhood shopping centers
- REAL ESTATE OFFICER: R. A. Pert
- UNITS PRESENTLY OPERATED: 980 franchised units; 60 co-owned stores
- RENTAL: Dependent upon location conditions; 3% of sales

EXHIBIT 13-1 (Contd.)

COLONIAL DRUG CO., INC. (DRUG)
7207 Indianapolis Blvd.
Hammond, Indiana

    BASIC LEASE PERIOD: 10 years
    TYPE LOCATION PREFERRED: Medical center pharmacy
    REAL ESTATE OFFICER: Raymond Lennertz
    UNITS PRESENTLY OPERATED: 6
    RENTAL: $5 per square foot or 10% of sales

COLONIAL STORES, INC. (SUPERMARKET)
Post Office Box 4358
Atlanta, Georgia

    BASIC LEASE PERIOD: Negotiable
    TYPE LOCATION PREFERRED: Varies
    REAL ESTATE OFFICER: Lewis B. Allen
    UNITS PRESENTLY OPERATED: 434
    RENTAL: Negotiable

COLONY SHOPS (CLOTHING)
301 North Howard
Tampa, Florida

    BASIC LEASE PERIOD: 10 years
    TYPE LOCATION PREFERRED: Shopping center
    REAL ESTATE OFFICER: M. Garnett
    UNITS PRESENTLY OPERATED: 13
    RENTAL: 5%

COMMUNITY DISCOUNT CENTERS, INC. (DISCOUNT)
227 South Seeley Avenue
Chicago, Illinois

    BASIC LEASE PERIOD: 5–10 years
    TYPE LOCATION PREFERRED: Good automobile traffic
    REAL ESTATE OFFICER: Lewis Engel
    UNITS PRESENTLY OPERATED: 26
    RENTAL: Open

COUNTRY STYLE DONUTS (RESTAURANT)
PETERS FAMILY HOLDINGS, INC.
406 East Broad Street
Richmond, Virginia

    BASIC LEASE PERIOD: Long term
    TYPE LOCATION PREFERRED: Drive-in of heavy walking traffic

EXHIBIT 13-1 (Contd.)

REAL ESTATE OFFICER:	Mrs. Diane Barbuto
UNITS PRESENTLY OPERATED:	29
RENTAL:	$300 to $1,100 per month

D & C STORES, INC. (VARIETY)
Stockbridge, Michigan

BASIC LEASE PERIOD:	10 years
TYPE LOCATION PREFERRED:	Downtown or shopping center (small community)
REAL ESTATE OFFICER:	E. E. Kistler
UNITS PRESENTLY OPERATED:	35
RENTAL:	$1.25–$1.35/square foot—4% to 4½%

DAIRY GOLD, INC. (CANDY)
310 South Palisades Drive
Signal Mountain, Tennessee

BASIC LEASE PERIOD:	10 years with option for two more 10's
TYPE LOCATION PREFERRED:	Corner lots on leading thoroughfares
REAL ESTATE OFFICER:	Att: real estate dept.
UNITS PRESENTLY OPERATED:	2
RENTAL:	$360 per month ground lease

DALY DRIVE-INS (RESTAURANT)
273 South Evangeline
Dearborn Heights, Michigan

BASIC LEASE PERIOD:	15 years with two 5-year options
TYPE LOCATION PREFERRED:	Near shopping; good highway; residential
REAL ESTATE OFFICER:	Care of real estate dept.
UNITS PRESENTLY OPERATED:	11
RENTAL:	12% of investment yearly (gross)

DEE'S, INC. (RESTAURANT)
437 South Main Street
Salt Lake City, Utah

BASIC LEASE PERIOD:	10 years; 5- to 10-year options
TYPE LOCATION PREFERRED:	Open
REAL ESTATE OFFICER:	Dee F. Anderson
UNITS PRESENTLY OPERATED:	9
RENTAL:	5% gross sale

EXHIBIT 13-1 (Contd.)

J.L. DEVENPORT & CO., INC. (VARIETY)
Drawer 751
Jacksonville, Texas

    BASIC LEASE PERIOD: 5–10 years
    TYPE LOCATION PREFERRED: Shopping center and downtown
    REAL ESTATE OFFICER: R. C. Davenport
    UNITS PRESENTLY OPERATED: 11
    RENTAL: 6%

DIXIE STORES (DEPT. STORE)
Post Office Box 1507
Shreveport, Louisiana

    BASIC LEASE PERIOD: 5 years and 5-year renewal option or 10 years
    TYPE LOCATION PREFERRED: Middle of block or next to grocery
    REAL ESTATE OFFICER: J. Weinberg
    UNITS PRESENTLY OPERATED: 14
    RENTAL: 3% volume

DOG-N-SUDS, INC. (FOOD)
Post Office Box 748
Arlington Heights, Illinois

    BASIC LEASE PERIOD: 10 years with a 10-year option at same terms
    TYPE LOCATION PREFERRED: On main thoroughfare, supported by residential area and businesses
    REAL ESTATE OFFICER: Fred Coffman
    UNITS PRESENTLY OPERATED: 450
    RENTAL: Based on 12% improved and 8% on land

DUNKIN DONUTS (RESTAURANT)
440 Hancock Street
Quincy, Massachusetts

    BASIC LEASE PERIOD: 20 years
    TYPE LOCATION PREFERRED: Top commercial locations only—minimum standards—10,000 cars—traffic under 40 miles per hour; 10,000-foot lot—100-foot frontage
    REAL ESTATE OFFICER: David Segal
    UNITS PRESENTLY OPERATED: Over 200
    RENTAL: Varies

EXHIBIT 13-1 (Contd.)

EAGLE BAKING CO., INC. (BAKERY)
1126 East Sixth Street
Tuscon, Arizona

BASIC LEASE PERIOD:	Indefinite
TYPE LOCATION PREFERRED:	Near market
REAL ESTATE OFFICER:	Care of real estate dept.
UNITS PRESENTLY OPERATED:	7
RENTAL:	Percentage lease

EBINGER BAKING CO. (BAKERY)
2290 Bedford Avenue
Brooklyn, New York

BASIC LEASE PERIOD:	10–15 years, with or without option
TYPE LOCATION PREFERRED:	Food shopping
REAL ESTATE OFFICER:	Leon Beltzer
UNITS PRESENTLY OPERATED:	60
RENTAL:	Depends on location; no percentage rent

ECHOLS MAJIK MARKETS (SUPERMARKET)
(ATLANTIC CO.)
68 Brookwood Drive, N.E.
Atlanta, Georgia

BASIC LEASE PERIOD:	10 years; 5-year option
TYPE LOCATION PREFERRED:	Shopping center area
REAL ESTATE OFFICER:	Homer Jones, Gen. Manager
UNITS PRESENTLY OPERATED:	21
RENTAL:	1% on building; ½ of 1% on ground

ECKERD DRUGS OF FLORIDA (DRUG)
2120 South U.S. 19
Clearwater, Florida

BASIC LEASE PERIOD:	15 years
TYPE LOCATION PREFERRED:	Shopping centers
REAL ESTATE OFFICER:	H. B. Hendrick
UNITS PRESENTLY OPERATED:	231
RENTAL:	Open

ECONOMY CLEANERS (CLEANER)
1915 W. San Carlos Street
San Jose, California

BASIC LEASE PERIOD:	3–5 years

EXHIBIT 13-1 (Contd.)

TYPE LOCATION PREFERRED:	Neighborhood or community shopping center
REAL ESTATE OFFICER:	David H. Rosenthal
UNITS PRESENTLY OPERATED:	45
RENTAL:	$150–$200; 5% to 8%

THE 88¢ STORES (VARIETY)
252 Madison Street
Corvallis, Oregon

BASIC LEASE PERIOD:	5 years
TYPE LOCATION PREFERRED:	Downtown or free-standing with heavy car traffic
REAL ESTATE OFFICER:	Dale F. Miller
UNITS PRESENTLY OPERATED:	10
RENTAL:	$740/month or 4%

ENDICOTT JOHNSON CORP. (SHOES)
1100 East Main Street
Endicott, New York

BASIC LEASE PERIOD:	10 years with options
TYPE LOCATION PREFERRED:	Community and regional shopping center
REAL ESTATE OFFICER:	D. C. McCarthy
UNITS PRESENTLY OPERATED:	500 plus
RENTAL:	No fixed minimum or maximum

ENLOE DRUG CO., INC. (DRUG)
Post Office Box 12333
Rome, Georgia

BASIC LEASE PERIOD:	Open
TYPE LOCATION PREFERRED:	Shopping center
REAL ESTATE OFFICER:	Van P. Enloe, III
UNITS PRESENTLY OPERATED:	7
RENTAL:	Varies

EPKO SHOES, INC. (SHOES)
1401 Summit Street
Toledo, Ohio

BASIC LEASE PERIOD:	5 years
TYPE LOCATION PREFERRED:	Drive-in, highway location
REAL ESTATE OFFICER:	Robert D. Gersten
RENTAL:	8% yearly on land value; 12% yearly on improvements. $2.80 to $3.10 per sq. ft.
UNITS PRESENTLY OPERATED:	43

EXHIBIT 13-1 (Contd.)

ERICKSON PHARMACY (DRUG)
1059 E. 21st St.
Salt Lake City, Utah

    BASIC LEASE PERIOD: 10 years or 10 years and 5-year option
    TYPE LOCATION PREFERRED: Shopping center
    REAL ESTATE OFFICER: R. E. Erickson
    UNITS PRESENTLY OPERATED: 5
    RENTAL: $300+5% declining

ERLICH'S THRIFT DRUGS, INC. (DRUG)
554 North Avenue
Glendale Heights, Illinois

    BASIC LEASE PERIOD: 10 years
    TYPE LOCATION PREFERRED: Shopping centers
    REAL ESTATE OFFICER: Ben Kaufman
    UNITS PRESENTLY OPERATED: 7
    RENTAL: Varies

FAMILY BOOTERIES (SHOES)
500 Exchange Building
Nashville, Tennessee

    BASIC LEASE PERIOD: 10–15 years
    TYPE LOCATION PREFERRED: Shopping centers
    REAL ESTATE OFFICER: Marvin M. Jacobs
    UNITS PRESENTLY OPERATED: 7
    RENTAL: 5% maximum

FISHER BROS. DRY GOODS CO. (DRY GOODS)
Post Office Box 1528
New Castle, Pennsylvania

    BASIC LEASE PERIOD: 10 years
    TYPE LOCATION PREFERRED: Shopping center, free standing
    REAL ESTATE OFFICER: M. Hess
    UNITS PRESENTLY OPERATED: 30
    RENTAL: $1.00 to $1.10 per square foot; 45,000 to 60,000 square feet

M.H. FISHMAN, CO., INC. (VARIETY)
300 Park Avenue South
New York, N.Y.

    BASIC LEASE PERIOD: Varies
    TYPE LOCATION PREFERRED: Suburban location for discount department stores

EXHIBIT 13-1 (Contd.)

    REAL ESTATE OFFICER: Sanford H. Goldstein
    UNITS PRESENTLY OPERATED: 45
    RENTAL: Open

FOOD FAIR STORES, INC. (SUPERMARKET)
3175 John F. Kennedy Building
Philadelphia, Pennsylvania

    BASIC LEASE PERIOD: Generally 15 years, plus options
    TYPE LOCATION PREFERRED: Shopping center; urban, free standing
    REAL ESTATE OFFICER: Sidney Tucker, Director Northern Division
    UNITS PRESENTLY OPERATED: 619
    RENTAL: Varies $2 to $4 per square foot

FOOD MART, INC. (SUPERMARKET)
3250 West Seminary Drive
Fort Worth, Texas

    BASIC LEASE PERIOD: 12–15 years
    TYPE LOCATION PREFERRED: Free standing
    REAL ESTATE OFFICER: B. Blair, Vice-President
    UNITS PRESENTLY OPERATED: 76
    RENTAL: $1.50/square foot against 1%

FOUNTAIN CUT-RATE STORES (DRUG)
Post Office Box 1530
Clarksburg, West Virginia

    BASIC LEASE PERIOD: 10 years
    TYPE LOCATION PREFERRED: Downtown 100%
    REAL ESTATE OFFICER: Leonard Gotlieb
    UNITS PRESENTLY OPERATED: 10
    RENTAL: Variable

FREMAC'S (CLOTHING)
Post Office Box 4647
Tampa, Florida

    BASIC LEASE PERIOD: 5 years
    TYPE LOCATION PREFERRED: Medium and larger shopping centers
    REAL ESTATE OFFICER: Fred Pearlman
    UNITS PRESENTLY OPERATED: 22
    RENTAL: 5%

EXHIBIT 13-1 (Contd.)

FRIENDLY ICE CREAM CORP. (RESTAURANT)
North Wilbaham, Massachusetts

BASIC LEASE PERIOD:	10 years or buy
TYPE LOCATION PREFERRED:	Suburban, malls
REAL ESTATE OFFICER:	David M. Blair
UNITS PRESENTLY OPERATED:	95+
RENTAL:	Open

GENERAL CINEMA CORP. (THEATRE)
480 Baylston Street
Boston, Massachusetts

BASIC LEASE PERIOD:	20 years plus options
TYPE LOCATION PREFERRED:	Regional shopping centers
REAL ESTATE OFFICER:	Richard A. Smith
UNITS PRESENTLY OPERATED:	95
RENTAL:	$2 to $3 per square foot vs. 10% of sales

GENERAL DISCOUNT CENTERS (DISCOUNT)
DIVISION OF DRUG CENTERS, INC.
Post Office Box 3352
Hampton, Virginia

BASIC LEASE PERIOD:	10 years
TYPE LOCATION PREFERRED:	High automobile traffic and/or high foot traffic
REAL ESTATE OFFICER:	F. G. Woodall
UNITS PRESENTLY OPERATED:	4
RENTAL:	Variable

GENESCO (SHOES)
Post Office Box 1090
Nashville, Tennessee

BASIC LEASE PERIOD:	10 to 15 years
TYPE LOCATION PREFERRED:	100% shopping center
REAL ESTATE OFFICER:	E. L. Britain
UNITS PRESENTLY OPERATED:	About 1,500
RENTAL:	Depending on type store

GILBERT 5–10–25¢ STORES, INC. (VARIETY)
534 South Union Avenue
Los Angeles, California

BASIC LEASE PERIOD:	20 years
TYPE LOCATION PREFERRED:	Shopping center
REAL ESTATE OFFICER:	L. N. Gilbert
UNITS PRESENTLY OPERATED:	12
RENTAL:	$1.25 per foot or 4% sales

EXHIBIT 13-1 (Contd.)

GORDON JEWELRY CORP. (JEWELRY)
700 Stewart Building
Houston, Texas

    BASIC LEASE PERIOD: 5 to 10 years
    TYPE LOCATION PREFERRED: Regional shopping center
    REAL ESTATE OFFICER: Harry B. Gordon
    UNITS PRESENTLY OPERATED: 152
    RENTAL: $3.50 per square foot or 4% sales

GOUBAUD DE PARIS, INC. (BEAUTY BARS)
580 Fifth Avenue
New York, N.Y.

    BASIC LEASE PERIOD: 5–10 years (lease)
    TYPE LOCATION PREFERRED: Main street
    REAL ESTATE OFFICER: Walter Ornstein
    UNITS PRESENTLY OPERATED: About 40
    RENTAL: Depends on location and size

W.T. GRANT (DEPT. STORE)
1441 Broadway
New York, N.Y.

    BASIC LEASE PERIOD: 15 years
    TYPE LOCATION PREFERRED: Shopping centers
    REAL ESTATE OFFICER: H. S. Hopkins, Real Estate Director
    UNITS PRESENTLY OPERATED: 1,085
    RENTAL: Varies (usually $1.10 per square foot vs. %)

GRAY DRUGSTORES, INC. (DRUG)
2400 Superior Avenue
Cleveland 14, Ohio

    BASIC LEASE PERIOD: 10–20 years
    TYPE LOCATION PREFERRED: Shopping center
    REAL ESTATE OFFICER: Jerome A. Weinberger, Executive Vice-President
    RENTAL: Negotiable

GREEN MOTOR PARTS (AUTOMOTIVE)
151 North K Street
Tulare, California

    BASIC LEASE PERIOD: 10 years with 5-, 7-, or 10-year option

EXHIBIT 13-1 (Contd.)

TYPE LOCATION PREFERRED: Close to auto dealers
REAL ESTATE OFFICER: E. E. Green
UNITS PRESENTLY OPERATED: 10
RENTAL: 2% fixed rent varies from locality to locality; from $150 to $625 base rental

GRISTEDE BROS., INC. (GROCERY)
1601 Bronsdale Avenue
Bronx, N.Y.

BASIC LEASE PERIOD: 10 years
TYPE LOCATION PREFERRED: High income areas
REAL ESTATE OFFICER: F. J. Nugent
UNITS PRESENTLY OPERATED: 120
RENTAL: Will pay going rate

GUY'S DRUGSTORES (DRUG)
1600 Factor Avenue
San Leandro, California

BASIC LEASE PERIOD: 10 years
TYPE LOCATION PREFERRED: Corner—50' to 75' × 100' to 150'
REAL ESTATE OFFICER: T. Guy Shafer
UNITS PRESENTLY OPERATED: 12
RENTAL: Maximum $470

H. & N. RESTAURANTS, INC. (RESTAURANT)
11711 Woodward Avenue
Detroit, Michigan

BASIC LEASE PERIOD: 5-year to 10-year option
TYPE LOCATION PREFERRED: Downtown or shopping centers
REAL ESTATE OFFICER: William Q. Neu
UNITS PRESENTLY OPERATED: 19
RENTAL: $500 per month vs. 7%

HAAG DRUG CO. (DRUG)
506 North Davidson Street
Indianapolis, Indiana

BASIC LEASE PERIOD: 15 years with two 5-year options
TYPE LOCATION PREFERRED: Associated with high-volume supermarket
REAL ESTATE OFFICER: Care of real estate dept.
UNITS PRESENTLY OPERATED: 42

EXHIBIT 13-1 (Contd.)

RENTAL: $1.65–$3 per square foot; 2–3% of sales

HABICHT & HABICHT (DEPT. STORES)
274 Dakota Avenue South
Huron, South Dakota

    BASIC LEASE PERIOD: 5–10 years
    TYPE LOCATION PREFERRED: Downtown first floor; 50′ × 150′
    REAL ESTATE OFFICER: S. C. Habicht
    UNITS PRESENTLY OPERATED: 5
    RENTAL: $300–$500 a month

HAFFNER'S 5¢ to $1 STORES, INC. (VARIETY)
214 South Randolph Street
Garrett, Indiana

    BASIC LEASE PERIOD: 10 years, with option
    TYPE LOCATION PREFERRED: Shopping centers or small towns in Ohio, Michigan, Illinois, and Indiana
    REAL ESTATE OFFICER: A. J. Nielsen, Vice-President
    UNITS PRESENTLY OPERATED: 43
    RENTAL: Will pay going rate

HARLEE MANUFACTURING CO. (RESTAURANT)
1200 North Horman Avenue
Chicago, Illinois

    BASIC LEASE PERIOD: 10 years with 5-year option
    TYPE LOCATION PREFERRED: Traffic and pedestrian location
    REAL ESTATE OFFICER: Bernard J. Spira
    UNITS PRESENTLY OPERATED: 1,600
    RENTAL: $300 per month against 5%

JOSEPH B. HARRIS (DEPT. STORE)
1224 F. Street
Washington, D.C.

    BASIC LEASE PERIOD: 15 years
    TYPE LOCATION PREFERRED: Major regional shopping center
    REAL ESTATE OFFICER: J. Robert Harris, Jr.
    UNITS PRESENTLY OPERATED: 6
    RENTAL: $3/square foot vs. 4% overage

EXHIBIT 13-1 (Contd.)

HECTOR'S, INC. (RESTAURANT)
205 West Lake Street
Chicago 6, Illinois

BASIC LEASE PERIOD:	5 years, with options
TYPE LOCATION PREFERRED:	High traffic
REAL ESTATE OFFICER:	Edward A. Gorenstein
UNITS PRESENTLY OPERATED:	4
RENTAL:	Varies

HOBBY CENTER, INC. (HOBBY SHOPS)
7856 Hill Avenue
Holland, Ohio

BASIC LEASE PERIOD:	10 years
TYPE LOCATION PREFERRED:	Shopping centers with malls
REAL ESTATE OFFICER:	Attention: real estate dept.
UNITS PRESENTLY OPERATED:	17
RENTAL:	$500 vs. 5%

HONOLULU BOOKSHOPS (BOOKS)
1450 Ala Mana Boulevard
Honolulu, Hawaii

BASIC LEASE PERIOD:	20 years
TYPE LOCATION PREFERRED:	Major shopping centers
REAL ESTATE OFFICER:	Care of real estate dept.
UNITS PRESENTLY OPERATED:	3
RENTAL:	25¢/square foot per month or 5% sales

HOOK DRUGS, INC. (DRUGS)
2800 Enterprise Street
Indianapolis, Indiana

BASIC LEASE PERIOD:	15–20 years
TYPE LOCATION PREFERRED:	With parking at front door
REAL ESTATE OFFICER:	August F. Hook
UNITS PRESENTLY OPERATED:	76; Indiana only
RENTAL:	$1.65/square foot vs. 2%

HOUSE OF NINE (CLOTHING)
1929 West Pico Boulevard
Los Angeles, California

BASIC LEASE PERIOD:	5 years
TYPE LOCATION PREFERRED:	Regional shopping center—main mall
REAL ESTATE OFFICER:	Irving Anekstein
UNITS PRESENTLY OPERATED:	40
RENTAL:	$7 per square foot vs. 6%

EXHIBIT 13-1 (Contd.)

HOWARD STORES CORP. (MEN'S WEAR)
40 Flatbush Avenue Expressway
Brooklyn, New York

    BASIC LEASE PERIOD: 10–15 years
    TYPE LOCATION PREFERRED: Shopping centers and 100% downtown
    REAL ESTATE OFFICER: Marcel Weiss, President
    UNITS PRESENTLY OPERATED: 140
    RENTAL: 4% of gross

HOWELL'S (CLOTHING)
1961 South Federal Boulevard
Denver, Colorado

    BASIC LEASE PERIOD: 10 years—10-year option
    TYPE LOCATION PREFERRED: Suburban city
    REAL ESTATE OFFICER: Paul W. Howell, Jr.
    UNITS PRESENTLY OPERATED: 4
    RENTAL: $1.50/square foot or 3%, graduating down as volume increases

HYDE PARK RESTAURANT, INC. (RESTAURANT)
998 Madison Avenue
New York, N.Y.

    BASIC LEASE PERIOD: 21 years
    TYPE LOCATION PREFERRED: Any active area
    REAL ESTATE OFFICER: Larry Lowersten
    UNITS PRESENTLY OPERATED: 8
    RENTAL: Varies

INTERSTATE DEPT. STORES (DEPT. STORE)
111 Eighth Avenue, Room 511
New York, N.Y.

    BASIC LEASE PERIOD: 20 years
    TYPE LOCATION PREFERRED: Prime sites only
    REAL ESTATE OFFICER: Barry Golden, Vice-President
    UNITS PRESENTLY OPERATED: 90
    RENTAL: Open

JACK'S DEPT. STORE (DEPT. STORE)
Post Office Box 789
Sumter, South Carolina

    BASIC LEASE PERIOD: 3–10 years
    TYPE LOCATION PREFERRED: Out of downtown districts
    REAL ESTATE OFFICER: A. Stern

EXHIBIT 13-1 (Contd.)

UNITS PRESENTLY OPERATED: 3
RENTAL: No; percentage lease—will pay going rate

JOE, THE MOTORIST'S FRIEND, INC. (AUTO SUPPLY)
3101 North Seventh Street
Harrisburg, Pennsylvania

BASIC LEASE PERIOD: 15 years—15-year option
TYPE LOCATION PREFERRED: Shopping center
REAL ESTATE OFFICER: Joseph R. Stine
UNITS PRESENTLY OPERATED: 36
RENTAL: $800 vs. 4%

JOHN'S BARGAIN STORES (VARIETY)
134 Jackson Street
Hempstead, New York

BASIC LEASE PERIOD: 10–15 years
TYPE LOCATION PREFERRED: Main street; shopping center
REAL ESTATE OFFICER: Care of real estate dept.
UNITS PRESENTLY OPERATED: Over 400
RENTAL: Open

JOHNNY-ON-THE-SPOT (DRY CLEANING)
830 Central Avenue
Scarsdale, New York

BASIC LEASE PERIOD: 21 years
TYPE LOCATION PREFERRED: Drive-ins or shopping centers
REAL ESTATE OFFICER: Morris Freidman
UNITS PRESENTLY OPERATED: 43
RENTAL: From $2.50/square foot vs. 10% sales

KATZ DRUG CO. (DRUG)
Kansas City, Missouri

BASIC LEASE PERIOD: Varies 5 to 20 years
TYPE LOCATION PREFERRED: Varies greatly by city; some regional centers, some free standing
REAL ESTATE OFFICER: Earl S. Katz
UNITS PRESENTLY OPERATED: 45
RENTAL: Open

KENMORE BOOT SHOP (SHOES)
2872 Delaware Avenue
Kenmore, New York

BASIC LEASE PERIOD: 3 years, with 2-year option

EXHIBIT 13-1 (Contd.)

TYPE LOCATION PREFERRED:	Close to a plaza
REAL ESTATE OFFICER:	None
UNITS PRESENTLY OPERATED:	4
RENTAL:	Varies

KENNEDY'S, INC. (CLOTHING)
Sunner and Hawley Street
Boston, Massachusetts

BASIC LEASE PERIOD:	Not to exceed 15 years
TYPE LOCATION PREFERRED:	12,000–15,000 feet; regional shopping center
REAL ESTATE OFFICER:	Herbert M. Weiss
UNITS PRESENTLY OPERATED:	35
RENTAL:	Negotiable

KENT CLEANERS (CLEANERS)
17–45 Clintonville Street
Whitestone, New York

BASIC LEASE PERIOD:	5–10 years
TYPE LOCATION PREFERRED:	Shopping centers or main streets
REAL ESTATE OFFICER:	Michael Onarado
UNITS PRESENTLY OPERATED:	125
RENTAL:	8% of gross, with guaranteed minimum

KENWIN SHOPS, INC. (CLOTHING)
505 Eighth Avenue
New York, N.Y.

BASIC LEASE PERIOD:	5–10 years
TYPE LOCATION PREFERRED:	Main street; shopping center
REAL ESTATE OFFICER:	Philip Abramson
UNITS PRESENTLY OPERATED:	56
RENTAL:	Open

KEY DRUG CO. (DRUGS)
Post Office Box 712
Rochester, New York

BASIC LEASE PERIOD:	15 years—15-year option
TYPE LOCATION PREFERRED:	Any place in shopping center
REAL ESTATE OFFICER:	Harry Achter
UNITS PRESENTLY OPERATED:	19
RENTAL:	$2.50/square foot vs. 2% of sales, whichever is greater

EXHIBIT 13-1 (Contd.)

KIMBERLING'S (SUPERMARKET)
Twenty-Third and Meridian
Oklahoma City, Oklahoma

> BASIC LEASE PERIOD: 10 years
> TYPE LOCATION PREFERRED: Shopping center
> REAL ESTATE OFFICER: C. J. Kimberling
> UNITS PRESENTLY OPERATED: 3
> RENTAL: 1½%

KING CLOTHING CO., INC. (CLOTHING)
460 West 34th St.
New York, N.Y.

> BASIC LEASE PERIOD: 10 to 15 years
> TYPE LOCATION PREFERRED: Shopping center of 300,000 to 400,000 feet
> REAL ESTATE OFFICER: William M. Wolff
> UNITS PRESENTLY OPERATED: 16
> RENTAL: Open

KING HARDWARE CO. (HARDWARE)
4555 Frederick Drive, S.W.
Atlanta, Georgia

> BASIC LEASE PERIOD: 10 years
> TYPE LOCATION PREFERRED: Shopping centers
> REAL ESTATE OFFICER: W. W. McManus
> UNITS PRESENTLY OPERATED: 18
> RENTAL: 4%

KOHL'S FOOD STORES (SUPERMARKET)
Post Office Box 295
Milwaukee, Wisconsin

> BASIC LEASE PERIOD: 15 years
> TYPE LOCATION PREFERRED: New areas
> REAL ESTATE OFFICER: Dan Dary
> UNITS PRESENTLY OPERATED: 50 +
> RENTAL: $2 per sq. ft.

SIGMOND KOHN & SONS (DEPT. STORE)
Box 206
Logan, West Virginia

> BASIC LEASE PERIOD: Open
> TYPE LOCATION PREFERRED: Open
> REAL ESTATE OFFICER: Raymond Kohn
> UNITS PRESENTLY OPERATED: 8
> RENTAL: Varies

EXHIBIT 13-1 (Contd.)

KUHN'S BIG K STORES CORP. (VARIETY)
Post Office Box 9248
3040 Sidco Drive
Nashville, Tennessee

    BASIC LEASE PERIOD: 10 years
    TYPE LOCATION PREFERRED: Shopping center
    REAL ESTATE OFFICER: C. L. Goldstein
    UNITS PRESENTLY OPERATED: 30
    RENTAL: $1.25 vs. 3%

LANE DRUGSTORES, INC. (DRUG)
696 Washington Street
Lynn, Massachusetts

    BASIC LEASE PERIOD: 10 years
    TYPE LOCATION PREFERRED: Shopping center
    REAL ESTATE OFFICER: R. F. Delaney
    UNITS PRESENTLY OPERATED: 7
    RENTAL: $1.80/square foot vs. 3%

HARRY V. LANE PERFUME, INC. (DRUG)
Hollywood Beach Hotel
Hollywood, Florida

    BASIC LEASE PERIOD: 3–5 years
    TYPE LOCATION PREFERRED: Large, busy hotel
    REAL ESTATE OFFICER: Ben Gardner
    UNITS PRESENTLY OPERATED: 4
    RENTAL: Up to 10% of gross receipts

LANZ OF CALIFORNIA, INC. (CLOTHING)
6150 Wilshire Boulevard
Los Angeles, California

    BASIC LEASE PERIOD: 5–10 years
    TYPE LOCATION PREFERRED: High-class shopping area
    REAL ESTATE OFFICER: Emanuel H. Rand
    UNITS PRESENTLY OPERATED: 15
    RENTAL: $4/square foot vs. 6%

C.H. LARKINS' CLOTHING STORE (CLOTHING)
Kinston, North Carolina

    BASIC LEASE PERIOD: 5 years
    TYPE LOCATION PREFERRED: Downtown; 85 to 100% block
    REAL ESTATE OFFICER: L. H. Larkins, Jr.
    UNITS PRESENTLY OPERATED: 21

EXHIBIT 13-1 (Contd.)

RENTAL: $500 to $700/month; percentage lease

LA ROSE CLEANERS (DRY CLEANERS)
515 North Seventy-Fifth Street
Houston, Texas

- BASIC LEASE PERIOD: 5–10 years
- TYPE LOCATION PREFERRED: Corner location with large driveways
- REAL ESTATE OFFICER: Joe Thompson, Jr.
- UNITS PRESENTLY OPERATED: 26
- RENTAL: $200 per month

LEEDS SHOES, INC. (SHOES)
1310 North 22nd Street
Tampa, Florida

- BASIC LEASE PERIOD: 5 years; some 10 years
- TYPE LOCATION PREFERRED: Shopping center
- REAL ESTATE OFFICER: F. Garcia
- UNITS PRESENTLY OPERATED: 51
- RENTAL: $170 to $225

LEVINE'S, INC. (DEPT. STORE)
8908 Ambassador Row
Dallas, Texas

- BASIC LEASE PERIOD: 7–10 years
- TYPE LOCATION PREFERRED: Shopping center
- REAL ESTATE OFFICER: Pat Smith, Vice-President
- UNITS PRESENTLY OPERATED: 150
- RENTAL: $1.00 to $1.10 per foot vs. 2% (turnkey)

LEWIS DRUGS (DRUGS)
3095 Phillips Avenue
Sioux Falls, South Dakota

- BASIC LEASE PERIOD: 15 years; 5 and 5
- TYPE LOCATION PREFERRED: Downtown and suburban on highways
- REAL ESTATE OFFICER: J. E. Griffin
- RENTAL: $1.50 vs. $2\frac{1}{2}$%

LIBERTY BAKERIES (BAKERY)
799 Liberty Street
Springfield 4, Massachusetts

- BASIC LEASE PERIOD: 5–10 years
- TYPE LOCATION PREFERRED: High foot traffic and shopping centers

EXHIBIT 13-1 (Contd.)

REAL ESTATE OFFICER: B. J. Silver
UNITS PRESENTLY OPERATED: 23
RENTAL: $400–$500 per month; 10% of gross

LI'L GENERAL STORES, INC. (SUPERMARKET)
5303 South McDill Avenue
Tampa, Florida

BASIC LEASE PERIOD: 10–15 years, with 2- to 5-year options
TYPE LOCATION PREFERRED: Corner
REAL ESTATE OFFICER: Mr. Roy Riedel
UNITS PRESENTLY OPERATED: 250
RENTAL: Standard lease $350 per month; choice location runs higher

LORY'S FASHION SHOP (CLOTHING)
6112 Northwest Seventh Avenue
Miami, Florida

BASIC LEASE PERIOD: 5 years
TYPE LOCATION PREFERRED: Active traffic
REAL ESTATE OFFICER: Martin W. Smith
UNITS PRESENTLY OPERATED: 10
RENTAL: Minimum rental against percentage

LUCKY AUTO SUPPLY (AUTOMOTIVE)
620 East 111th Place
Los Angeles California

BASIC LEASE PERIOD: Sale-leaseback
TYPE LOCATION PREFERRED: Corner adjacent to or across from shopping centers
REAL ESTATE OFFICER: Maurice Getz
UNITS PRESENTLY OPERATED: 16
RENTAL: Variable

LYNN'S DISCOUNT CENTERS, INC. (CLOTHING)
601 West Twenty-Sixth Street
New York, N.Y.

BASIC LEASE PERIOD: 10 years
TYPE LOCATION PREFERRED: Around corner from 100%
REAL ESTATE OFFICER: George Nodelman
UNITS PRESENTLY OPERATED: 60
RENTAL: $2 per square foot; no percentage

EXHIBIT 13-1 (Contd.)

MACK'S 5, 10, 25¢ STORES, INC. (VARIETY)
Drawer 2010
Sanford, North Carolina

    BASIC LEASE PERIOD: 15 years
    TYPE LOCATION PREFERRED: Shopping center, uptown
    REAL ESTATE OFFICER: O. T. Sloan
    UNITS PRESENTLY OPERATED: 62
    RENTAL: $1.50 per square foot or 3%, whichever is greater

MAGNIN JOSEPH, CO. (CLOTHING)
Stockton at O'Farrell
San Francisco, California

    BASIC LEASE PERIOD: 15 years
    TYPE LOCATION PREFERRED: Shopping centers, downtown
    REAL ESTATE OFFICER: Walter S. Newman
    UNITS PRESENTLY OPERATED: 22
    RENTAL: Variable

MAJESTIC PAINT CENTERS, INC. (PAINT)
1920 Leonard Avenue
Columbus, Ohio

    BASIC LEASE PERIOD: Variable
    TYPE LOCATION PREFERRED: Open
    REAL ESTATE OFFICER: B. K. Ynekin
    UNITS PRESENTLY OPERATED: 30
    RENTAL: Open

MARCH SUPERMARKETS, INC. (SUPERMARKET)
Yorktown, Indiana

    BASIC LEASE PERIOD: 20 years
    TYPE LOCATION PREFERRED: Near good residential area
    REAL ESTATE OFFICER: C. Alan Marsh
    UNITS PRESENTLY OPERATED: 69
    RENTAL: $2.13 per sq. ft. rental

MARILONIS PASTRY SHOP (BAKERY)
1730 South Boston Street
Tulsa 14, Oklahoma

    BASIC LEASE PERIOD: 5 years
    TYPE LOCATION PREFERRED: Next door to grocery store
    REAL ESTATE OFFICER: Care of real estate dept.

EXHIBIT 13-1 (Contd.)

    UNITS PRESENTLY OPERATED: 8
    RENTAL: Minimum vs. percentage

MARKS BROS. JEWELERS, INC. (JEWELRY)
29 East Madison Avenue
Chicago 2, Illinois

    BASIC LEASE PERIOD: 5 years
    TYPE LOCATION PREFERRED: 100% shopping center; regional, only Chicago area
    REAL ESTATE OFFICER: Ira G. Marks
    UNITS PRESENTLY OPERATED: 7
    RENTAL: Open

MARRIOTT HOT SHOPPES, INC. (RESTAURANT)
5161 River Road
Washington, D.C.

    BASIC LEASE PERIOD: 15 years
    TYPE LOCATION PREFERRED: Cafeterias in large shopping centers
    REAL ESTATE OFFICER: James Mitchell
    UNITS PRESENTLY OPERATED: 120
    RENTAL: $2–$3 per square foot vs. 5% of sales

MARTIN'S PAINT (PAINT)
153–22 Jamaica Avenue
Jamaica, New York

    BASIC LEASE PERIOD: 15-year minimum
    TYPE LOCATION PREFERRED: Shopping center or main street
    REAL ESTATE OFFICER: Att: real estate dept.
    UNITS PRESENTLY OPERATED: 60 plus
    RENTAL: Varies in area

JACK MASHBURN, INC. (AUTO SUPPLY)
1203 West Thomas Street
Hammond, Louisiana

    BASIC LEASE PERIOD: 10 years
    TYPE LOCATION PREFERRED: Near Supermarket in shopping center
    REAL ESTATE OFFICER: J. S. Mashburn
    UNITS PRESENTLY OPERATED: 5
    RENTAL: $1.65 per square foot

EXHIBIT 13-1 (Contd.)

MAURICE'S APPAREL, INC. (CLOTHING)
Duluth 2, Minnesota

- BASIC LEASE PERIOD: 5–10 years
- TYPE LOCATION PREFERRED: Downtown—100% on well-developed shopping centers
- REAL ESTATE OFFICER: E. M. Labovitz
- UNITS PRESENTLY OPERATED: 6
- RENTAL: Open

MAXWELL BROTHERS (FURNITURE)
933 Broad Street
Augusta, Georgia

- BASIC LEASE PERIOD: 10 years
- TYPE LOCATION PREFERRED: Downtown, 80% areas
- REAL ESTATE OFFICER: Maxwell Brothers
- UNITS PRESENTLY OPERATED: 32—3 more in prospect
- RENTAL: 3% on overage

MAYFAIR MARKETS (SUPERMARKETS)
Post Office Box 2256
Terminal Annex
Los Angeles, California

- BASIC LEASE PERIOD: 20 years
- TYPE LOCATION PREFERRED: Shopping center
- UNITS PRESENTLY OPERATED: 225
- REAL ESTATE OFFICER: Care of real estate dept.
- RENTAL: $1\frac{1}{2}\%$ and have gone as high as $4 per foot on the building

J.W. MAYS, INC. (DEPT. STORE)
510 Fulton Street
Brooklyn, N.Y.

- BASIC LEASE PERIOD: 21 years plus options
- TYPE LOCATION PREFERRED: High traffic
- REAL ESTATE OFFICER: Aaron London, Esq.
- UNITS PRESENTLY OPERATED: 6
- RENTAL: $1.75 per square foot against $1\frac{1}{2}\%$

McBRIDE'S DRUGS, INC. (DRUGS)
801 South Lincoln Avenue
Urbana, Illinois

- BASIC LEASE PERIOD: 10 years
- TYPE LOCATION PREFERRED: Shopping center
- REAL ESTATE OFFICER: David McBride
- UNITS PRESENTLY OPERATED: 5

EXHIBIT 13-1 (Contd.)

MERCHANTS' FIRESTONE, INC. (AUTO SUPPLY)
Manassas, Virginia

    BASIC LEASE PERIOD: 10 years
    TYPE LOCATION PREFERRED: Brick building
    REAL ESTATE OFFICER: E. P. Dixon
    UNITS PRESENTLY OPERATED: 11
    RENTAL: $1,000 per month or 3% sales

MILLER AUTO SUPPLY (AUTO SUPPLY)
200 South Eighteenth Street
Harrisburg, Pennsylvania

    BASIC LEASE PERIOD: 20 years
    TYPE LOCATION PREFERRED: Shopping center or roadside
    REAL ESTATE OFFICER: I. Donnayry
    UNITS PRESENTLY OPERATED: 19
    RENTAL: Minimum vs. 4%

MINYARD'S FOOD STORES (SUPERMARKET)
6100 Cedar Springs
Dallas, Texas

    BASIC LEASE PERIOD: 20 years
    TYPE LOCATION PREFERRED: Free-standing
    REAL ESTATE OFFICER: H. L. Minyard
    UNITS PRESENTLY OPERATED: 16
    RENTAL: $1.25 to $1.50 per square foot

MISTER DONUT (RESTAURANT)
89 Providence Highway
Westwood, Massachusetts

    BASIC LEASE PERIOD: 20 years, with two 10-year options to extend
    TYPE LOCATION PREFERRED: Suburban with shopping
    REAL ESTATE OFFICER: Donald S. King
    UNITS PRESENTLY OPERATED: 200 plus
    RENTAL: Negotiated

MODERN WOMAN STORES (CLOTHING)
4314 East Gage Avenue
Bell, California

    BASIC LEASE PERIOD: 10 years up
    TYPE LOCATION PREFERRED: 100% shopping centers
    REAL ESTATE OFFICER: M. E. Gardner
    UNITS PRESENTLY OPERATED: 12
    RENTAL: Depending on locations

EXHIBIT 13-1 (Contd.)

MOORE'S (AUTO SUPPLY)
Box 550
Newark, Ohio

    BASIC LEASE PERIOD: 10 years
    TYPE LOCATION PREFERRED: 90% downtown or shopping center
    REAL ESTATE OFFICER: W. S. Moore, III
    UNITS PRESENTLY OPERATED: 112
    RENTAL: 3% vs. minimum

MO-RAY FROCKS (CLOTHING)
505 Eighth Avenue
New York, N.Y.

    BASIC LEASE PERIOD: 10 years
    TYPE LOCATION PREFERRED: Downtown area
    REAL ESTATE OFFICER: Irving Moss
    UNITS PRESENTLY OPERATED: 6
    RENTAL: Open

MOSS CLOTHING STORE (CLOTHING)
601 Clematis Street
West Palm Beach, Florida

    BASIC LEASE PERIOD: 5 years
    TYPE LOCATION PREFERRED: Downtown
    REAL ESTATE OFFICER: Walter Moss
    UNITS PRESENTLY OPERATED: 6
    RENTAL: $100 to $200; no percentage

NAHAS DEPT. STORES (VARIETY)
4520 Van Nuys Boulevard
Sherman Oaks, California

    BASIC LEASE PERIOD: 20–25 years
    TYPE LOCATION PREFERRED: Shopping centers
    REAL ESTATE OFFICER: A. S. Nahas
    UNITS PRESENTLY OPERATED: 9
    RENTAL: $2/square foot vs. 4%

NATIONAL 5 & 10 to $3 STORES, INC. (VARIETY)
Store No. 1
Newark, Delaware

    BASIC LEASE PERIOD: 10 to 20 years
    TYPE LOCATION PREFERRED: Center or city
    REAL ESTATE OFFICER: Alvin I. Handloff

EXHIBIT 13-1 (Contd.)

UNITS PRESENTLY OPERATED:	7
RENTAL:	Varies

NATIONAL SHIRT STORES (HABERDASHERY)
19 West Thirty-Fourth Street
New York, N.Y.

BASIC LEASE PERIOD:	10 years—two 5-year options
TYPE LOCATION PREFERRED:	Prominent corner; 3,000′ regional center, 100% downtown
REAL ESTATE OFFICER:	F. J. Tyrrell
UNITS PRESENTLY OPERATED:	160
RENTAL:	Too variable; 4–5% depending on fixed rent

NATIONAL SHOE CO., LTD. (HABERDASHERY)
3515 East Sixth Street
Topeka, Kansas

BASIC LEASE PERIOD:	10–20 years
TYPE LOCATION PREFERRED:	100% downtown or good shopping centers
REAL ESTATE OFFICER:	Bently Pritsker
UNITS PRESENTLY OPERATED:	32
RENTAL:	$3/square foot vs. 5% and 6%

NATIONWIDE SAFTI-BRAKE CENTERS (AUTOMOTIVE)
7301 Wisconsin Avenue
Bethesda, Maryland

BASIC LEASE PERIOD:	15 years
TYPE LOCATION PREFERRED:	In heavy automotive use area
REAL ESTATE OFFICER:	David Lawson
UNITS PRESENTLY OPERATED:	70
RENTAL:	$500 to $700

NELLI DAVIS PHARMACY, INC. (DRUG)
424 East Fourth Street
Royal Oak, Michigan

BASIC LEASE PERIOD:	5 years and 5-year option
TYPE LOCATION PREFERRED:	Neighborhood
REAL ESTATE OFFICER:	Henry A. Sehwagn
UNITS PRESENTLY OPERATED:	4
RENTAL:	Fixed rent; negotiated

EXHIBIT 13-1 (Contd.)

NEUMODE HOSIERY CO.   (CLOTHING)
131 South Wabash Avenue
Chicago, Illinois

    BASIC LEASE PERIOD: 3–5 years
    TYPE LOCATION PREFERRED: 100% female traffic
    REAL ESTATE OFFICER: A. T. Koos
    UNITS PRESENTLY OPERATED: About 100
    RENTAL: Minimum based on traffic against 7%

NEW YORK BAKERY, INC.   (BAKERY)
5820 Mayfield Road
Mayfield Heights, Ohio

    BASIC LEASE PERIOD: 5 years with 5-year option
    TYPE LOCATION PREFERRED: Shopping centers next to supermarkets
    REAL ESTATE OFFICER: Sigmond Penn
    UNITS PRESENTLY OPERATED: 26
    RENTAL: $500 and 5% over $120,000

NEW YORK LAUNDRY   (DRY CLEANING)
400 East Forsythe Street
Jacksonville 2, Florida

    BASIC LEASE PERIOD: 5 years with options
    TYPE LOCATION PREFERRED: End store in small neighborhood shopping center
    UNITS PRESENTLY OPERATED: 18
    REAL ESTATE OFFICER: T. C. Allin
    RENTAL: $150–$250 or 8% of sales

S.E. NICHOLS   (VARIETY)
500 Eighth Avenue
New York, N.Y.

    BASIC LEASE PERIOD: 20 years with two 5-year options
    TYPE LOCATION PREFERRED: Shopping center bypass and good road pattern
    REAL ESTATE OFFICER: Max Brecker
    UNITS PRESENTLY OPERATED: 23
    RENTAL: $1.95–$2.10 per square foot vs. 2½% of gross

NOBBY KNIT SHOPS   (CLOTHING)
6328 Hollywood Boulevard
Hollywood 28, California

EXHIBIT 13-1 (Contd.)

BASIC LEASE PERIOD:	10 years
TYPE LOCATION PREFERRED:	Varies
REAL ESTATE OFFICER:	Irwin Meyer
UNITS PRESENTLY OPERATED:	7
RENTAL:	6%

ONMAN HOUSE CORP. (RESTAURANT)
Post Office Box 5891
Memphis, Tennessee

BASIC LEASE PERIOD:	10 years with 10-year option
TYPE LOCATION PREFERRED:	Depends on traffic and street surroundings
REAL ESTATE OFFICER:	Ira Sachs
UNITS PRESENTLY OPERATED:	10
RENTAL:	If building, only $175; if building, and fixtures furnished, $275

PARIS STYLE (CLOTHING)
Seymour, Indiana

BASIC LEASE PERIOD:	Varies
TYPE LOCATION PREFERRED:	Open
REAL ESTATE OFFICER:	A. W. Osife
UNITS PRESENTLY OPERATED:	7
RENTAL:	Varies

PEARL'S DEPT. STORES, INC. (DEPT. STORE)
153 Maple Street
Glen's Falls, New York

BASIC LEASE PERIOD:	Varies
TYPE LOCATION PREFERRED:	Small towns—downtown
REAL ESTATE OFFICER:	Att: real estate dept.
UNITS PRESENTLY OPERATED:	15
RENTAL:	Fixed—varies

PECK & PECK (CLOTHING)
221 Fifth Avenue
New York, N.Y.

BASIC LEASE PERIOD:	10 years
TYPE LOCATION PREFERRED:	Shopping centers
REAL ESTATE OFFICER:	Frederick C. Peck
UNITS PRESENTLY OPERATED:	65
RENTAL:	Minimum rent plus % above agreed volume

EXHIBIT 13-1 (Contd.)

W.S. PEEBLER & CO., INC. (DEPT. STORE)
Box 225
Lawrenceville, Virginia

    BASIC LEASE PERIOD: 10 years
    TYPE LOCATION PREFERRED: Shopping center of 100,000 square feet
    REAL ESTATE OFFICER: W. S. Peebles, III
    UNITS PRESENTLY OPERATED: 25
    RENTAL: Up to $2.50 per sq. ft.

I. PERLIS & SONS (DEPT. STORE)
123 Eighth Street South
Gordele, Georgia

    BASIC LEASE PERIOD: Open
    TYPE LOCATION PREFERRED: Open
    REAL ESTATE OFFICER: Lamar J. Perlis
    UNITS PRESENTLY OPERATED: 7
    RENTAL: Varies

PERRY'S SHOES (SHOES)
93-41 One Hundred-Seventieth Street
Jamaica 33, New York

    BASIC LEASE PERIOD: 10-21 years
    TYPE LOCATION PREFERRED: Downtown
    REAL ESTATE OFFICER: Martin A. Samowitz
    UNITS PRESENTLY OPERATED: 29
    RENTAL: No fixed

PETERS FAMILY HOLDINGS, INC. (RESTAURANT)
406 East Broad Street
Richmond, Virginia

    BASIC LEASE PERIOD: 10 years
    TYPE LOCATION PREFERRED: Main thoroughfare or free-standing unit
    REAL ESTATE OFFICER: Mrs. Diane Barbuto
    UNITS PRESENTLY OPERATED: 29
    RENTAL: Open

PIXLEY AND EHLER'S (RESTAURANT)
205 West Lake Street
Chicago 6, Illinois

    BASIC LEASE PERIOD: 5 years with options
    TYPE LOCATION PREFERRED: High traffic
    REAL ESTATE OFFICER: W. Goodman
    UNITS PRESENTLY OPERATED: 11
    RENTAL: Varies

EXHIBIT 13-1 (Contd.)

POPE'S CATERING CO. (RESTAURANT)
805 St. Charles Street
St. Louis, Missouri

    BASIC LEASE PERIOD: 10–15 years
    TYPE LOCATION PREFERRED: Suburban shopping centers
    REAL ESTATE OFFICER: H. H. Pope
    UNITS PRESENTLY OPERATED: 45
    RENTAL: $3/square foot vs. 6% to 8%

PRINCESS SHOPS, INC. (CLOTHING)
1118 Light Street
Baltimore, Maryland

    BASIC LEASE PERIOD: 5 years with 5-year option
    TYPE LOCATION PREFERRED: 100% downtown, or shopping center not less than 100,000 square feet
    UNITS PRESENTLY OPERATED: 7
    RENTAL: $200 vs. 3%

PROSPERITY CLEANERS (DRY CLEANERS)
48–12 Twenty-Fifth Avenue
Long Island City, New York

    BASIC LEASE PERIOD: 5–10 years
    TYPE LOCATION PREFERRED: Shopping centers
    REAL ESTATE OFFICER: John Pardi
    UNITS PRESENTLY OPERATED: 28
    RENTAL: 8% of gross with fixed minimum (under $10,000)

PUCKETT'S FOOD STORES (SUPERMARKET)
204 N. Third Street
Sayre, Oklahoma

    BASIC LEASE PERIOD: 5 years, with option
    TYPE LOCATION PREFERRED: Shopping centers
    REAL ESTATE OFFICER: J. B. Purckett
    UNITS PRESENTLY OPERATED: 11
    RENTAL: Maximum, 1½% of sales

QUALITY MARKETS, INC. (SUPERMARKET)
101 Jackson Avenue
Post Office Box 30
Jamestown, New York

    BASIC LEASE PERIOD: Old building—5 years; new building 10–15 years, with three 5-year options to renew

EXHIBIT 13-1 (Contd.)

TYPE LOCATION PREFERRED: Shopping center
REAL ESTATE OFFICER: Rollin J. Reading
UNITS PRESENTLY OPERATED: 40
RENTAL: 1% of sales; fixed rent depends on volume potential

QUISENBERRY'S (DEPT. STORE)
Post Office Box 40
Vale, Oregon

BASIC LEASE PERIOD: 15 years
TYPE LOCATION PREFERRED: Shopping center
REAL ESTATE OFFICER: W. B. Quisenberry
UNITS PRESENTLY OPERATED: 6
RENTAL: 2½%

RALEY'S SUPERMARKETS (SUPERMARKET)
1515 Twentieth Street
Sacramento, California

BASIC LEASE PERIOD: 20 years, plus options
TYPE LOCATION PREFERRED: Shopping center
REAL ESTATE OFFICER: Care of real estate dept.
UNITS PRESENTLY OPERATED: 15
RENTAL: Fixed rent; 8% net, net, net return on total investment vs. 1%

RAMADA INNS, INC. (MOTEL)
Post Office Box 590
Phoenix, Arizona

BASIC LEASE PERIOD: 99 years with subordination
TYPE LOCATION PREFERRED: Highway sites
REAL ESTATE OFFICER: Real estate dept.
UNITS PRESENTLY OPERATED: 115
RENTAL: 6% of land value

RAYCO MFG. CO. (AUTOMOTIVE)
East 221 State Highway #4
Paramus, New Jersey

BASIC LEASE PERIOD: 15 years
TYPE LOCATION PREFERRED: Highway
REAL ESTATE OFFICER: John Randel
UNITS PRESENTLY OPERATED: 150
RENTAL: $1,000/month vs. 5%

EXHIBIT 13-1 (Contd.)

RAYLASS DEPT. STORE, INC. (DEPT. STORE)
370 Seventh Avenue
New York, N.Y.

    BASIC LEASE PERIOD: 5 years
    TYPE LOCATION PREFERRED: Downtown
    REAL ESTATE OFFICER: F. K. Baiff
    UNITS PRESENTLY OPERATED: 29
    RENTAL: $1.25/square foot to vs. 2½%

RECHTER BROS. CLOTHING CO. (DEPT. STORE)
1908 Washington Avenue
St. Louis, Missouri

    BASIC LEASE PERIOD: 5 years, usually with option to renew
    TYPE LOCATION PREFERRED: Downtown or shopping center
    REAL ESTATE OFFICER: I. J. Rechter
    UNITS PRESENTLY OPERATED: 16
    RENTAL: $125 per square foot to $1.75 per square foot

THE RED BARN SYSTEM, INC. (RESTAURANT)
2701 East Sunrise Boulevard
Fort Lauderdale, Florida

    BASIC LEASE PERIOD: 15 years and two 5-year options
    TYPE LOCATION PREFERRED: Corner or inside location with minimum of 150-foot frontage
    REAL ESTATE OFFICER: Willard C. Eichenberger
    UNITS PRESENTLY OPERATED: 75
    RENTAL: $12,000 per year; no percentage

RED OWL STORES, INC. (SUPERMARKET)
Post Office Box 329
Minneapolis, Minnesota

    BASIC LEASE PERIOD: 15 years, three 5-year options
    TYPE LOCATION PREFERRED: Shopping center and free-standing
    REAL ESTATE OFFICER: Charles M. Upham, Jr.
    UNITS PRESENTLY OPERATED: 200
    RENTAL: Varies $1.50–$2.00/square foot vs. percentage

EXHIBIT 13-1 (Contd.)

REMAR'S (CLOTHING)
417 East Pico Boulevard
Los Angeles, California

> BASIC LEASE PERIOD: 10 years
> TYPE LOCATION PREFERRED: 100% retail
> REAL ESTATE OFFICER: Adolph B. Remar
> UNITS PRESENTLY OPERATED: 18
> RENTAL: 6%

R.H. RENY, INC. (DEPT. STORE)
Damariscott, Maine

> BASIC LEASE PERIOD: 2–3–5, at our option
> TYPE LOCATION PREFERRED: Downtown—5,000 to 8,000 square feet
> REAL ESTATE OFFICER: R. H. Reny
> UNITS PRESENTLY OPERATED: 8
> RENTAL: $250/month

RESTAURANT ASSOCIATES, INC. (RESTAURANT)
515 West Fifty-Seventh Street
New York, N.Y.

> BASIC LEASE PERIOD: Varies, around 20 years
> TYPE LOCATION PREFERRED: High traffic
> REAL ESTATE OFFICER: S. L. Sleeper
> UNITS PRESENTLY OPERATED: 42
> RENTAL: 5%

RICE FOOD MARKETS (SUPERMARKET)
5333 Gulfton Street
Houston, Texas

> BASIC LEASE PERIOD: 15 years with options
> TYPE LOCATION PREFERRED: 7- to 10-acre center
> REAL ESTATE OFFICER: William H. Levy
> UNITS PRESENTLY OPERATED: 13; 2 more under construction
> RENTAL: $150 or 1½% maximum

RICELLI CANDIES, INC. (CANDY)
1612 East 11 Mile Road
Royal Oak, Michigan

> BASIC LEASE PERIOD: 3 years
> TYPE LOCATION PREFERRED: Downtown or/and suburban shopping centers
> REAL ESTATE OFFICER: Leon Ricelli
> UNITS PRESENTLY OPERATED: 5
> RENTAL: $400 vs. 9%

Chain Stores—Location and Leasing Information / 235

EXHIBIT 13-1 (Contd.)

THE RICHMAN BROTHERS CO. (CLOTHING AND FURNITURE)
Post Office Box 5999
Cleveland, Ohio

    BASIC LEASE PERIOD: 10 years
    TYPE LOCATION PREFERRED: Regional shopping centers and good downtown locations
    REAL ESTATE OFFICER: William F. Kennedy, Vice-President
    UNITS PRESENTLY OPERATED: 313
    RENTAL: Varies

RICH'S (CLOTHING)
6406 Fair Oaks Boulevard
Carmichael, California

    BASIC LEASE PERIOD: 10 years
    TYPE LOCATION PREFERRED: Discount—concession, women's and children's apparel
    REAL ESTATE OFFICER: J. Rich
    UNITS PRESENTLY OPERATED: 4
    RENTAL: 25¢ a foot per month

RISCH DRUGSTORES (DRUG)
24 West Main Street
Logan, Ohio

    BASIC LEASE PERIOD: 10–15 years
    TYPE LOCATION PREFERRED: Neighborhood with off-street parking
    REAL ESTATE OFFICER: Lester V. Risch
    UNITS PRESENTLY OPERATED: 6
    RENTAL: $2\frac{1}{2}\%$

ROLLNICK SHOE CO. (SHOES)
544 Acoma Street
Denver, Colorado

    BASIC LEASE PERIOD: 5 years plus options
    TYPE LOCATION PREFERRED: Regional shopping centers
    REAL ESTATE OFFICER: Norman Gray
    UNITS PRESENTLY OPERATED: 9

ROOS-ATKINS (CLOTHING)
798 Market Street
San Francisco, California

    BASIC LEASE PERIOD: 20 years
    TYPE LOCATION PREFERRED: Shopping center

EXHIBIT 13-1 (Contd.)

    REAL ESTATE OFFICER: G. A. Somers
    UNITS PRESENTLY OPERATED: 27
    RENTAL: $1.75/square foot vs. 4%

ROYAL'S INC. (DEPT. STORE)
324 S.W. Sixteenth Street
Belle Glade, Florida

    BASIC LEASE PERIOD: Own all their buildings or 15 years
    TYPE LOCATION PREFERRED: Varies
    REAL ESTATE OFFICER: Charles Royal
    UNITS PRESENTLY OPERATED: 5
    RENTAL: Open

ROYAL CROWN HOSIERY CO., INC. (HOSIERY)
3516 West Fond du Lac Avenue
Milwaukee, Wisconsin

    BASIC LEASE PERIOD: 3 years with 2-year option
    TYPE LOCATION PREFERRED: Shopping center
    REAL ESTATE OFFICER: F. H. Fischer
    UNITS PRESENTLY OPERATED: 12
    RENTAL: $250 vs. 5%

SAFEWAY STORES (SO. CALIF.) (SUPERMARKET)
P.O. Box 3399 Terminal Annex
Los Angeles, California

    BASIC LEASE PERIOD: 20 years
    TYPE LOCATION PREFERRED: Neighborhood or community shopping center
    REAL ESTATE OFFICER: E. J. Penprase, W. A. Vollmer
    UNITS PRESENTLY OPERATED: 240
    RENTAL: Varies

SALLY SHOPS OF CALIFORNIA, INC. (CLOTHING)
2222 South Finnoa Street
Los Angeles, California

    BASIC LEASE PERIOD: 10–20 years
    TYPE LOCATION PREFERRED: 100% only in shopping centers
    REAL ESTATE OFFICER: H. Lew Zuckerman
    UNITS PRESENTLY OPERATED: 40
    RENTAL: $1.75/square foot vs. 4%

THE SAMPLE, INC. (DEPT. STORE)
Buffalo 16, New York

EXHIBIT 13-1 (Contd.)

BASIC LEASE PERIOD:	10–15 years
TYPE LOCATION PREFERRED:	Mall
REAL ESTATE OFFICER:	Louis M. Bunis
UNITS PRESENTLY OPERATED:	9
RENTAL:	4%

SAVEMART (APPLIANCES)
334 East One Hundred Forty-Ninth Street
Bronx, N.Y.

BASIC LEASE PERIOD:	10–15 years
TYPE LOCATION PREFERRED:	Prime shopping district within the metropolitan area
REAL ESTATE OFFICER:	Ben Blank
UNITS PRESENTLY OPERATED:	14
RENTAL:	3% of gross

SCHUCART SHOES (SHOES)
225 Collinsville Avenue
East St. Louis, Illinois

BASIC LEASE PERIOD:	5–20 years
TYPE LOCATION PREFERRED:	100%
REAL ESTATE OFFICER:	A. O. Schucart
UNITS PRESENTLY OPERATED:	3
RENTAL:	$500 against 5 or 6%

SEKULOW BROS., INC. (CLOTHING)
36–38 South Placa Street
Baltimore, Maryland

BASIC LEASE PERIOD:	5 years or less
TYPE LOCATION PREFERRED:	As close to 100% as possible
REAL ESTATE OFFICER:	J. Sekulow
UNITS PRESENTLY OPERATED:	50
RENTAL:	6 or 7%

SHARPE DEPT. STORE (DEPT. STORE)
Post Office Box 328
Checotah, Oklahoma

BASIC LEASE PERIOD:	3 years with two 5-year options
TYPE LOCATION PREFERRED:	Small towns to 10,000 population
REAL ESTATE OFFICER:	J. M. Le Masters

EXHIBIT 13-1 (Contd.)

UNITS PRESENTLY OPERATED:	17
RENTAL:	$150 per month on $75,000 sales—2½% for all over $75,000

SHELBRO, INC. (SHOES)
47 South Fifth Avenue
Mt. Vernon, N.Y.

BASIC LEASE PERIOD:	5 years
TYPE LOCATION PREFERRED:	Leased retail shoe departments
REAL ESTATE OFFICER:	Joseph J. Shell
UNITS PRESENTLY OPERATED:	27
RENTAL:	12%

SIDNEY'S INC. (RESTAURANT)
501–03 South Jefferson Street
Roanoke, Virginia

BASIC LEASE PERIOD:	10 years
TYPE LOCATION PREFERRED:	Shopping center
REAL ESTATE OFFICER:	Sidney A. Weinstein
UNITS PRESENTLY OPERATED:	6
RENTAL:	2%

SILBEY'S SHOES (SHOES)
2235 Woodward Avenue
Detroit, Michigan

BASIC LEASE PERIOD:	10 years to 15 years
TYPE LOCATION PREFERRED:	Shopping center—major department store
REAL ESTATE OFFICER:	Norman H. Rosenfeld
UNITS PRESENTLY OPERATED:	8
RENTAL:	$4/square foot men's stores; $3/square foot family stores; 5% overage

SILVER BRAND CLOTHES, INC. (CLOTHING)
108–110 Capitol Street
Charlestown, West Virginia

BASIC LEASE PERIOD:	10 years
TYPE LOCATION PREFERRED:	Downtown
REAL ESTATE OFFICER:	Ben Sherman
UNITS PRESENTLY OPERATED:	4
RENTAL:	Fixed rent

EXHIBIT 13-1 (Contd.)

N. SINKIN (DEPT. STORE)
718 North Cherry Street
San Antonio, Texas

    BASIC LEASE PERIOD: 5–10 years
    TYPE LOCATION PREFERRED: Suburban
    REAL ESTATE OFFICER: William Sinkin
    UNITS PRESENTLY OPERATED: 7
    RENTAL: Maximum, vs. 3%

SMITH'S CLOTHIERS OF CALIFORNIA (CLOTHING)
Fourteenth and Broadway
Oakland, California

    BASIC LEASE PERIOD: 10–20 years
    TYPE LOCATION PREFERRED: Shopping centers
    REAL ESTATE OFFICER: Harold Smith
    UNITS PRESENTLY OPERATED: 16
    RENTAL: $3–$4 per sq. ft.

SNYDER'S DRUGSTORES, INC. (DRUG)
215 Excelsior Street
Hopkins, Minnesota

    BASIC LEASE PERIOD: 20 years
    TYPE LOCATION PREFERRED: Center—urban
    REAL ESTATE OFFICER: James Gottleib
    UNITS PRESENTLY OPERATED: 43
    RENTAL: $3 vs. %

SPIES' SUPERMARKETS (SUPERMARKETS)
Post Office Box 137
Watertown, South Dakota

    BASIC LEASE PERIOD: 12–15 years
    TYPE LOCATION PREFERRED: Shopping center or free standing; at least 3 to 1 parking
    REAL ESTATE OFFICER: B. E. Spies
    UNITS PRESENTLY OPERATED: 11
    RENTAL: 1% or 8 1/3% net, net

SPORT FISCHER (SPORTING GOODS)
699 Main Street
Buffalo, New York

    BASIC LEASE PERIOD: 15 years
    TYPE LOCATION PREFERRED: Enclosed mall
    REAL ESTATE OFFICER: Bernard Tuchman
    UNITS PRESENTLY OPERATED: 7
    RENTAL: 4% to 5%

EXHIBIT 13-1 (Contd.)

SPOTLESS STORES (DRY CLEANING)
317 Ninth Avenue
Paterson, New Jersey

    BASIC LEASE PERIOD: 5–10 years
    TYPE LOCATION PREFERRED: Main street locations
    REAL ESTATE OFFICER: I. Denberg
    UNITS PRESENTLY OPERATED: 200
    RENTAL: 8% of gross with fixed minimum

SPURGEION MERCANTILE CO. (DEPT. STORE)
822 West Washington Boulevard
Chicago, Illinois

    BASIC LEASE PERIOD: 10 years
    TYPE LOCATION PREFERRED: 10,000 to 20,000 population towns in midwestern state
    REAL ESTATE OFFICER: A. W. Graham
    UNITS PRESENTLY OPERATED: 56
    RENTAL: 3%

STAFF, BUSINESS & DATA AIDS, INC. (BUSINESS AIDS)
122 E. Forty-Second Street
New York, N.Y.

    BASIC LEASE PERIOD: 3 years with options
    TYPE LOCATION PREFERRED: Prime office building
    REAL ESTATE OFFICER: M. Radlauer
    UNITS PRESENTLY OPERATED: 3
    RENTAL: $2.50 per square foot

STEVENS (CLOTHING)
159 Newark Avenue
Jersey City, N.J.

    BASIC LEASE PERIOD: 10 years
    TYPE LOCATION PREFERRED: 90 to 100%
    REAL ESTATE OFFICER: B. Wallis
    UNITS PRESENTLY OPERATED: 15
    RENTAL: $750 per month

STINEWAY-FORD HOPKINS CO. (DRUG)
1950 North Mannheim Road
Melrose Park, Illinois

    BASIC LEASE PERIOD: 10–20 years
    TYPE LOCATION PREFERRED: Midwest area only; downtown office building; shopping center and discount stores

EXHIBIT 13-1 (Contd.)

    REAL ESTATE OFFICER: Walter F. Osborn
    UNITS PRESENTLY OPERATED: 56
    RENTAL: $4 to $5—percentage varies; downtown stores 8% to 9%; downtown office building 4–5%; shopping center 2½ to 3%

SWIFT SERVICE STORES (DRY CLEANING)
8920 Euclid Avenue
Cleveland, Ohio

    BASIC LEASE PERIOD: 5 years
    TYPE LOCATION PREFERRED: Corner retail shopping area
    REAL ESTATE OFFICER: E. D. Friedman
    UNITS PRESENTLY OPERATED: 77
    RENTAL: $300/month vs. 6%

TAGGURT SHOES, INC. (SHOES)
734 Eighth Street
Portsmouth, Ohio

    BASIC LEASE PERIOD: Flexible
    TYPE LOCATION PREFERRED: Shoe department in department store
    REAL ESTATE OFFICER: A. H. Yeary
    UNITS PRESENTLY OPERATED: 16
    RENTAL: Flexible

T. G. & Y. STORES CO. (VARIETY)
Post Office Box 1967
Oklahoma City, Oklahoma

    BASIC LEASE PERIOD: To be negotiated
    TYPE LOCATION PREFERRED: Shopping center
    REAL ESTATE OFFICER: V. L. Helt
    UNITS PRESENTLY OPERATED: 386
    RENTAL: To be negotiated

JOHN R. THOMPSON CO. (RESTAURANT)
29 West Randolph Street
Chicago, Illinois

    BASIC LEASE PERIOD: 20 years
    TYPE LOCATION PREFERRED: Shopping centers and motels
    REAL ESTATE OFFICER: R. C. Dickman
    UNITS PRESENTLY OPERATED: 40
    RENTAL: 6% land; 8½% building plus % rent

EXHIBIT 13-1 (Contd.)

THRIFT SHOE STORES   (SHOES)
62 South Main Street
Wilkes-Barre, Pennsylvania

BASIC LEASE PERIOD:	5–10 years
TYPE LOCATION PREFERRED:	Shopping centers
REAL ESTATE OFFICER:	Harvey S. Klein
UNITS PRESENTLY OPERATED:	30
RENTAL:	5% of sales

TREND STORES, INC.   (DISCOUNT)
1235 North Moseley
Wichita 5, Kansas

BASIC LEASE PERIOD:	5–10 years
TYPE LOCATION PREFERRED:	4,000 to 6,000 square feet
REAL ESTATE OFFICER:	Gene Friedman
UNITS PRESENTLY OPERATED:	10
RENTAL:	$2.50 per square foot or 5%

TRIANGLE SHOE CO.   (SHOES)
Narrows Shopping Center
Kingston, Pennsylvania

BASIC LEASE PERIOD:	10 years or less
TYPE LOCATION PREFERRED:	Shopping centers plus departments in discount stores
REAL ESTATE OFFICER:	Norman D. Weiss
UNITS PRESENTLY OPERATED:	130
RENTAL:	Depends on location

TRIANGLE STORES   (SPORTING GOODS)
182 Flatbush Avenue
Brooklyn, New York

BASIC LEASE PERIOD:	10–15 years
TYPE LOCATION PREFERRED:	Busy
REAL ESTATE OFFICER:	Leon Shapiro
UNITS PRESENTLY OPERATED:	7
RENTAL:	4½%

UNCLE SAM'S SHOE STORES   (SHOES)
339 East Forty-First Street
Paterson, 4, New Jersey

BASIC LEASE PERIOD:	5–10 years
TYPE LOCATION PREFERRED:	Leased departments in volume promotional department store
REAL ESTATE OFFICER:	Samuel M. Levine

EXHIBIT 13-1 (Contd.)

UNITS PRESENTLY OPERATED: 4
RENTAL: $5/square foot vs. 6%

UNITS SHOE STORES CO. of LA., INC. (SHOES)
Post Office Box 1567
Shreveport, Louisiana
  BASIC LEASE PERIOD: 10 years plus 5-year option
  TYPE LOCATION PREFERRED: 100% downtown or selected regional shopping centers
  REAL ESTATE OFFICER: Frank Katzenstein
  UNITS PRESENTLY OPERATED: 48
  RENTAL: Fixed rent is variable, not over 5%

UTOPIA CLEANERS & DYERS, INC. (DRY CLEANER)
916 South Fifteenth Street
Birmingham, Alabama
  BASIC LEASE PERIOD: 1–5 years
  TYPE LOCATION PREFERRED: In or adjoining shopping centers
  REAL ESTATE OFFICER: P.N. Plylar
  UNITS PRESENTLY OPERATED: 38
  RENTAL: As nearly 7% of volume as possible

VALLINS ADDIE, INC.
75 East One Hundred Sixty-First Street
Bronx, New York
  BASIC LEASE PERIOD: 21 years
  TYPE LOCATION PREFERRED: 80–100%
  REAL ESTATE OFFICER: J. D. Assail
  UNITS PRESENTLY OPERATED: 4
  RENTAL: $12,000/year vs. 5%

VILLAGE INN PANCAKE HOUSE, INC. (RESTAURANT)
1111 South Colorado Boulevard
Denver, Colorado
  BASIC LEASE PERIOD: 10–15 years with two 5-year options
  TYPE LOCATION PREFERRED: Corner location on busy streets near good motel and restaurant area, free standing
  REAL ESTATE OFFICER: L. A. Fisher
  UNITS PRESENTLY OPERATED: 54
  RENTAL: $22–24,000 net, net rental

EXHIBIT 13-1 (Contd.)

VOGUE SHOES, INC. (SHOES)
Post Office Box 412
Houston, Texas

    BASIC LEASE PERIOD: 15 years
    TYPE LOCATION PREFERRED: Shopping centers—regional
    REAL ESTATE OFFICER: Harry Susman
    UNITS PRESENTLY OPERATED: 8
    RENTAL: $2.40 per square foot based on 5% of gross

THE VOGUE SHOPS (CLOTHING)
6225 Powers Avenue
Jacksonville, Florida

    BASIC LEASE PERIOD: 10- to 5-year option
    TYPE LOCATION PREFERRED: Shopping centers
    REAL ESTATE OFFICER: Ben Friedman
    UNITS PRESENTLY OPERATED: 21
    RENTAL: $1–$2/square foot vs. 4–5%

WAID'S RESTAURANT (RESTAURANT)
3054 Southwest Boulevard
Kansas City, Missouri

    BASIC LEASE PERIOD: 15 years
    TYPE LOCATION PREFERRED: Highway
    REAL ESTATE OFFICER: Real estate department
    UNITS PRESENTLY OPERATED: 12
    RENTAL: $750/month vs. 5% over $300,000

WALDORF SYSTEM, INC. (RESTAURANT)
512 West Fifty-Eighth Street
New York, N.Y.

    BASIC LEASE PERIOD: 10 years
    TYPE LOCATION PREFERRED: In city or periphery of downtown
    REAL ESTATE OFFICER: Nathaniel Frommartz
    UNITS PRESENTLY OPERATED: 104
    RENTAL: 4% to 5%

WALTERSDORF FURNITURE ENTERPRISES (FURNITURE)
330 West Market Street
York, Pennsylvania

    BASIC LEASE PERIOD: 5–10 years
    TYPE LOCATION PREFERRED: Varies greatly
    REAL ESTATE OFFICER: Att: real estate dept.

EXHIBIT 13-1 (Contd.)

UNITS PRESENTLY OPERATED: 15
RENTAL: 4 to 5%

WARD & WARD, INC. (MANHATTAN WARD) (CLOTHING)
2333 Fairmont Avenue
Philadelphia, Pennsylvania

    BASIC LEASE PERIOD: 10 years
    TYPE LOCATION PREFERRED: Shopping center
    REAL ESTATE OFFICER: Hubert Jauk
    UNITS PRESENTLY OPERATED: 12
    RENTAL: $1.72/square foot vs. 5%

WASHINGTON DISTRIBUTORS (DISCOUNT)
1225 Indiana Avenue
Toledo, Ohio

    BASIC LEASE PERIOD: 15 years
    TYPE LOCATION PREFERRED: Primary highway, edge of city
    REAL ESTATE OFFICER: H. R. Swolsky
    UNITS PRESENTLY OPERATED: 10
    RENTAL: $1.25 per square foot

WAVERLY B. WATKINS (RESTAURANT)
14256 East Firestone Boulevard
La Mirada, California

    BASIC LEASE PERIOD: 20 years
    TYPE LOCATION PREFERRED: Heavily populated
    REAL ESTATE OFFICER: Waverly Watkins
    UNITS PRESENTLY OPERATED: 85
    RENTAL: Minimum fixed or percentage

WEATHERWAX'S (DRUG)
4600 Francis Street
Jackson, Michigan

    BASIC LEASE PERIOD: 10 years
    TYPE LOCATION PREFERRED: Shopping center residential
    REAL ESTATE OFFICER: Alan Weatherwax
    UNITS PRESENTLY OPERATED: 4
    RENTAL: $300 to $700, plus 3% of sales

WEBSTER CLOTHIERS (CLOTHING)
1800 Woodlawn Drive
Baltimore, Maryland

    BASIC LEASE PERIOD: Varies
    TYPE LOCATION PREFERRED: Shopping center

EXHIBIT 13-1 (Contd.)

REAL ESTATE OFFICER: Samuel M. Feldman
UNITS PRESENTLY OPERATED: 27
RENTAL: Open

WEINER'S STORES, INC. (DEPT. STORE)
Post Office Box 2612
Houston, Texas

BASIC LEASE PERIOD: 10 years, with renewal options
TYPE LOCATION PREFERRED: Neighborhood shopping centers; adequate parking
REAL ESTATE OFFICER: Leon Weiner
UNITS PRESENTLY OPERATED: 24
RENTAL: No minimum rent; 2% to 3% of sales

J. WEINGARTEN, INC. (SUPERMARKET)
P.O. Box 1698
Houston Texas

BASIC LEASE PERIOD: Long term
TYPE LOCATION PREFERRED: Shopping center or free standing
REAL ESTATE OFFICER: Stanford Alexander
UNITS PRESENTLY OPERATED: 63
RENTAL: Varies

WEISFIELD'S (JEWELRY)
800 South Michigan Street
Seattle, Washington

BASIC LEASE PERIOD: Negotiable
TYPE LOCATION PREFERRED: 100% downtown or shopping center
REAL ESTATE OFFICER: Phil Bogugh
UNITS PRESENTLY OPERATED: 46

WEST & CO. OF LA. INC. (DEPT. STORE)
Miden, Louisiana

BASIC LEASE PERIOD: 10 years
TYPE LOCATION PREFERRED: In cities of 10,000 to 40,000 and in shopping centers 65,000 square feet total leased area and larger
REAL ESTATE OFFICER: R. A. Simmons
UNITS PRESENTLY OPERATED: 29
RENTAL: To be negotiated

EXHIBIT 13-1 (Contd.)

WESTERN AUTO SUPPLY (AUTO SUPPLY)
2107 Grand Avenue
Kansas City 8, Missouri

    NOTE: Have both franchise and company stores; high-volume traffic
    RENTAL: Open

WHITE WAY CLEANERS (DRY CLEANERS)
113 East Twenty-Sixth Street
Minneapolis, Minnesota

    BASIC LEASE PERIOD: 10 years
    TYPE LOCATION PREFERRED: Shopping center
    REAL ESTATE OFFICER: P. M. Raven
    UNITS PRESENTLY OPERATED: 34
    RENTAL: 7% of gross with minimum

WHITE WAY LAUNDRY (DRY CLEANING)
Twenty-First Street and Colby Avenue
Norfolk, Virginia

    BASIC LEASE PERIOD: 5 years and 5-year option
    TYPE LOCATION PREFERRED: Shopping center
    REAL ESTATE OFFICER: Paul L. Strassberg
    UNITS PRESENTLY OPERATED: 15
    RENTAL: $250 against 8%

WIDMAN, L.F., INC. (DRUG)
738 Bellefonte Avenue
Lock Haven, Pennsylvania

    BASIC LEASE PERIOD: 5–10 years
    TYPE LOCATION PREFERRED: Shopping center
    REAL ESTATE OFFICER: L. F. Widman
    UNITS PRESENTLY OPERATED: 14
    RENTAL: 3–4%

WILLIAMS 5 & 10¢ STORES, INC. (VARIETY)
418 Main Street
Tarboro, North Carolina

    BASIC LEASE PERIOD: 5 and 10 (5 on old, 10 on new)
    TYPE LOCATION PREFERRED: Renewed downtown or good shopping center
    REAL ESTATE OFFICER: H. W. Hull
    UNITS PRESENTLY OPERATED: 9
    RENTAL: $1/square foot or 4%

EXHIBIT 13-1 (Contd.)

WILLNER M. CO., INC. (DEPT. STORE)
2212 South Jackson Street
Seattle, Washington

    BASIC LEASE PERIOD: 2–3–5 years; 2–3 preferred on new locations
    TYPE LOCATION PREFERRED: Small-income settlements and district shopping areas
    REAL ESTATE OFFICER: Real estate department
    UNITS PRESENTLY OPERATED: 7
    RENTAL: $300 to $500 on new rents and locations to $600 (old)

YANKEE DISTRIBUTORS, INC. (DISCOUNT)
P.O. Box 4415
Detroit, Michigan

    BASIC LEASE PERIOD: 15 years
    TYPE LOCATION PREFERRED: 60,000 to 80,000 square feet
    REAL ESTATE OFFICER: Joseph Megsell
    UNITS PRESENTLY OPERATED: 18
    RENTAL: $1.35 to 2%

EXHIBIT 13-2. Additional Chain Store Sources to Be Contacted.

Alpha-Beta-Acme Markets, Inc., 777 S. Harbor Blvd., La Hobra, Calif.
Andrews, Stanley, Sporting Goods, 840 B St., San Diego, Calif.
Austin Shoe Stores, 1715 N. Industrial St., Dallas, Tex.
Ayres, L.S. and Co., 25 Meridian St., Indianapolis, Ind.
Bailey's of Boston, Inc., 26 Temple Pl., Boston, Mass.
Bargain Town U.S.A., Inc., 222 6th Ave., Birmingham, Ala.
Bartell Drug Co., 1906–16 Boren Blvd., Seattle, Wash.
Be-Lo Markets, 4603 Cape Henry Ave., Norfolk, Va.
Bernstein Bros., 1280 Flatbush Ave., Brooklyn, N.Y.
Big Apple Supermarkets, Inc., Hemlock Street and Boulevard Ave., Central Islip, N.Y.
Bowman Shoe Co., 61 Public Sq., Monmouth, Ill.
Brewer, J.W. Tire Co., Inc., 2346 Grant Ave., Ogden, U.
Brigham's, Inc., 30 Mill St., Arlington, Mass.
Broward Sport Shops, 15 S. Andrews Ave., Ft. Lauderdale, Fla.
Builder's Emporium, 12500 E. Slavson Ave., Santa Fe Springs, Calif.
Calico Cottage Candies, 1163 Broadway, Hewlett, N.Y.
Cannon Shoe Co., Lafayette Ave. and Dickson St., Baltimore, Md.
Carousel Snack Bars, Inc., 9549 Penn Ave. S., Minneapolis, Minn.

EXHIBIT 13-2 (Contd.)

Carr's Food Center, Inc., 145th and Gambell Sts., Anchorage, Alask.
Central Markets, Inc., Box 1074, Schenectady, N.Y.
Cornet Stores, 411 S. Arroyo Parkway, Pasadena, Calif.
Craft's Drugstores, Box 5808, Spartanburg, S.C.
Crane's-Mayo's Clothes, 588 Broadway, New York, N.Y.
Cumberland Farms Dairy, Inc., 777 Dedham St., Canton, Mass.
Danner Bros. Co., Inc., 257 S. Meridian St., Indianapolis, Ind.
Dan's Supreme Supermarkets, Inc., 120 Jackson St., Hempstead, N.Y.
Delchamps Food Stores, 305 N. Water St., Mobile, Ala.
Dixieland Food Stores, Inc., P.O. Box 398, Geneva, Ala.
Dominion Stores, Ltd., 605 Roger Rd., Toronto, Can.
Eagle Army-Navy Stores, 1 Eagle Plaza, Opa-Locka, Fla.
Eagle Midwestern Region (Lucky Stores, Inc.), Route 67 and Knoxville Rd., Milan, Ill.
Eleanor Shops, Inc., 621 Sixth Ave., New York, N.Y.
Ellner & Pike, 437 Railroad Ave., Westbury, N.Y.
Fabric Tree, Inc., 18 E. 41st St., New York, N.Y.
Fedco Foods Corp., 540 E. 170th St., Bronx, N.Y.
Federal Market Co., Inc., 968 Kenmore Ave., Buffalo, N.Y.
Fernwood Candy & Ice Cream Co., 150 W. Commonwealth St., Salt Lake City, U.
Fisher Foods, Inc., 5300 Richmond Rd., Bedford Heights, O.
Food Giant Markets, Inc., 12500 E. Slauson Ave., Santa Fe, Calif.
Frank's Shoes, Inc., 2249 N. Wayne Ave., Chicago, Ill.
Friedman Jewelers, 4 W State St., Savannah, Ga.
Gallenkamp Stores, Inc. (A part of Shoe Corp. of America), 8300 Santa Monica Blvd., Los Angeles, Calif.
Giant Food, Inc., 6900 Sheriff Rd., Landover, Md.
Giant Food, Inc., Box 1804, Washington, D.C.
Giant Tiger Stores, Inc., 12825 Taft Ave., Cleveland, O.
Giltex Corp., for Gilberg's Fabrics, 1516 S. Monroe St., Talahassee, Fla.
Ginn, M.S. & Co., 919 E St. N.W., Washington, D.C.
Glen-Joe, Inc., 1877 Penn Mar Ave., S. El Monte, Calif.
Green Hills Supermarkets, Inc., 1122 Penn St., St. Joseph, Mo.
Greyhound Food Management Corp., 2301 W. Lafayette Blvd., Detroit, Mich.
Grossman, L. Sons., Inc., S.E. Express and Union Sts., Braintree, Mass.
Harrison's Shoe Stores, 221 E. Center St., Kingsport, Tenn.
Harvey's, 455 W. Lincolnway St., Valpariso, Ind.
Hickory Farms, 1021 N. Reynolds Rd., Toledo, O.
Hillman's, Inc., 28 W. Washington St., Chicago, Ill.
Hobby-Center, Inc., 1514 S. Detroit St., Toledo, O.

EXHIBIT 13-2 (Contd.)

Home Stores, Inc., Middle St., Chattanooga, Tenn.
Home Trading Co., Inc., 548 W. Diversey Parkway, Chicago, Ill.
Homestead House, Inc., 999 S. Jason St., Denver, Colo.
Hornsby's 5¢ to $1 Stores, Inc., 301 Liberty St., Morris, Ill.
House of Fabrics, 11250 Sherman Way, Sun Valley, Calif.
Hy-Vee Food Stores, Inc., 1801 Osceola Ave., Chariton, Io.
In & Out Corporation, Old Warren Rd., Pine Bluff, Ark.
Jack's Hamburgers, Inc., 2719 S. 19th St., Birmingham, Ala.
Jewel Box Stores Corp., Guilford Bldg., Greensboro, N.C.
Jewel Food Stores, 1955 W. North Ave., Melrose Pk., Ill.
Johnson's 5–10 to $1 Stores, Inc., P.O. Box 248, St. Paul, Va.
Kash N' Carry Wholesale Supermarkets, 5015 E. Hillsborough Ave., Tampa, Fla.
Katz & Besqhoff, Inc., 900 Camp St., New Orleans, La.
Kaufman & Chernick, Inc., 80 Fountain St., Pawtucket, Rhode Is.
Kay Jewelry Stores, Inc., 1328 New York Ave., N. W. Washington, D.C.
King, M.H. Co., 110 West 13th St., Burley, Id.
Kinney Shoe Corp., 221 Park Ave., S., New York, N.Y.
Kirby's Shoe Stores, 1114 S. Los Angeles St., Los Angeles, Calif.
Knapp Shoes, 173 Spark St., Brockton, Mass.
Kobacker Shoe Co., Inc., 998 McKee Ave., McKee Rocks, Pa.
Kohler-McLiester Paint Co., P.O. Box 546 Denver, Colo.
Kostel Corp., 1314 N. Milwaukee Ave., Chicago, Ill.
Larkin's, C.H. Clothing Stores, Inc., Kinston, N.C.
La Verdiere's Super Drugstores, 160 Main St., Fairfield, Me.
Lerner Shops, 354 Park Ave. S., New York, N.Y.
Lewis and Lewis, 1721 Broadway, Oakland, Calif.
Liberal Market, Inc., 230 Concord St., Dayton, O.
Libson Shops, Inc., 1209 Washington Blvd., St. Louis, Mo.
Lowe's Companies, Inc., 922 C St., North Wilkersboro, N.C.
Mae-Moon Associates, Inc., 407 3rd Ave., Brooklyn, N.Y.
Malone & Hyde, Inc., 1700 Dunn Ave., Memphis, Tenn.
Martin Co., Inc., 124 W. Emma St., Springdale, Arkansas.
May, Fannie Candy Shops, Inc., 1137 W. Jackson St., Chicago, Ill.
McDonald, J.M. Co., 2635 W. 2nd St., Hastings Neb.
Metropolitan Paint Stores, Inc., 1200 U St. N.W., Washington, D.C.
Mill End Shops, Inc., 417 15th St., Denver, Colo.
Mode O' Day Co., 2130 N. Hollywood Way, Burbank, Calif.
Moore's Super Stores, 44 Reserve Ave., Roanoke, Va.
Moses, M.E. Co., 2919 Hansboro Ave., Dallas, Tex.
Motherhood Maternity Shops, 1712 21st St., Santa Monica, Calif.
National Auto, 523 Baltimore Ave., Clarksburg, W. Va.

EXHIBIT 13-2 (Contd.)

National Stores Co., 929 Market St., San Francisco, Calif.
Neisner Bros., Inc., 49 East Ave., Rochester, N.Y.
Newport Creamery, Inc., 208 W. Main St., Newport, R.I.
Nichol's 5¢ to $1, Inc., 636 W. Liberty St., Hubbard, O.
Olan Mills, Inc., 1101 Carter St., Chattanooga, Tenn.
Ormond Shops, Inc., 381 Park Ave. S., New York, N.Y.
Ostroy, Louis, Shoe Co., 2775 Barber St., Akron, O.
Parklane Hosiery Co., Inc., 343 Great Neck Rd., Great Neck, N.Y.
Pay N' Save Corp., 1511 6th Ave., Seattle, Wash.
Peoples Drugstores, Inc., 60 Florida Ave. N.E., Washington, D.C.
Petric Stores Corp., 45 W. 18th St., New York, N.Y.
Piedmont Fabrics of Charlotte, Inc., 3800 Silabert Ave., Charlotte, N.C.
Pix Shoes, 4140 S.W. 74th St., Miami, Fla.
Pope's Cafeterias, Inc., 805 St. Charles St., St. Louis, Mo.
Pope's 5¢ to $5 Stores, P.O. Box 478, Fuquay-Varina, N.C.
Publix Supermarkets, Inc., P.O. Box 407, Lakeland, Fla.
Puritan Confectionery Co., Inc., 897 Elm St., Manchester, N.H.
Raff's Shoes, 401 E. Hine St., Seattle, Wash.
Rainbow Shops, 357 Empire Blvd., Brooklyn, N.Y.
Regis Beauty Salons, Inc., 415 1st Ave. N., Minneapolis, Minn.
Revco D.S., Inc., 3030 Quigley Rd. Cleveland, O.
Reynolds, F.T. Co., Glendive, Mont.
Rhodes, Inc., 10 N. Rhodes, Center N.W., Atlanta, Ga.
Rite Aid Centers, Trindle Rd. and Railroad Ave., Shiremanstown, Pa.
Roe E.P. Stores, Inc., 1220 W. 6th St., Cleveland, O.
Rogers Clothes, 113 Broad St., Elizabeth, N.J.
Rosen, George, & Sons, P.O. Box 551, Clarksburg, W. Va.
Savemart, Inc., 332 E. 149th St., Bronx, N.Y.
Save Way Food Markets, Inc., 3075 Broadway, Schenectady, N.Y.
Savitt Bros., Inc., 1021 Hennepin Ave., Minneapolis, Minn.
Schensul's Cafeterias, Inc., 1036 W. 38th St., Wyoming, Mich.
Seaman Store Co., 301 Garrison St., Fort Smith, Ark.
Self-Service Shoe Stores, Inc., 4507 S. Pale Mabry H'Way, Tampa, Fla.
7-11 Fashions, Inc., 3120 S. Highland Dr., Las Vegas, Nev.
Sharp Dry Goods Co., Inc., P.O. Box 328, Checota 4, Okla.
Shelbro, Inc., 47 S. 5th Ave., Mt. Vernon, N.Y.
Shinner, E.G. Co., Inc., 9320 So. Ashland Ave., Chicago, Ill.
Sibley's Shoes, 2234 Woodward Ave., Detroit, Mich.
Sidney's, Inc., 501-03 S. Jefferson St., Roanoke, Va.

EXHIBIT 13-2 (Contd.)

Siesta Sleep Shop, Hildreth St., Westford, Mass.
Silco Cut Price Stores, Inc., Tomlinson Rd. and Jamison Ave., Philadelphia, Pa.
Simon, I. Co., Inc., 385 Gerard Ave., Bronx, N.Y.
Smith Food King, 672 S. Main St., Brigham City, U.
Smith's Clothiers of California, B'way and 14th St., Oakland, Calif.
Snelling & Snelling Co., 1530 Chestnut St., Philadelphia, Pa.
Sno-White Co., Inc., 205 E. Kettleman La., Lodi, Calif.
South Carolina Drive-ins, Inc., c/o Burger Castle, 3120 Beltline Ave., Columbia, S.C.
Spartan Dept. Stores, 111 8th Ave., New York, N.Y.
Sport & Fischer, 5 Boylston Pl., Boston, Mass.
Sprouse-Reitz Co., Inc., 2175 N.W. Upshur St., Portland, Ore.
Stacey, J.T. & Co., Inc., 2000 N.E. Alberta St., Portland, Ore.
Stambough-Thompson Co., 114 W. Federal St., Youngstown, O.
Stark, F.M. & Co., 1830 Palmer Park Blvd., Colorado Springs, Colo.
Stop & Shop, Inc., 383 D St., Boston, Mass.
Stop N' Shop, Inc., 1000 Vine St., Sacramento, Calif.
Sun Ray Cleaners, Inc., 2324 W. Madison Ave., Chicago, Ill.
Super Stores, Inc., P.O. Box 333, Chickasaw, Ala.
Supermarkets General Corp., 3 Gommerce Dr., Cranford, N.J.
Thrifty Drugstores of Washington, 16175 W. Roxbury St., Seattle, Wash.
Tuchman Cleaners, 4401 N. Keystone St., Indianapolis, Ind.
Unimart, 12500 E. Slawson Ave., Santa Fe Springs, Calif.
Union News Co., 131 Varick St., New York, N.Y.
Vogue Shoes, Inc., P.O. Box 412 Houston, Tex.
Volume Shoe Corp., 3231 E. 6th St., Topeka, Kan.
Walden Book Co., 179 Ludlow St., Stamford, Conn.
Weigel's Inc., Emory Road, Powell, Tenn.
Weiner Shoe Co., 2612 McKenney Ave., Box 2612, Houston, Tex.
Weis Markets, Inc., 1000 S. Second St., Sunbury, Pa.
Weiss & Neuman Shoe Co., 1209 Washington Ave., St. Louis, Mo.
White Drug, 205 First Ave. S., Jamestown, N. Dakota.
Wolfe's Camera Shop, 116 W. 8th St., Topeka, Kan.
Wyatt Cafeterias, Inc., 2361 W. Northwest Highway, Dallas, Tex.
Yankee Distributors, Inc., 3086 E. Court St., Flint, Mich.
Zercher Photo, Inc., 104 W. 11th St., Topeka, Kan.
Zippy Car Rentals, Inc., 439 S. Grove St., Freeport, N.Y.

SOURCES FOR LEASING AND PURCHASING FEDERAL PROPERTIES

14

Government surplus and real property may be secured by bidding. Write to the Department of the Army Corps of Engineers and ask to be placed on the mailing list of bidders. The federal government submits plans and specifications to builders, agents, etc. Whoever agrees to build on a low bid will get the job. Also, the government leases space in communities and asks for submissions (area and price). These are bids which are later acted upon. Write to the district office nearest to the area you are interested in. See Exhibit 14-1.

EXHIBIT 14-1. Government Leasing and Purchasing Agencies (District Offices of Dept. of the Army Corps of Engineers).

P.O. Box 1169, Mobile, Alabama

P.O. Box 7002, Anchorage, Alaska

P.O. Box 867, Little Rock, Arkansas

P.O. Box 17277, Foy Station, Los Angeles, California

P.O. Box 1739, Sacramento, California

First and Douglas Sts., Washington, D.C.

P.O. Box 4970, Jacksonville, 1, Florida

P.O. Box 889, Savannah, Georgia

536 So. Clark St., Chicago 5, Illinois

Clock Tower Bldg., Rock Island, Illinois

P.O. Box 59, Louisville 1, Kentucky

P.O. Box 277, Foot of Prytania St., New Orleans 9, Louisiana

EXHIBIT 14-1 (Contd.)

P.O. Box 1715, Baltimore 3, Maryland
424 Trapelo Rd., Waltham 54, Massachusetts
P.O. Box 1027, Detroit 31, Michigan
180 E. Kellog Blvd., St. Paul 1, Minnesota
1800 Federal Office Bldg., Kansas City, Missouri
420 Locust St., St. Louis 2, Missouri
6012 U.S. Post Office Bldg., Omaha 2, Nebraska
P.O. Box 1538, Albuquerque, New Mexico
Foot of Bridge St., Buffalo 7, New York
111 E. 16th St., New York 3, New York
P.O. Box 61, Tulsa, Oklahoma
628 Pittock Block S.W., Portland 5, Oregon
925 New Federal Bldg., Pittsburgh 19, Pennsylvania
P.O. Box 97, Memphis 1, Tennessee
P.O. Box 1070, Nashville, Tennessee
P.O. Box 1600, Fort Worth, Texas
P.O. Box 1229, Galveston, Texas
P.O. Box 119, Norfolk, Virginia
1519 Alaskan Way, Seattle 4, Washington
Bldg. 602, City-County Airport, Walla Walla, Washington
P.O. Box 2127, Huntington 18, W. Virginia

PROPERTY OWNED BY INDIVIDUAL STATES

Individual states own much of the land that is offered to the public for sale. The types of property vary. However, it is a good idea to contact the various states periodically and inquire relative to property available. Write to the state that you are interested in and it will comply with your request. See Exhibit 14-2.

EXHIBIT 14-2. State Leasing and Purchasing Agencies.

STATE	ADDRESS
Alaska	Rural Rehabilitation Corp., Palmer, Alaska
Alaska	Land Office Manager, Anchorage, Alaska
Alaska	Dept. of Agriculture, Fairbanks, Alaska
Alabama	Secretary of State, Montgomery, Alabama
Arizona	State Land Commissioner, Phoenix, Arizona
Arkansas	Commissioner of State Lands, Little Rock, Arkansas

Sources for Leasing and Purchasing Federal Properties / 255

EXHIBIT 14-2 (Contd.)

California	State Land Dept., Sacramento, California
Colorado	State Land Dept., Denver, Colorado
Connecticut	State Treasurer, Hartford, Connecticut
Delaware	State Park Commission, Dover, Delaware
Florida	Agriculture Commissioner, Tallahassee, Florida
Georgia	Secretary of State, Atlanta, Georgia
Idaho	Land Commissioner, Boise, Idaho
Illinois	Auditor of Public Accts., Springfield, Illinois
Indiana	State Auditor, Indianapolis, Indiana
Kansas	State Land Registrar, Topeka, Kansas
Kentucky	State Auditor, Frankfort, Kentucky
Louisiana	State Land Office, Baton Rouge, Louisiana
Maine	State Land Commissioner, Augusta, Maine
Maryland	State Land Commissioner, Annapolis, Maryland
Massachusetts	Conservation Department, Boston, Massachusetts
Michigan	Conservation Department, Lansing, Michigan
Minnesota	Division of Land, St. Paul, Minnesota
Mississippi	Commissioner of Lands, Jackson, Mississippi
Missouri	Secretary of State, Jefferson City, Missouri
Montana	Commissioner of State Lands, Helena, Montana
Nebraska	Board of Educational Lands, Lincoln, Nebraska
Nevada	Land Registrar, Carson City, Nevada
New Hampshire	State Forest Dept., Concord, New Hampshire
New Jersey	Dept. of Conservation, Trenton, New Jersey
New Mexico	Commissioner of Public Lands, Santa Fe, New Mexico
New York	Dept. of Conservation, Albany, New York
North Carolina	Secretary of State, Raleigh, North Carolina
North Dakota	State Land Commissioner, Bismark, North Dakota
Ohio	State Auditor, Columbus, Ohio
Oklahoma	Commissioner of Land, Oklahoma City, Oklahoma

EXHIBIT 14-2 (Contd.)

Oregon	State Land Board, Salem, Oregon
Pennsylvania	Secretary of Internal Affairs, Harrisburg, Pennsylvania
South Carolina	Sinking Fund Commission, Columbia, South Carolina
South Dakota	Commissioner of Lands, Pierre, South Dakota
Tennessee	State Property Administration, Nashville, Tennessee
Texas	Commissioner Land Office, Austin, Texas
Utah	State Land Board, Salt Lake City, Utah
Virginia	State Librarian, Richmond, Virginia
Vermont	State Forester, Montpelier, Vermont
Washington	Dept. of Public Lands, Olympia, Washington
West Virginia	State Auditor, Charleston, West Virginia
Wisconsin	Commissioner of Public Lands, Madison, Wisconsin
Wyoming	Commissioner of Public Lands, Cheyenne, Wyoming

The U.S. Post Office Department is continually seeking new, additional locations for post office sites. The job for the commercial real estate broker is to find a builder interested in building for the Post Office, then submit locations for approval, and if the site is approved, negotiate a lease. To submit locations or get information, contact the nearest regional real estate office, as shown in Exhibit 14-3.

EXHIBIT 14-3. Post Office Regional Real Estate Offices.

Florida, Georgia, North Carolina, and South Carolina:
Chief, Real Estate Branch, Federal Annex Bldg., Atlanta 4, Georgia.

Maine, New Hampshire, Vermont, Massachusetts, Connecticut, and Rhode Island:
Chief, Real Estate Branch, Post Office & Courthouse Bldg., Boston 9, Massachusetts.

Illinois and Michigan:
Chief, Real Estate Branch, Main Post Office Bldg., Chicago 100, Illinois.

Indiana, Kentucky, and Ohio:
Chief, Real Estate Branch, P.O. Box 1999, Cincinnati 1, Ohio.

Texas and Louisiana:
Chief, Real Estate Branch, Box 3, Main Post Office Bldg., Dallas 21, Texas.

EXHIBIT 14-3 (Contd.)

Arizona, Colorado, New Mexico, Utah, and Wyoming:
Chief, Real Estate Branch, New Custom House Bldg., Denver 2, Colorado.

Alabama, Mississippi, and Tennessee:
Chief, Real Estate Branch, Post Office Bldg., Memphis 1, Tennessee.

Minnesota, North Dakota, South Dakota, and Wisconsin:
Chief, Real Estate Branch, 212 Nicollet Ave., Minneapolis 2, Minnesota.

New York, Puerto Rico, and Virgin Islands:
Chief, Real Estate Branch, Main Post Office Bldg., New York 1, N.Y.

Pennsylvania, New Jersey, and Delaware:
Chief, Real Estate Branch, Box 8687, Main Post Office, Philadelphia 1, Pennsylvania.

Arkansas, Iowa, and Missouri:
Chief, Real Estate Branch, U.S. Court House & Custom House, St. Louis 1, Missouri.

California, Nevada, and all Pacific possessions:
Chief, Real Estate Branch, 79 New Montgomery St., San Francisco 6, California.

Alaska, Idaho, Montana, Oregon, and Washington:
Chief, Real Estate Branch, New Republic Bldg., Seattle 24, Washington.

Washington, D.C., Maryland, Virginia, and West Virginia:
Chief, Real Estate Branch, Washington City Post Office Bldg., Washington 50, D.C.

Kansas, Nebraska, and Oklahoma:
Chief, Real Estate Branch, Post Office Bldg., Wichita 25, Kansas.

It is suggested that the commercial broker make himself familiar with the forms of leases used by the government. Exhibits 14-4 and 14-5 following, show a sample post office lease and an agreement to lease.

The Post Office Department maintains a policy of leasing rather than owning the majority of space used for postal operations. It operates out of approximately 30,000 buildings. Twenty-six thousand seven hundred buildings containing 55% of all space used is leased from private owners. The remaining 45% is found in 3,000 federally owned buildings.

The privately owned buildings contain actual post offices, garages, office space, etc. The rate of increase in mail is absolutely fantastic. The Post Office Department estimates that approximately 5,000 new post offices will be needed within the next five years. When a post office becomes overloaded, the Department makes feasibility studies to determine where it must place a new post office and what the size will be.

When it is determined that a post office is needed in a particular

258 / *Sources for Leasing and Purchasing Federal Properties*

Form courtesy of Bureau of Facilities, U. S. Post Office Dept.

EXHIBIT 14-4. Post Office Lease.

POST OFFICE DEPARTMENT

LEASE

MAIN OFFICE, STATION, BRANCH, ETC.

CITY, COUNTY, STATE AND ZIP CODE

1. This LEASE, made and entered into this _____ day of _____, 19___ by and between _____ whose address is _____ hereinafter called the Lessor, and the UNITED STATES of America hereinafter called the Government:

for Lessor and Lessor's heirs, executors, administrators, successors, and assigns

WITNESSETH: The parties hereto for the consideration hereinafter mentioned covenant and agree as follows:

2. The Lessor hereby leases to the Government the following described premises, viz:

EXHIBIT 14-4 (Contd.)

to be used for postal purposes.

3. TO HAVE AND TO HOLD the said premises with their appurtenances for:

THE TERM BEGINNING	AND ENDING WITH	TOTAL NUMBER OF YEARS

4. The Government shall pay the lessor an annual rental of: _____ Dollars. $ _____ payable in equal installments at the end of each calendar month. Rent for part of month shall be prorated.

5. This lease may be renewed, at the option of the Government, for the following separate and consecutive terms and at the following annual rentals:

NO. YEARS	AT (PER ANNUAL RENTAL)	NO. YEARS	AT (PER ANNUAL RENTAL)	NO. YEARS	AT (PER ANNUAL RENTAL)
(a)		(c)		(e)	
(b)		(d)		(f)	

provided notice be given in writing to the Lessor at least _____ days before the end of the original lease term or any renewal term. All other terms and conditions of this lease shall remain the same during any renewal term unless stated otherwise herein.

6. The Lessor shall furnish to the Government under the terms of this lease, as part of the rental consideration, the following:

POD Form 1449
May 1966

Exception to Standard Form 2
Approved by Bureau of the Budget
August 1964

PAGE 1

EXHIBIT 14-4 (Contd.)

7. The lessor shall, unless herein specified to the contrary, maintain the demised premises, including the building and any and all equipment, fixtures, and appurtenances, whether severable or non-severable, furnished by the lessor under this lease in good repair and tenantable condition, except in case of damage arising from the act or the negligence of the Government's agents or employees. During the continuance of the lease, the interior of the building, including, but not limited to, the walls and ceilings, shall be repainted at least once every five (5) years unless required more often because of damage from fire or other casualty, or unless the five year period is specifically extended in writing by the Contracting Officer. The required painting shall be completed not later than six (6) months following the end of the first and each successive five (5) year period during the continuance of the lease. For the purpose of so maintaining said premises and property, the lessor may at reasonable times enter and inspect the same and make any necessary repairs thereto. Additionally, the lessor shall designate maintenance repairmen for electrical emergencies, for plumbing emergencies, for heating, ventilating and air conditioning emergencies and other emergencies (windows, doors, locks, etc.), to be called in the event of an emergency situation involving maintenance of the leased property and/or equipment when the lessor or his agent cannot be contacted within a reasonable time.

8. The Government may sublet all or any part of the premises or assign this lease but shall not be relieved from any obligation under this lease by reason of any such subletting or assignment.

9. The Government shall have the right to make alterations, attach fixtures and erect additions, structures or signs in or upon the premises hereby leased (provided such alterations, additions, structures or signs shall not be detrimental to or inconsistent with the rights granted to other tenants on the property or in the building in which said premises are located); which fixtures, additions or structures so placed in, upon or attached to the said premises shall be and remain the property of the Government and may be removed or otherwise disposed of by the Government. Prior to expiration or termination of this lease the Government shall, if required by the Lessor by notice in writing sixty days in advance of such expiration or termination, restore the premises to as good condition as that existing at the time of entering upon the same under this lease, reasonable and ordinary wear and tear and damages by the elements or by circumstances over which the Government has no control, excepted.

10. (a) This lease may be terminated upon ninety days' notice in writing to the Lessor whenever the Post Office Department shall decide to move the office into a Government-owned building which shall have been provided for it.

(b) This lease may be terminated upon ninety days' notice in writing to the Lessor whenever, in the judgment of the Post Office Department, the growth of the service at that office renders additional room necessary and the Lessor is unable or unwilling to furnish suitable and sufficient additional space at an additional rental satisfactory to the Department.

(c) If any building or any part of it on the leased property becomes unfit for use for the purposes leased, the lessor shall put the same in a satisfactory condition, as determined by the Post Office Department, for the purposes leased. If the lessor does not do so with reasonable diligence, the Post Office Department in its discretion may cancel the lease. For any period said building or any part thereof is unfit for use for the purposes leased, the rent shall be abated in proportion to the area determined by the Post Office Department to have been rendered unavailable to the Post Office Department by reason of such condition. Unfitness for use does not include subsequent unsuitability arising from such matters as design, size or location of the building.

(d) If conditions should occur which would otherwise give the Government the right to cancel this lease or to incur a cost for which it could obtain reimbursement under this lease, the Government shall not have said rights unless it gives:

(1) written notice of said occurrence by certified or registered mail to the mortgagee and the assignee of moneys due or to become due under this lease whose names and addresses are furnished to the Government by Lessor.

and the Lessor shall at Lessor's expense record this lease in the proper recording office.

EXHIBIT 14-4 (Contd.)

(2) said mortgagee and assignee not less than 45 days' opportunity to cure the default by the Lessor and the condition or conditions giving rise to said cancellation or reimbursement rights. Additional time may also be granted the above parties at the discretion of the Government. The curative period set out in this paragraph does not control or govern the curative period which has been or may be determined upon as proper in connection with any equal opportunity clauses, herein.

11. No member of or Delegate to Congress or Resident Commissioner shall be admitted to any share or part of this lease or to any benefit to arise therefrom. Nothing, however, herein contained shall be construed to extend to any incorporated company, if the lease be for the general benefit of such corporation or company.

12. (The following clause is applicable unless this contract is exempt under the rules and regulations of the Secretary of Labor issued pursuant to Executive Order No. 11246, dated September 24, 1965 (30 F.R.12319)).

During the performance of this contract, the contractor agrees as follows:

(a) The contractor will not discriminate against any employee or applicant for employment because of race, creed, color, or national origin. The contractor will take affirmative action to ensure that applicants are employed, and that employees are treated during employment, without regard to their race, creed, color, or national origin. Such action shall include, but not be limited to the following: employment, upgrading, demotion, or transfer; recruitment or recruitment advertising; layoff or termination; rates of pay or other forms of compensation; and selection for training, including apprenticeship. The contractor agrees to post in conspicuous places, available to employees and applicants for employment, notices to be provided by the contracting officer setting forth the provisions of this nondiscrimination clause.

(b) The contractor will, in all solicitations or advertisements for employees placed by or on behalf of the contractor, state that all qualified applicants will receive consideration for employment without regard to race, creed, color, or national origin.

(c) The contractor will send to each labor union or representative of workers with which he has a collective bargaining agreement or other contract or understanding, a notice, to be provided by the agency contracting officer, advising the labor union or workers' representative of the contractor's commitments under Section 202 of Executive Order No. 11246 of September 24, 1965, and shall post copies of the notice in conspicuous places available to employees and applicants for employment.

(d) The contractor will comply with all provisions of Executive Order No. 11246 of Sept. 24, 1965, and of the rules, regulations, and relevant orders of the Secretary of Labor.

(e) The contractor will furnish all information and reports required by Executive Order No. 11246 of September 24, 1965, and by the rules, regulations, and orders of the Secretary of Labor, or pursuant thereto, and will permit access to his books, records, and accounts by the contracting agency and the Secretary of Labor for purposes of investigation to ascertain compliance with such rules, regulations, and orders.

EXHIBIT 14-4 (Contd.)

(f) In the event of the contractor's noncompliance with the nondiscrimination clauses of this contract or with any of such rules, regulations, or orders, this contract may be cancelled, terminated or suspended in whole or in part and the contractor may be declared ineligible for further Government contracts in accordance with procedures authorized in Executive Order No. 11246 of Sept. 24, 1965, and such other sanctions may be imposed and remedies involved as provided in Executive Order No. 11246 of September 24, 1965, or by rule, regulation, or order of the Secretary of Labor, or as otherwise provided by law.

(g) The contractor will include the provisions of Paragraphs (1) through (7) in every subcontract or purchase order unless exempted by rules, regulations, or orders of the Secretary of Labor issued pursuant to Section 204 of Executive Order No.11246 of Sept. 24, 1965, so that such provisions will be binding upon each subcontractor or vendor. The contractor will take such action with respect to any subcontract or purchase order as the contracting agency may direct as a means of enforcing such provisions including sanctions for noncompliance: *Provided, however,* That in the event the contractor becomes involved in, or is threatened with, litigation with a subcontractor or vendor as a result of such direction by the contracting agency, the contractor may request the United States to enter into such litigation to protect the interests of the United States.

13. (The following clause is applicable when the leased space is in a building occupied by tenants or concessionaires in addition to the Government and if the total rental under this lease exceeds $10,000 per year, or, at the sole election of the Government, if the total rental under this lease combined with the total rental under all other Federal Government leases of space in the building which the space covered by this lease is located exceeds $10,000 per year, the lessor agrees to comply with the following provision:)

(a) As used in this section, the term "facility" means stores, shops, restaurants, cafeterias, rest-rooms, and any other facility of a public nature in the building in which the space covered by this lease is located.

(b) The lessor agrees that he will not discriminate by segregation or otherwise against any person or persons because of race, creed, color, or national origin in furnishing, or by refusing to furnish to such person or persons the use of any facility, including any and all services, privileges, accomodations, and activities provided thereby.

(c) It is agreed that the lessor's noncompliance with the provisions of this section shall constitute a material breach of this lease. In the event of such noncompliance, the Government may take appropriate action to enforce compliance, may terminate this lease, or may pursue such other remedies as may be provided by law. In the event of termination, the lessor shall be liable for all excess costs of the Government in acquiring substitute space, including but not limited to the cost of moving to such space.

(d) The lessor agrees to include, or to require the inclusion of, the foregoing provisions of this section (with the terms "lessor" and "lease" appropriately modified) in every agreement or concession pursuant to which any person other than the lessor operates or has the right to operate any facility. The lessor also agrees that it will take such action with respect to any such agreement as the Department may direct as a means of enforcing this section, including but not limited to termination of the agreement or concession.

14. The following paragraphs were deleted before execution:

15. The following paragraphs were added before execution:

EXHIBIT 14-4 (Contd.)

It is expressly understood between the parties hereto that the terms and conditions of the Agreement to Lease executed by the Government on _____, 19___, including any amendments or modifications thereto, are made and accepted by _____ part of this lease and are to be complied with as though fully set forth herein.

IN WITNESS WHEREOF, the parties hereto have hereunto signed and sealed these presents as of the date first written above.

SEAL

_____
(Company, Corporate or Partnership Name)

(A _____ Corporation)
    (State)

By _____

Its _____
    (Title)

By _____

Its _____
    (Title)

WITNESSES:

_____

_____

EXHIBIT 14-4 (Contd.)

GOVERNMENT:

THE UNITED STATES OF AMERICA

By _____

Title _____
      Contracting Officer

WITNESSES:

PAGE

POD Form 1449
May 1966

Sources for Leasing and Purchasing Federal Properties / 265

Form courtesy of Bureau of Facilities, U. S. Post Office Dept.

EXHIBIT 14-5. Post Office Agreement to Lease.

FORM OF ACKNOWLEDGMENT FOR INDIVIDUALS

State of _____)
) SS:
County of _____)

  Personally appeared before me, a Notary Public in and for the County and State aforesaid, _____
            (Identify individual party to the lease)
who is known to me to be the same person who executed the foregoing lease, and who acknowledged that _____ signed, sealed and delivered the
            (he)(she)
same as _____ free and voluntary act for the uses and purposes
    (his)(her)
therein set forth.

  Witness my hand and notarial seal, in the County and State aforesaid, this _____ day of _____, 19_____.

               _____
                   Notary Public

(Notarial Seal)

             My commission expires _____

OD Form 1455a
Dec. 1964

EXHIBIT 14-5 (Contd.)

FORM OF ACKNOWLEDGMENT FOR HUSBAND AND WIFE

State of _____)
) SS:
County of _____)

    Personally appeared before me, a Notary Public in and for the County and State aforesaid, _____ who is known to me to be the same person who executed the foregoing lease, and who acknowledged that he signed, sealed, and delivered the same as his free and voluntary act for the uses and purposes therein set forth.

    And on the same day also voluntarily appeared before me _____ _____, wife of the said _____ to me well known as the person signing said lease, and in the absence of _____ _____, said _____ declared that she had of her own free will signed and sealed the foregoing lease for the purposes therein contained and set forth, including the release of homestead and dower therein, of which she had full knowledge, without compulsion or undue influence of her said husband.

    Witness my hand and notarial seal, in the County and State aforesaid, this _____ day of _____, 19____.

                                                   _____
                                                   Notary Public

(Notarial Seal)

                My commission expires _____

POD Form **1438**
Dec. 1964

EXHIBIT 14-5 (Contd.)

FORM OF ACKNOWLEDGMENT FOR CORPORATIONS

STATE OF ....
COUNTY OF .... } ss:

Personally appeared before me, a notary public in and for the county and State aforesaid,..................

....

....

and .... who .... known to me to be the

.... and .... of the ....

.... and

to be the same person who executed the foregoing lease, who deposes and says that he knows the seal of the said corporation, that the seal affixed to the above instrument is the seal of said corporation, and that it was affixed, and that he signed .... name thereto, by authority of the said corporation, for the purposes set forth, and as .... own free and voluntary act.

....

Done at ...., in the county and State aforesaid, this........................ day of ...., 19 ....

[NOTARIAL SEAL]

....
Notary Public.

My commission expires ....

NOTE.—If the corporation is without a seal, that portion of the acknowledgment referring to a seal should be stricken out, and on the blank line following this statement should be made: "and that the said corporation has no corporate seal."

EXHIBIT 14-5 (Contd.)

FORM OF ACKNOWLEDGMENT FOR ATTORNEYS IN FACT

State of ....} ss:
County of ....

On this .... day of ...., in the year one thousand nine hundred and ...., before me personally came ...., to me known and known by me to be the Attorney in Fact of ...., known to me to be the individual described in, and who by said Attorney in Fact executed, the within instrument, and he acknowledged that he executed the same as the act and deed of ...., therein described, and for the purposes therein mentioned, by virtue of a power of attorney duly executed by the said ...., bearing date the .... day of ...., in the year .... hundred and ...., and recorded in the office of the .... for the County of ...., State of ...., on the .... day of ...., 19 , in Liber ...., of ...., page ....

Done at ...., in the County and State aforesaid, this .... day of ...., 19

{ NOTARIAL SEAL }

....
Notary Public.

My commission expires ....

1455

EXHIBIT 14-5 (Contd.)

Post Office Department

LEASE

FOR

POST OFFICE QUARTERS

Post Office:

Lessor:

Date:

Term: years

Beginning

Rent: $ per annum.

Lease includes:

GOVERNMENT PRINTING OFFICE   5—3142

Form courtesy of Bureau of Facilities, U. S. Post Office Dept.

EXHIBIT 14-6. Post Office Lease Bidder's Qualifications Form.

POST OFFICE DEPARTMENT **LEASE BIDDER'S QUALIFICATIONS** (See Instructions on Reverse)	FORM APPROVED BUDGET BUREAU NO. 46-R037

1. BID IDENTIFICATION

POST OFFICE (Branch, station, main PO, etc.)

LOCATION (City, state, ZIP code)

DATE OF BID (Month, day, year)

INSTRUCTIONS: The bidder shall answer all questions on this form, inserting "none" or "not applicable" where appropriate. Use "REMARKS" or attach additional sheets if more space is required. Questions concerning this form should be directed to the office designated in the advertisement to receive the bids.

2. NAME OF BIDDER

3. ADDRESS (Street, City, State & ZIP Code)

4. HAVE YOU OR THE PARTNERSHIP, CORPORATION, ETC. YOU REPRESENT, SUBMITTED ANY BIDS ON POST OFFICES WHICH ARE NOW PENDING AWARD AND/OR HAVE YOU OR THE FIRM YOU REPRESENT PARTICIPATED AS A PRINCIPAL IN CONSTRUCTION AND LEASE OF POST OFFICES?
☐ YES   ☐ NO.

5. IF ITEM 4 IS YES, GIVE NUMBER OF AND NAME OF STATE WHERE POST OFFICES ARE OR WILL BE LOCATED, EXAMPLE 1. N.Y.; 2. FLA.

BIDS ON POST OFFICES NOW PENDING AWARD. _____
POST OFFICE CONSTRUCTION WITHIN PAST YEAR. _____
POST OFFICE CONSTRUCTION WITHIN PRIOR YEAR. _____
POST OFFICE CONSTRUCTION WITHIN PRIOR TWO YEARS. _____

6. ARE YOU, ANY MEMBERS OF YOUR IMMEDIATE FAMILY, OR ANY OF THE PRINCIPALS, OFFICERS, DIRECTORS, OR STOCKHOLDERS OF THE FIRM YOU REPRESENT, IN THE EMPLOY OF THE POST OFFICE DEPARTMENT?
☐ YES   ☐ NO   *(See Instruction # 2 on reverse)*

7. IF ITEM 6 IS YES, GIVE NAME(S) OF INDIVIDUAL(S) AND NAME AND LOCATION OF POSTAL FACILITY WHERE EMPLOYED.

8. LIST ALL CONSTRUCTION CONTRACTS (INCLUDING POST OFFICES) CURRENTLY IN FORCE WITH YOU AS OWNER OR CONTRACTOR:

LOCATION AND TYPE OF BUILDINGS	OWNER'S NAME AND ADDRESS	CONTRACT AMOUNT	ESTIMATED COMPLETION DATE

POD Form **1413**
Mar. 1967

EXHIBIT 14-6 (Contd.)

9. LIST THE LAST 5 BANKS OR OTHER LENDING INSTITUTIONS FROM WHICH YOU HAVE BORROWED AND AMOUNTS OWING:		
NAME	ADDRESS (Street, City, State, ZIP Code)	AMOUNT NOW OWING

10. AMOUNT I/WE ARE WORTH IN REAL ESTATE AND PERSONAL PROPERTY: $

11. MY/OUR LIABILITIES OWING AND INCURRED DO NOT EXCEED THE AMOUNT OF: $

12. CHECK PROPER BOX IN ANSWER TO THE FOLLOWING QUESTIONS *(Attach explanation for each "YES" answer)*	YES	NO
A. HAVE YOU DURING THE PAST TWO YEARS BEEN CHARGED WITH A FAILURE TO MEET THE CLAIMS OF YOUR SUBCONTRACTORS, MATERIAL MEN, OR SUPPLIERS?		
B. HAVE YOU EVER FAILED TO QUALIFY AS A RESPONSIBLE BIDDER?		
C. HAVE YOU EVER FAILED TO ENTER INTO A CONTRACT AFTER AN AWARD WAS MADE?		
D. HAVE YOU EVER FAILED TO COMPLETE ANY WORK AWARDED?		
E. HAS YOUR APPLICATION FOR SURETY BOND EVER BEEN DECLINED?		

13. HOW WILL YOU FINANCE CONSTRUCTION OF THIS PROJECT?

14. WHEN A LOAN IS REQUIRED, ENTER THE NAME AND ADDRESS OF THE LENDING INSTITUTION FROM WHICH A COMMITMENT HAS OR WILL BE OBTAINED:

REMARKS

CERTIFICATION: For the purpose of establishing the qualification of the undersigned as a lease bidder with the Post Office Department, I (we) furnish the foregoing information and certify, as bidder, that it is true and correct.

SIGNATURE OF AUTHORIZED OFFICER	SIGNATURE OF AUTHORIZED OFFICER
TITLE	TITLE

DATE FORM EXECUTED

INSTRUCTIONS

1. This form must be used whenever a bid for construction and lease of a Postal Facility is submitted. One completed copy will accompany the bidder's executed bid and other related bid documents as required by the advertisement.

2. For purposes of completing items 6 and 7 of this form, "employ" means persons performing assigned duties at Headquarters or postal installations or facilities of the Department, including special Government officers, employees, or members of any committee appointed by the Postmaster General who are retained, designated, appointed, or employed to perform temporary duties either on a full-time or intermittent basis, with or without compensation, for not to exceed 130 days during any period of 365 consecutive days, and "immediate family" means spouse minor child, and other persons related to the employee by blood who are regular members of the employee's household.

suburban community, the Regional Real Estate Office will advertise for bids. The bids are based on standard plans and specifications plus the bidder's site. A contract is awarded to the most responsible bidder who submits the best bid in the government's opinion. When the building is completed, the post office occupies the premises as a tenant, the fee belonging to the bidder. The bidder may maintain ownership, sell the property, or finance same.

The larger post office buildings are handled slightly differently. The Regional Office will obtain an option on a suitable site. Building plans are then prepared. After that, bidders can make bids on the building construction requirements and the known land cost.

How will anyone interested in knowing about post office deals, to be bid upon, go about getting this information? Anyone interested should contact the nearest Regional Office covering the area that he may be interested in. He will then be placed upon the bidder's mailing list for postal projects. Invitations to bid are offered for each project in that area. Notices for bidders are placed in post offices and local newspapers. Those bidders interested in major facilities of 50,000 sq. ft. and over should seek to be placed on the bidder's list for major facilities. To do so, you must contact the Director, Realty Division, Bureau of Facilities, Post Office Dept., Washington, D.C. 20260.

The government is interested in knowing who they are doing business with. Consequently, they have a "lease bidder's qualifications" form that must be completed. Basically, the form requests the bidder's financial background and eligibility to bid. An example is shown in Exhibit 14-6.

The Post Office Department takes long-term leases generally for 20 years, plus options. There are various clauses that may differ. Leases may contain the following:

(1) Option to purchase by the government. (Not found in all leases.)
(2) Actual building maintenance is always the landlord's obligation. (Usually found in all leases.)
(3) Janitorial service is the responsibility of the tenant. (Usually found in all leases.)
(4) Tax clause—the government agrees to pay all taxes. (This is not found in all leases.)

The leasing program of the Post Office Department is similar to those used by private industry.

APPENDIX

APPENDIX A : The Basics of Commercial Leasing Law

APPENDIX B : Listing and Selling Pointers

APPENDIX C : Glossary of Terms

APPENDIX A

The Basics of Commercial Leasing Law

A basic knowledge of commercial law is definitely a prerequisite to becoming a store leasing broker. It cannot make you an expert, but a little knowledge is sometimes a good thing.

The basis of all real estate is property. Property is the interest that one has in anything that is subject to ownership. This interest may be tangible or intangible. The interest in property may be permanent, temporary, conditional, or legal. The rights to the use of property may be complete, limited, or partial.

Types of Property and Ownership

There are two types of property and each is classified according to its actual definition:

(1) Personal property.
(2) Real property.

Personal property is the term applied to interests in all movable objects. Specifically, this means objects that are not attached or affixed to the earth. Interest in personal property include furniture, books, clothing, stocks, bonds, jewelry, etc.

Real property may be defined as an interest in things that are permanently affixed to buildings or land. Interests in real property include land, trees, buildings, and anything permanently affixed to the buildings.

There are various forms of ownership and there are limitations of ownership. First, I will clarify the meaning of ownership. It is possible to be a limited, partial, restricted, or absolute owner. The highest form of ownership is absolute. The rights of absolute ownership include:

1. The right of use and enjoyment.
2. The right to sell, assign, or give away during life.
3. The right to sell, assign, or give away after death.
4. The right of inheritance.

But, even absolute ownership of property carries with it certain restrictions. Property may not be used in such a way as to annoy or injure neighbors. Barking dogs or television sets playing loudly all night are not rights that go with property ownership. A second restriction on property is the state's right to eminent domain. The state may condemn and take any real property that it deems warranted. Generally, property is taken for use as a state building or if it is in the path of a public highway. The owner of the building, however, must be paid just compensation. A third restriction against ownership is the right of the state to levy taxes, assessments, etc. against the property. This is done because real property taxes provide much of the state's income. The use of property is also controlled by the state. There are laws providing for percentage of use, height, type of use, and so forth. The last major restriction against real property is that of the property being liable for the debts of the owner. The property, by various legal methods, may be sold and the proceeds used to apply toward payment of obligations.

Real property may be owned through four principal methods which are:

1. Severalty.
2. Joint tenancy.
3. Tenancy in common.
4. Tenancy in partnership.

Ownership in severalty is the term applied to property owned by one person alone.

Joint tenancy applies to property owned by two or more persons having identical interests. When a joint tenancy partner dies, however, the surviving tenant or tenants take his share or interest. Surviving heirs, such as children, widow, etc., have no right to the interest.

Tenancy in common is nearly identical to joint tenancy, except that the survivorship factor is different. The heirs, in this case, do share in the interest and become tenants in common with other co-owners.

Tenancy in partnership is the term applied to property when a partnership acquires firm property. The partners have equal rights, and neither one may dispose of his interest alone.

How Real Property May Be Acquired

(A) There are many methods by which real property may be acquired by operation of law:

1. Occupancy —Abandoned property may be taken after statutory requirements have been met.
2. Succession —Transfer of real property of a deceased person to heirs by operation of law.

3. Marriage —Wife by dower rights acquires one-third interest in real property which husband owned during their marriage.
4. Accretion —Increase of land due to action of water.
5. Bankruptcy—If owner becomes a bankrupt, title may be transferred for the benefit of the creditors.

(B) Real property may also be acquired by the action of both principals:

1. Grants —Under the Homestead Act, the government may issue title.
2. Dedication —An owner may set land aside for public use.
3. Will —Upon death, owner may stipulate passing of title to heir.
4. Sale —Sale between willing buyer and willing seller.
5. Deed of Conveyance—Deed containing words of conveyance.
6. Gift —Voluntary transfer of title.

(C) Real property may be acquired by the act of the acquirer:

1. Eminent Domain —State has the right to take its property for its use and the owner is compensated.
2. Adverse Possession—Open and notorious claim against owner for a period of years (varies in different states).
3. Forfeiture —(Very rare) Applicable in instances of crime or breach of contract.
4. Judgement —To satisfy a lien by court decision.
5. Execution —Sale made by court order.

At this point, I would like to explain that certain laws, customs, legal terms, etc. will be discussed briefly. This is because the real estate managing agent must know enough law so that he may understand his business, and be prompted, when in doubt, to know when to consult an attorney. In this way, the managing agent is able to prevent his client, in many instances, from becoming involved in a lawsuit.

The Prime Importance of Commission Agreements

Another important phase of the law that deals directly with the interests of the broker is the question of commission agreements.

The value of a commission agreement is the end product or the "name of the game." It is entirely possible to earn your commission legally and yet deprive yourself just as legally of any right to collect this commission. If you prevent yourself from earning money, then you are a poor store leasing broker. I will give you a few tips that will make you a good commercial managing agent.

The intent of this appendix section is to help you benefit from reading about time and money loss mistakes I have made in the past. I have committed the error of signing "bad" commission agreements. The best way to prevent this from happening is to read and understand your agreement. Do not sign a commission agreement blindly. This is a must.

Many attorneys for the landlord are not working for, nor are they concerned in any way, with the interests of the commercial leasing broker. The newcomer in this business must realize that he has an obligation to protect himself. Commission agreements must be carefully read, digested, and, if necessary, reasonable and fair alterations should be demanded by the managing agent. Do not permit an attorney to submit an agreement that you cannot live with.

The commercial store leasing broker is an expert who performs a valuable service. This service should not be subject to the whims of some attorneys. I do not refer to the vast majority of attorneys, but rather to the few. These particular lawyers attempt to overprotect the landlord to the complete exclusion of the managing agent. This is a disservice, and the experienced leasing agent will not tolerate such tactics. Unless you are completely satisfied with a proposed commission agreement, *do not sign it*. I have found that the demands of lawyers are often overridden and appropriate changes inserted at the request of the landlord.

In very rare instances, the deal may break up because the managing agent does not agree to the terms of a commission agreement. Forget it; do not worry. It is possible, with an unreasonable agreement, for the deal to close without the agent ever receiving his commission. Yes, he cannot collect his commission because he has signed away his legal rights.

My intent is not to criticize the legal profession. I am only pointing out that the landlord's attorney does not have your interest at heart. This is entirely understandable. A lawyer's professional responsibility is to protect the interests of his client. At the same time, however, you have your own interests, and it is *your* responsibility to see to it that they are fully protected. Laudable as it is, lawyers are sometimes overprotective and overzealous in behalf of their client.

Never permit a lawyer to limit or restrict your right to obtain your commission or persuade or pressure you into any agreement which is unilaterally slanted in his client's favor. Obviously, you are in business to make money. Without your rightful commission, you cannot earn a living.

Terms of Commission Agreement

The customary leasing procedure is relatively simple. When all terms have been agreed upon verbally, an appointment is made for the purpose of reducing the understanding to writing. At this meeting, prior to presentation of the proposed lease, a commission agreement is presented to the broker for signature. In order to give you an idea of what you may be asked to sign, a typical commission agreement follows, (Exhibit A–1).

EXHIBIT A-1. Brokerage Agreement.

BROKER: DATE:
OWNER:
PROSPECTIVE TENANT:
PREMISES:

The above owner and broker mutually agree with each other as follows

1. This agreement is in accordance with the terms of the original hiring and constitutes the entire and only agreement between the owner and broker affecting the above premises. No modification of this agreement shall be valid unless made by an instrument in writing signed by both the owner and broker.

2. The broker represents that the broker is and has been a duly licensed real estate broker under the laws of the State of _____ during all of the times that said broker has been negotiating a possible sale of the above premises.

3. Said broker represents that he is the sole broker who has been negotiating a possible lease of the above premises to the above prospective tenant and said broker agrees to indemnify and save harmless the owner from any and all claims of any other broker in connection therewith.

4. The total amount of commission shall be _____ DOLLARS, and said sum shall be deemed to have been earned by said broker as, if and when and only in the event that a lease for premises described in the proposed lease shall actually be consummated.

5. If for any reason whatsoever, including the owner's fault or arbitrary action, a lease of said premises shall not be actually executed by both the owner and said prospective tenant, no commission shall be deemed to have been earned and the broker shall not be entitled to any payment whatsoever.

6. Anything to the contrary notwithstanding, the following shall prevail; except for wilful default on the part of the landlord, the understanding in previous paragraphs shall prevail. In the event of wilful default on the part of the lessor, the brokerage commission shall be due and payable.

7. The broker acknowledges that he did not have, does not have, and will not have an exclusive brokerage for the lease of said premises by said owner.

WITNESS: _____

(Owner)

_____

(Broker)

The opening parts of this agreement are self-explanatory. Date, broker, owner, prospective tenant, should present no problems. My only suggestion is that under the heading "prospective tenant," complete the applicant's name as follows:

Prospective Tenant: JOHN JONES, et al; or corporation in which they are beneficially interested. The particular working used will eliminate any misunderstanding or possible connivance. The owner cannot, if the tenant signs using a corporate name, claim that the individual and the corporation are separate and distinct and, consequently, attempt to avoid payment of a rightful commission.

Paragraph one is fair and equitable. This paragraph actually does help the broker and landlord. Any changes should be in writing. No change or alteration is required for this paragraph.

Paragraph two requires no change. A broker must be licensed in order to collect a commission. If neither of the parties to the lease comes from the state in which you are licensed, then you are taking a chance of not being paid. My only suggestion in this type of situation is to have a "personal service" contract drawn up by your attorney and agreed to by the landlord. This is a weak crutch, but it's better than nothing. The best protection is to work through a licensed local broker.

Paragraph three is a reasonable agreement. The only suggested addition would be "said indemnification to apply to brokerage claims arising, with relation to the aforementioned prospective tenant only."

Paragraph four is acceptable if the amount of commission entered is the correct amount. This is a bad paragraph for the broker, but it can be mitigated later.

Paragraph five is unreasonable. This particular paragraph can be a license to "steal." Much money has been taken from brokers through this particular paragraph. However, we will pass this up. No changes will be made at this time. The necessary alterations will be made later. The reason why this particular paragraph is unacceptable is obvious. The landlord may take a broker's deal and peddle it until he matches the deal. The landlord may then consummate his own deal without the broker. Because the managing agent signed this agreement, he actually placed himself in the position of having less legal rights than the law allowed prior to his signing.

Paragraph six is the all important one. Here, you can nullify much of the restrictive legal language of the attorney with the addition of, "Anything to the contrary notwithstanding, the following shall prevail; except for wilful default on the part of the landlord." If the landlord or his attorney will not accept this alteration, then terminate the deal and take your client elsewhere. I must mention that the question of "wilful default" is generally agreed to by most attorneys. A few lawyers reject the idea because they are overprotective. A very few tend to "showboat" and their acting may be costly to their client.

Paragraph seven is a fair paragraph and permits the landlord to look to other managing agents, in the event that you are not the "exclusive broker."

Make sure that the owner signs the agreement and as an artistic touch, have his lawyer witness the agreement and date same.

There are other types of agreements where the attorney does considerable repeating, legal dancing, and throws in everything but his fee. The lawyer does not worry about your fee, so be sure that you do.

Exhibit A-2, following, is another brokerage agreement you should peruse in order to give you the feel of reading these agreements. The most unacceptable paragraph in this agreement, is number one. It should be altered to contain the "wilful default" segment.

EXHIBIT A-2. Brokerage Agreement.

As a consideration moving to the parties to a certain lease to be made between _____, landlord, and _____ as tenant, for the letting of _____ _____ and before the signing of such lease and as a condition precedent to the consummating of all prior negotiations and to the creation of any lease and each and every term thereof, the undersigned broker does hereby covenant and agree to and with the said parties, their heirs, distributees, executors, administrators, successors, and assigns, as follows:

1. In the event that the lease herein referred to fails to be consummated, and/or received and accepted by the landlord, whether any such failure is by reason of any default or act of omission or commission, arbitrary, intentional, or otherwise, by either of the said parties to said lease, or by any of their heirs, distributees, executors, administrators, successors, or assigns, or by reason of any lack of any approval or consent that may be deemed necessary, appropriate, or advisable by either of such parties or by any of their heirs, distributees, executors, administrators, successors, or assigns, or for any other reason whatsoever, then and in that event, the undersigned will waive and does hereby waive all claims or demand, in law or in equity, for any commission whatever in connection with such lease and all negotiations prior thereto.

2. In the event that the lease and the full consideration therefor are actually delivered, received, and accepted in accordance with the terms of such lease, then and in that event, the undersigned does hereby agree to accept as commission in full in connection with such lease, including tenant's option to renew, if any, and all negotiations prior thereto.

The agreed commission is $_____, payable when tenant opens for business and pays rent therefor.

Due and Payable

3. The undersigned represents that the undersigned is the sole broker in any wise instrumental in consummating the within lease and the prior negotiations thereto and agrees to hold the landlord harmless against any claims by any other brokers.

This agreement cannot be changed orally.

DATED:

AGREED TO:

By: _____
          BROKER

_____
LESSOR

APPENDIX B

Listing and Selling Pointers

When a store is leased, it will generally take a tenant about three to four weeks to get it ready for business. This period of time enables the managing agent to continue his visual salesmanship by placing his name before the public. This is done by placing a "Rented By" strip over the old "For Rent" sign. Landlords are quick to appreciate a successful renting agent, and they will contact you when they have a vacancy.

Contact Property Owners for Listings

I have already stressed how the telephone is used constantly to contact landlords who have vacant stores. Another method is to send out mimeographed letters to all property owners in your town. Books containing these lists are available for some areas. In other areas, you will have to make up your own owners' manual from information contained at the local hall of records. I must stress that it is better to try to control a relatively small area and have information on all owners, rather than attempting to control an area that is too large to handle. When your owners' manual is completed, you should have the following information for each property:

1. Address of property.
2. Owner's name, address, and telephone number.
3. Assessed value of property.
4. Date of last transfer.
5. List of present tenancy.

Once the owners' manual has been completed, it is relatively simple to keep it up to date.

I suggest a form letter be sent to all landlords periodically, usually every six months. The suggested form is shown in Exhibit B–1.

EXHIBIT B-1. Listing Letter.

YO 6-2130   JOHN JONES REAL ESTATE
COMMERCIAL LEASING
102 MAIN STREET
YONKERS, N.Y.

Date

Mr. A. Atwood
1200 Main St.
Yonkers, N.Y.

Re: (Insert address of property
in this space)

Dear Sir:

Do you have any vacant stores for lease? We have a number of tenants who are looking for stores in your area. If you wish to lease at this time, we believe we can be of assistance to you. We post signs and do all advertising

Our services include:

1. Finding a tenant ready and able to rent your store.
2. Securing a legally binding deposit.
3. Assisting in all legal details, except where an attorney is required.
4. Financial reports on all prospective tenants.

Please phone us for an appointment. We will be glad to inspect your property and give you the benefit of our professional experience, without obligation.

Very truly yours,

John Jones

Letter courtesy of The Mines Press, 342 W. 14th St., New York, N.Y.

Continue Selling New Listings

A renting agent must always remember that salesmanship has a dual purpose. First, salesmanship must be used to secure a listing. Second, it must be used to sell or lease the listing after it has been secured. A common error made by many managing agents is to worry about leasing stores already on file, while completely forgetting about securing new listings. Before you can sell or lease you must secure.

Brochures are of some help in selling. If you secure a store that is large enough so that it will pay a good commission, do not hesitate to spend some money, if it is good enough to warrant the expenditure. All types of realty brochures are made up, some costing several dollars each and others costing a few cents each. I am not saying that an expensive brochure does not serve its purpose, because it does; however, I do feel that a clean, clear, well-thought-out and well-written, mimeographed brochure will serve almost as well.

An example of an inexpensive brochure is shown in Exhibit B-2. The reverse is seen in B-3, which are solicitation forms.

EXHIBIT B-2. Presentation of Listing.

John Jones Real Estate
4 Main Street
New York, N.Y.   MU 2-1000

2207 Linden Blvd., New York, N.Y.
  Entire Building for Lease

PRIME PRESTIGE INSTITUTIONAL-TYPE BUILDING
  Ultramodern in Every Respect

FULLY AIR-CONDITIONED   CENTRALLY HEATED   WELL-APPOINTED
  8,000 Square Feet on First (Ground) Floor.

LINDEN BOULEVARD

A most important business thoroughfare. The heaviest traffic artery in Queens. From 1940 to present, every inch of land both north and south of and on Linden Blvd. has been fully developed and utilized through the erection of apartment houses, homes, and retail stores.

This building is located at an intersection that is fast becoming an important pivotal point for this area.

FOR FULL DETAILS CALL MR. JONES, MU 2-1000

---

288 / *Appendix*

EXHIBIT B-3. Typical Solicitation Forms.

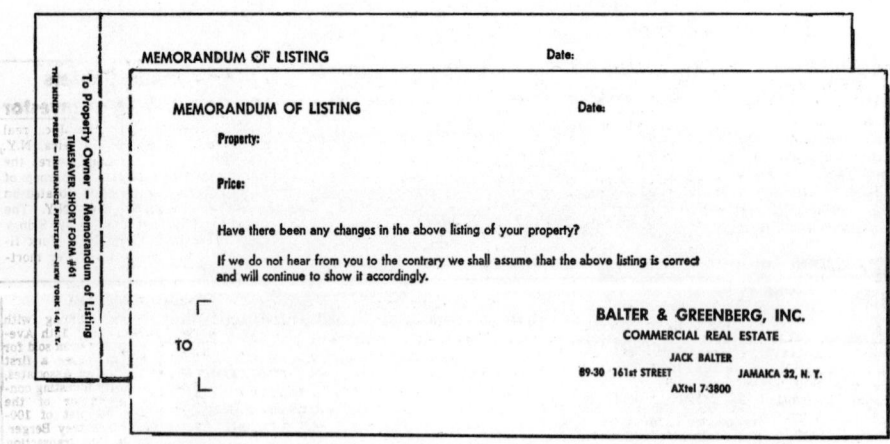

Forms courtesy of The Mines Press, 342 W. 14th St., New York, N.Y.

EXHIBIT B-4. Typical Publicity Pieces for Securing Taxpayers.

(212) AXtel 7-3800   Established 1946

Balter & Greenberg, Inc.
"THE NATIONS PRESTIGE REALTY FIRM"
89-30 161 STREET • JAMAICA, N. Y. 11432

CALVIN L. GREENBERG, C. S. A.
   Chairman of the Board
JACK BALTER
   President
LEE WEISINGER
   Vice Pres., Investments
SOLOMON GOODMAN
   Vice Pres., Leasing
SID LEVINE
   Vice Pres., Appraising

MEMBER
National Association of Real Estate Boards
Long Island Real Estate Board
Columbia Society of Real Estate Appraisers
New York State Appraisal Society
National Institute of Real Estate Brokers
International Traders Club
N. Y. S. Association of Real Estate Boards

Gentlemen:

    For many years (over 20) Balter & Greenberg have specialized in the sale of net leases, taxpayers and shopping centers. Perhaps at this time you may wish to sell. Possibly you may have used up your depreciation or wish to consolidate your holdings.

    We are not seeking listings for general mailings. We represent several groups of sophisticated investors who are experienced and financially able to purchase large properties. We are soliciting on behalf of these clients. Any information given us will be treated in a confidential manner.

Very truly yours,
BALTER & GREENBERG, INC.

Calvin L. Greenberg

CLG:re   Calvin L. Greenberg

...ter & Greenberg, Inc., Queens Realtors, ...nce the sale of the Plainedge Shopping ...r. The center, built in 1950, is located ...icksville Road and Boundary Avenue; ...edge, New York. The center contains ...r market and eight stores plus substan-...ront car parking. The purchasers were ...ing clients of Balter & Greenberg. The ...& Greenberg company was repre-...d by Calvin L. Greenberg. The seller ...enny Associates.

Shopping Center
...d at Auction
$911,000

...lter & Greenberg, Inc., real ...e brokers of Jamaica, N.Y. announced the sale at auc-... of the Carteret Shopping ...er containing 26 stores on a ... acre plot with a frontage of ... feet on Roosevelt Ave., just ... of the New Jersey Turnpike ... exit 12 in Middlesex County. ...ildings are one story, were ...ructed in 1957, and contain ...) sq. ft. General construction ... der block and brick. There is ...ng for approximately 1,500

Baltimore Store Site Sold

    The N.F.L. Corporation, a group of Manhattan investors, has purchased an Acme supermarket site in Baltimore for $450,000.
    The building of 26,800 square feet is on a plot of two and one-half acres at Stevenson Lane and Charles Street.
    The property was bought from the Buckeye Development Corporation of Baltimore for cash on a free and clear basis. Balter & Greenberg was the broker.

Shopping Center Sold

    The Fall River Shopping Center at 548 Pleasant Street in Fall River, Mass., which has the A & P. as a major tenant, has been purchased by the Benenson Realty Company of Buffalo, N.Y. The sale was arranged by Balter & Greenberg, Inc., brokers of Jamaica, Queens. The Moss Construction Company, which built the center in 1962, was the seller. The sales price was about $500,000.

Balter & Greenberg, Inc., has announced the sale of a free standing single tenant 20 year net lease to Circle K Supermarkets located in Winslow, Arizona. Circle K is a west coast super market chain with over 150 stores. The buyer from Providence, R.I. was represented by Lowenstein, Pitcher, Hotchkiss & Parr, New York attorneys. Saul Diskin was the seller.

* * *

    Balter & Greenberg, Inc., announced sale of a free standing, single tenant, net deal. The Pancake House, on a plot 125 x 100, located at Parsonage Road adjacent to the Menlo Park Shopping Center, was sold. The tenant is the AAA-1 rated International Industries. The property was sold for approximately $100,000 over financing. The seller was represented by W. Landberg, Esq. The purchaser was represented by Eugene Hionas, Esq. Balter & Greenberg was represented by Lee Weisinger.

Four Retail Centers
On L.I. Sold to Investor

    Balter & Greenberg, Inc., real estate brokers of Jamaica, N.Y., announce that they were the brokers in the sale of a group of four shopping centers located in Valley Stream, L.I., N.Y. The properties were sold by Sidney Weiderlight, noted New York financier, for all cash over mortgages.

Brooklyn Parcel Sold

    A one-story building with eight stores at 4001 13th Avenue, Brooklyn, has been sold for $155,000 in cash over a first mortgage by Steven Associates, a Brooklyn realty investing concern. The purchaser of the building and its plot of 100- by 60 feet was Sidney Berger. The broker in the transaction was Lee Weisinger of Balter & Greenberg, Inc. The lawyer for the seller was Edward A. Segal. Gene Wollin, represented the buyer.

    Clippings courtesy of *Real Estate Weekly*, 614 E. 14th St., New York, N.Y.; *Realty*, 264 W. 40th St., New York, N.Y.; and *National Real Estate Investor*, 132 W. 31st St., New York, N.Y.

11 STORE BUILDINGS BOUGHT FOR MILLION

The A. S. W. Holding Corporation, a real estate investing company, has bought 11 store buildings in the metropolitan area in a transaction involving about $1,000,000. The one-story taxpayers were acquired from the Greenwich Estate, a realty holding company.

The properties, which are in Queens, Brooklyn, the Bronx and Nassau County, were sold through Balter & Greenberg, Inc., brokers of Jamaica, Queens, who were represented

BALTER & GREENBERG, INC.

Balter & Greenberg, Inc., leading investment firm, announced the recent sale of 12 commercial buildings for aggregate sales of $4,837,000.

St. Louis Store Sold to Investor

Balter & Greenberg, Inc., New York brokers, have announced the sale of the F. W. Woolworth building at Olive and Grand Sts., St. Louis. The property is a 3-story reinforced concrete store building with a total sales area over 60,000 sq. ft. The property was sold for $1 million to an investor.

Calvin Greenberg, chairman of the board for Balter & Greenberg, Inc., Queens investment brokers, announced that during the past 12 months his firm sold 23 parcels totalling $19,000,000 in sales prices. Of this total, 11 deals totaling $7,500,000 were sold on a co-brokerage basis. Each was made in a different state. Mr. Greenberg announced that his company is planning to expand its co-brokerage department with the addition of two more men.

Recent Sales

MERRICK & NIEMAN, LYNBROOK, L.I.
424 ATLANTIC, E. ROCKAWAY, L.I.
324 POST, WESTBURY, L.I.
40-01 13th AVENUE, BROOKLYN, N.Y.
PLAINEDGE S.C., PLAINEDGE, L.I.
NOR. BLVD. & 157 ST., FLUSHING, N.Y.
349 KNICKERBOCKER, BROOKLYN, N.Y.
SUN RAY STATION, WATERLOO, IOWA
PANCAKE HOUSE, MENLO PK., N.J.
FALL RIVER S.C., FALL RIVER, MASS.

Bay State Store Parcel Sold

The Gateside Corporation has contracted to buy a four-story and basement department store building in Springfield, Mass. The property, which is assessed at $430,000, is being sold for all cash by Maslin & Moslin through Balter & Greenberg, Inc., chain-store brokers, of Jamaica, Queens.

BALTER & GREENBERG, INC.

Balter & Greenberg, Inc., New York Investment brokers recently announced sale of the Sunray D-X Service Station located in Parkersburg, Iowa.

SHOPPING CENTER IN QUEENS BOUGHT

Investor Gets Grand Union Building in Laurelton

The Grand Union Shopping Center at the intersection of Merrick Road and Laurelton Parkway, Queens, has been purchased by an investing client of Balter & Greenberg, commercial property brokers of Jamaica.

Sale of Retail Center In Northport Announced

Calvin L. Greenberg, chairman of the board of Balter & Greenberg, Inc., real estate brokers announced the sale of the He Shopping Center.

LICENSED IN STATES OF NEW YORK, NEW JERSEY, PENNSYLVANIA, MASSACHUSETTS, CONNECTICUT, ILLINOIS, MARYLAND

In conformity with Balter & Greenberg, Inc., code of ethics, every effort has been made to verify the accuracy of the information herein presented, however no warranty or guarantee of such accuracy is expressed or implied.

The preceding exhibit, B–4, is of prime importance. Publicity creates in the mind of the owner the feeling of: "Here is an organization that makes deals. If they have been successful for others, then they should also be for me."

A managing agent must constantly secure new merchandise. He must also check to see if the old merchandise is still available. The form shown in Exhibit B-4 helps to provide this.

APPENDIX C

Glossary of Terms*

Abstract of Title:	A short history of the title.
Acceleration Lease:	Periodic increases.
Accessibility:	Ease with which a site may be reached.
Acknowledgement:	Statement and execution before authorized officer that such statement and execution is his act.
Acquisition:	Process of procuring property.
Acre:	Land—43,560 sq. ft.
Administrator:	One who handles affairs of an estate.
Ad Valorem:	According to the valuation.
Adverse Possession:	To acquire title by possession.
Affidavit:	Written statement sworn to before an officer having authority to administer oath.
Affirm:	Act of confirming or ratifying.
Agent:	One who is employed to represent another.
Agreement of Sale:	Contract to sell and to purchase.
Alienation:	Transfer of property from one person to another.
Alluvion:	Increase of earth along riverbank shores.
Amortization:	Paying of a financial debt on a regular basis.
Appraisal:	Process for obtaining conclusions of values.
Approved Plans:	Those passed by municipality.
Assessment:	A municipal charge against real estate on a proportionate basis.
Assignment:	Transfer of an agreement to another.
Assigns:	Those to whom property shall have been transferred.

---

* Information listed here was taken from *Real Estate Primer*, State Real Estate Dept., Phoenix, Arizona and *Georgia Real Estate License Law with Rules and Regulations*, Georgia Real Estate Commission, 166 Pryor St. S.W., Atlanta, Georgia.

Assumption of Mortgage:	Purchaser taking title to property that is mortgaged and assuming liability for payments of the existing mortgage.
Attachment:	To seize property and bring it into custody of law because of an action.
Avulsion:	Removal of land by action of water.
Bequeath:	To leave or give, by will.
Bill of Sale:	Written instrument used to establish ownership of personal property.
Binder:	See Earnest Money.
Bargain and Sale Deed:	Conveys all interest of grantor, but with no warranties.
Blanket Mortgage:	One mortgage covering two or more properties.
Blighted Area:	A declining area: changes for the worse.
Bona Fide:	In good faith.
Bond:	Evidence of personal debt secured by a mortgage.
Broker:	Employed for a commission or fee to represent another.
Builder's Terms:	One-third cash, balance short-term mortgage.
Building Area:	Gross area of first floor of building.
Building Code:	Regulation of construction.
Building Line:	Line beyond which a building may not be erected.
Cancellation Clause:	Agreement invalid upon certain conditions.
Capitalization:	Return estimated by net income and investment, to determine value of property.
Capitalization Rate:	Property value based upon net income.
Caveat Emptor:	Let the buyer beware. Buyer makes purchases at his own risk.
Chain:	Four or more stores under one management.
Chattel Mortgage:	Conditional transfer of title to personal property.
Cloud on Title:	A claim against property.
C.O.:	Certificate of Occupancy.
Collusion:	An agreement to defraud.
Commercial Acre:	Balance of land after taking out streets, sidewalks, and curbs
Commercial Paper:	Bill of exchange used in trade.
Commission:	Payment for employment; agent compensation.
Commitment:	Written statement from lending institution that monies are being reserved for mortgage loan.
Common Law:	Law that grew from customs used in England.
Community Property:	Real and personal property belonging to husband and wife.

Condemnation:	Taking private property for public use and compensating for it.
Conditional Sales Contract:	Contract of sale, but not transferring title until contract conditions have been met, although delivery has already been made.
Consideration:	An adequate promise used in an exchange.
Constructive Eviction:	Breach of lease.
Constructive Notice:	Notice given in public records.
Contract of Sale:	See Agreement of Sale.
Conversation:	Change from one use to another.
Conveying:	Written transfer of title.
Corporation:	Created by law with powers of natural person and may continue active for any length of time prescribed by law, with rights and liabilities apart from persons composing it.
Covenant:	Agreements written into deeds and other instruments stipulating uses or nonuses of property.
Courtesy:	Husband's right to half of wife's estate.
Dedication:	Private land given to municipality for public use.
Deed:	Written instrument conveying title.
Default:	Failure to meet obligation.
Defendant:	Party being sued in legal action.
Deposit:	Earnest-money down payment prior to formal contract.
Depreciation:	Loss in value by wear and tear.
Devise:	Gift or property by will.
Dispossess:	To deprive of possession.
Docketed Judgement:	Judgement listed in records.
Dower:	Wife's half interest in husband's estate.
Duress:	When a person is forced to do something against his will.
Earnest Money:	Binds deal subject to more formal contract.
Easement:	Sharing right-of-way.
Effective Income:	Actual collectable income less vacancies.
Ejectment:	Action to gain possession because of unlawful use.
Eminent Domain:	The right of government to take private property upon payment of compensation.
Encumbrance:	A claim against real property.
Encroachment:	Structure on land of another.
Equity:	Value above claims against property.
Erosion:	Loss of land by nature.

Escheat:	Reverting to state because of lack of heirs.
Escrow:	Held in trust subject to condition.
Estate:	Property ownership.
Eviction:	Action to gain possession of real property.
Exclusive:	Unrestricted right to sell.
Execute:	To make or perform; as to execute a contract.
Executor:	Carries out provision of will.
Exterior:	Outside; as used in exterior repairs.
Fee Simple:	Largest form of realty ownership.
Fiduciary:	A position of trust.
Fixture:	Personal property, apart from realty.
Foreclosure:	Creditor's action to defeat redemption.
Forfeit:	Loss due to failure to perform.
Fraud:	Successful employment of and intentional deception to deceive another.
Front Foot:	A price unit of lease, purchase, or sale.
Graduated Lease:	Rent increases at specified intervals.
Grantee:	The buyer.
Grantor:	The seller.
Gross Lease:	All operating charges paid by landlord.
Ground Rent:	Tenant does not own fee, but pays for right to use same.
Habendum Clause:	"To have and to hold the above granted premises unto the party of second part—his heirs and assigns forever."
Holder in Due Course:	One who has taken a note in good faith, before due.
Hundred Per Cent Location:	Retail location considered best in city.
Improved:	A building erected upon vacant land.
Incompetent:	Unable to take care of property acceptably.
Incorporate:	To form a corporation; limits personal liability.
Industrial:	Manufacturing.
Injunction:	Restraining order.
Instrument:	Written legal document.
Installment Contract:	Title conveyed upon final payment.
Interest:	The percentage of a sum of money charged for its use.
Interior:	Inside; as interior repairs.
Intestate:	Dying without a will.
Investment:	Capital spent for profit.
Joint Tenancy:	Property held by two or more persons with right of survivorship.

Judgement:	Court action declaring indebtedness.
Laches:	Delay in asserting one's legal rights.
Landlord:	One who leases to another.
Lease:	An agreement by landlord to lease real estate and for tenant to use and pay for same.
Leasehold:	Realty held under lease.
Legal Description:	Given in metes and bounds.
Lessee:	Tenant.
Lessor:	Landlord.
Liability Insurance:	Accident policy.
Lien:	Claim against property; mortgage, taxes.
Life Estate:	Interest confined to duration of life.
Lispendens:	Suit pending; recorded to give notice.
Listing:	Real estate for sale or lease.
Maintenance:	Act of upkeeping physical condition of real estate.
Mall:	Pedestrian walk flanked by stores.
Marketable Title:	Court would force purchaser to accept.
Market Value:	Willing buyer and willing seller create same.
Meeting of Minds:	Willing buyer and willing seller.
Mortgage:	Conditional transfer of real property as security for debt.
Mortgagee:	Party who lends money.
Mortgagor:	Party who borrows money.
Multiple Listing:	A cooperative listing.
Net Income:	Revenue paid by tenant, less expenses.
Net Lease:	Tenant pays expenses.
Net Listing:	All remaining after net price of agent's commission is deducted.
Note:	Acknowledging a debt.
Obsolescence:	Changes causing outdating.
Occupancy:	Taking possession.
Option:	Right to lease or purchase at a specified date.
Parking Ratio:	Relationship between building and parking area.
Party Wall:	On line of adjoining properties for mutual use.
Percentage Lease:	Based upon percentage of gross business in order to determine rent.
Plat:	Land map.
Prepayment Privilege:	Permission to pay before maturity.
Prima Facie:	Presumptive on its face.
Prime:	Best available; top-quality location.
Property:	An individual interest in real estate.

Purchase-Money Mortgage:	Given as part payment of purchase.
Specific Performance:	Court order compelling defendant to carry out terms of agreement.
Square-Foot Content:	Area within outer measurements.
Statute of Frauds:	Certain contracts must be in writing in order to be enforceable.
Structural:	Major construction.
Sublease:	A lease given by lessee.
Subordination:	To take a secondary position.
Suburban:	Outlying district.
Survey:	Determine boundary lines of property.
Taxpayer:	A one- or two-story commercial building with stores occupying street level. Formerly built as interim improvement, but not today.
Tenancy in Common:	Estate held by two or more; no survivorship.
Tenant:	One who leases space for a period of time.
Time Is of the Essence:	Agreement cannot be extended.
Title:	Ownership.
Title Insurance:	Protect owner against loss by bad title.
Tort:	A wrongful act.
Twilight Zone:	Diminishing economic value.
Underimprovement:	Bad economic use.
Unimproved:	Vacant land.
Urban:	City real estate.
Use Clause:	States use tenant may make of leased premises.
User:	Purchaser who will tenant the property himself.
Usury:	Charging more than legal rate of interest.
Value:	Bona-fide price property will bring at a sale between a willing buyer and a willing seller.
Vendee:	The purchaser of real estate.
Vendor:	The seller of real estate.
Waiver:	To forego a right.
Warranty Deed:	Conveys property with guarantees.
Water Table:	Distance from surface of ground to a depth at which natural groundwater is found.
Zoning:	Municipal regulation relating to percentage and type of use.

This glossary should be used often. Try to memorize four or five words daily. If you follow this suggestion, within 30 days it is possible to have a good, workable real estate background of understandable terms. Try not only to memorize the meaning of the various terms, but also to make an effort to use the words in sentences. Many of these terms do not have a direct bearing on commercial leases, but all may be used indirectly or in conjunction with commercial leasing.

INDEX

A

Accountant, 89
Accretion, 279
Adverse possession, 279
Advertising space, 43
Agent, managing, 55, 63
Appendix, 273-297
Articles:
  double-spaced, 43
  how to write, 44
  lengthy, 44
  little-known facts, 44
  plain, white paper, 43
  proper form, 43
  subjects, 44

B

Bakery, 85
Balloon, definition, 96
Bankruptcy, 279
Beauty salons, 85
Benefits, 17
Booklets, 25-32
Books, 24-39
Brochures, 75-77

C

Calendars, 45
Capitalization, inadequate, 74, 90
Cards store, 85
Cash, minimum investment, 72-73
Cash reserve, 72
Chain stores:
  "Approximate Income," 172
  "Approximate Support," 172
  "Att.," 171
  "Basement," 171-172
  "Checked," 171
  "Competition," 172
  "Future Planning," 172
  index by state, 182-191
  index by type, 173-182
  leasing formula, 193-248
  "Location," 171
  location and leasing information, 193-252
  "Remarks," 172
  sources to be contacted, 248-252
  "Store Location Report," 171, 172-173
  submitting locations, 171-173
  "Type of Neighborhood," 172
  "Type of Storefront," 172
  types listed, 173
Checklist, 21-22
Christmas, 44-45
Classified section of telephone book, 44
Clients, attract:
  article, 43-44 (see also Articles)
  be well known, 43-44
  calendars, 45
  Christmas, gadgets, 44-45
  coin-op business, 49-50
  commercial supplies, 45-48
  diploma type papers, 41
  floors, carpeted, 41
  furniture, wood, 41
  government, 48-49
  license on display, 41
  list of taxpayer sales, 43
  location, 45
  name before public, 43
  newspapers, 43-44
  office, 41

Clients, attract (Cont'd.)
　photographs, framed, 41
　professional dignity, 41
　publicity, 43
　purchase advertising space, 43
　Red Book, not for neophyte, 44
　shopping center owners, 43
　signs, 45
　Small Business Administration Services, 50–52
　telephone book, 44
　trade papers, 43
　visual aids, 41–43
　walls, 41
Coin-op business, 49–50
Commercial law:
　accretion, 279
　acquisition of real property, 278–279
　adverse possession, 279
　bankruptcy, 279
　commission agreements, 279–284
　dedication, 279
　deed of conveyance, 279
　eminent domain, 279
　execution, 279
　forfeiture, 279
　gift, 279
　grants, 278
　joint tenancy, 278
　judgement, 279
　marriage, 279
　occupancy, 278
　personal property, definition, 277
　real property, definition, 277
　sale, 279
　severalty, 278
　succession, 278
　tenancy in common, 278
　tenancy in partnership, 278
　types of property and ownership, 277–278
　will, 279
Commercial leasing:
　AAA-1 credit rating, 95, 98
　"expired buildings," 96–99
　　approval for lease guarantees, 98
　　balloon (remaining balance), 96
　　Bonanza Formula, 96–97
　　chain supermarket, 98
　　check comparative rentals, 97
　　definition, 96
　　drop in market value, 96
　　example, 96–97
　　fears of owner, 96
　　increased financing, 98
　　individual tenancies, 98, 99
　　knowledge, 96
　　long-term leases, 96
　　long-term mortgage, 96
　　money made, 97–99
　　mortgage secured, 98
　　new setup, 98
　　picturing property, 96
　　prevailing rentals, 96
　　raise rent and/or mortgage, 96
　　rentals on downgrade, 97
　　rentals on upswing, 98
　　secure new leases, 97
　　total value increase, 99
　government, 95, 98
　rent guarantee policies, 95–96
　　advance rent monies, 96
　　federal guarantees, 95
　　partial loan, 96
　　premiums, 95
　　private insurance companies, 95
　　procedure, 95
　　tenant not in default, 96
　　termination of lease, 96
　rent payments guaranteed, 95
　Small Business Administration, 95, 98
Commercial supplies, 45–48
Commission agreements, 279–284
Commissions, 18
Comparables, 90
Conveyance, deed, 279
Cost, 23–39
Customer file, 24

D

Dedication, 279
Deed of Conveyance, 279
Department stores, 85
Deposits, 80
Dignity, professional, 41
Directory of Leading Chain Stores, 25
Directory of Shopping Centers, 25
Discount stores, 85
Drug stores, 85
Dry cleaners, 85

E

Eminent domain, 279

Exclusive agreement, 80–81
Execution, acquisition of real property, 279
"Expired buildings," 96–99

F

Failure of stores, 74
Federal properties:
   leasing and purchasing agencies, 253–254
   owned by individual states, 254–256
   Post Office regional real estate offices, 256–272
File:
   customer, 24
   listing, 24
Financing, institutional, 92
Firms, 28–32
Floors, carpeted, 41
Forfeiture, 279
Forms, leasing aids, 77–78
Franchising:
   cost, 125
   franchise, 125
   index of franchises by name, 113–118
   index of franchises by state, 118–124
   index of franchises by type, 107–113
   lease, 125
   location and leasing information, 125–170
   plot, 126
   "purchasing percentage," 105
   questionnaire form, 101–102
   realty officer, 125
   rental, 126
   requirements, 101–102
   site evaluation method, 102–106
   sources, 126–170
   special building, 125
   store size, 125
   street and traffic information, 103–104
   total units, 125
   type, 126
   type location, 125
   types of franchises listed, 106–107
Furniture, wood, 41

G

Gadgets, 44–45
Gas stations, 85
Gift, acquiring real property, 279

Gift store, 85
Government, 48–49, 89, 95
Government property, 253–272 (*see also* Federal properties)
Graduated lease, 55
Grants, 279

H

Hardware stores, 86
Homestead Act, 279
Hours, 17, 18

I

Income, 17, 18
Information, 24–39
Institutional financing, 92

J

Joint tenancy, 278
Judgement, acquisition of real property, 279

L

Laundromats, 86
Leasehold, 91, 93, 94
Leases:
   agent, managing, 55, 63
   chain stores, 53, 193–252
   commercial, 95–99 (*see also* Commercial leasing)
   commercial law, 277–284 (*see also* Commercial law)
   franchising, 101–170 (*see also* Franchising)
   government property, 253–272 (*see also* Federal properties)
   graduated, 55
   individual merchants, 53
   negotiating, 53–69
   "ordinary taxpayer lease," 53, 54
   percentage (*see* Shopping center lease)
   renewal, 91
   right of assignment, 55
   sale or transfer, 55
   schedule, leasing, 67–68
   securing, 83–88
      always be professional, 86–87
      bakery, 85
      beauty salon, 85
      brokerage step, 84

Leases (Cont'd.)
  securing (Cont'd.)
    building, cost, 84
    cash in job, 84
    client, find, 83
    department store, 85
    discount store, 85
    drug store, 85
    dry cleaner, 85
    estimating, 84
    expenses, 84
    first mortgage, 84
    gas station, 85
    gifts and cards store, 85
    insurance (estimated), 84
    interest and amortization, 84
      and, cost, 84
    laundromat, 86
    listing, 83
    location for client, 83-85
    luncheonette, 86
    majority of commercial vacancies, 84
    paint and hardware store, 86
    presentation to property owner, 84
    prime locations, 84
    rated tenants, 84
    rebates, 86-87
    secret method of leasing, 85-86
    shoe stores, 86
    supermarket, 86
    taxes (estimated), 84
    total cost, 84
    water and sewer (estimated), 84
  shopping center, 53 (see also Shopping center lease)
  supermarket lease specifications, 58-63 (see also Supermarket lease specifications)
  types, 53
Library, 24-39
License, display, 41
Listing file, 24
Listing information, 74-75, 285-290
Location, office, 45
Luncheonettes, 86

M

Managing agent, 55, 63, 89, 90
Marriage, acquisition of real property, 279
Methods, explanation, 21-22
Money, 18, 24
Mortgage, advantageous, 90

N

Negotiating:
  deposits, 80
  exclusive agreement, 80-81
  forms and brochures, 77-78
  leases, 53-69 (see also Leases)
  listing information, 74-75
  rental costs, 71-72
  telephone, 78-79
Newspapers, 43-44

O

Occupancy, 278
Office, 41
Operator, personality, 74
Outright sale, 91, 92, 94
"Overrented" buildings, 90
Ownership, 277-279

P

Paint stores, 86
People, necessary to business, 73
Percentage lease, defined, 53, 64
Percentage rental rates, 64-66
Personal property, definition, 277
Photographs, framed, 41
Population backing, 73-74
Post Office Department, 256-272
Property:
  acquisition of real property, 278-279
  government, 253-272 (see also Federal properties)
  ownership, 277-278
  personal property, definition, 277
  real property, definition, 277
  types, 277
Publicity, 43, 44
"Purchasing percentage," 105

R

Real property, definition, 277
Rebates, 86-87
Recording machines, 79
Red Book, 44
Reference checklist, 21-22
Rent guarantee policies, 95-96
Rental costs:
  chart, 71, 72
  frontage, 71

Rental costs (Cont'd.)
  price per front foot, 71
Rental value, 90
Retail trade organizations, 32–36

S

Sale, acquiring real property, 279
Sale-leaseback, 91, 92–93, 94
Sales methods:
  leasehold, 91, 93, 94
  outright, 91, 92, 94
  sale-leaseback, 91, 92–93, 94
S.B.A., 50, 95, 98
Selling pointers, 285–290
Severalty, 278
Shoe stores, 86
Shopping center lease:
  additional rent, 55
  agent, 55
  agreements in writing, 58
  alterations, 57
  basement space, 54, 55, 56
  charges, additional, 55–56
  condemnation, 54, 55
  differs from ordinary taxpayer lease, 54
  drawn up in advance, 54
  electrical outlets, 54, 56
  electricity, 56
  fire, 54, 55, 58
  form lease, 54
  graduated, 55
  heat clause, 57
  insurance rates, increase, 58
  location of store, 54
  options, 57
  parking, 54
  parking area maintenance, 55
  percentage lease, defined, 53, 64
  percentage rental rates, 64–66
  rent increases, 55
  repairs, 56
  right of assignment, 55
  rubbish removal, 56
  sale or transfer, 55
  schedule, leasing, 67–68
  security, 57
  signs, 57
  size and lease requirements, 68
  small, unrated tenant, 54
  supermarket lease specifications 58–63
    (see also Supermarket lease specifications)
  tax increases, 55
  types of stores, 68–69
  use clause, 54, 56–57
  water clause, 57
  work to be done, 54
Shopping center owners, 43
Shoulder rest, telephone, 79
Signs, 45
Small Business Administration, 50–52, 95, 98
Sponsor, definition, 37
State leasing information sources, 25–28
Succession, 278
Supermarket lease specifications:
  air-conditioning, 62
  architect, 58
  "as built" drawings, 59
  building certificate of occupancy, 59
  cellar, 59
  certificates, electrical and plumbing, 59
  changes in structure, 59
  column spacing, 60
  doors, 59, 60, 63
  drainage of fixtures, 59
  dustproofing of floors, 59
  electric facilities, 60–61
  fixture layout, 58
  floor drains, 59
  foundation walls, 60
  garbage room, 59
  general provisions, 62–63
  ground floor, 60
  heat, 62
  lessee's requirements, 58
  materials used, 59
  painting, 63
  parking area, 63
  plumbing, 61
  roof insulation, 60
  sales floor, 60
  stairs, 59
  survey, 58
  toilet facilities, 59
  ventilating, 62
  water for cooling, 59
  windows, 59
  work area floor, 60
Supermarkets, 86
Supplies, commercial, 45–48

T

Tax facts, 89, 90, 91

Taxpayer sales, list, 43
Telephone, 78–79
Telephone-amplifying machine, 79
Telephone book, classified, 44
Tenancy, 278

U

Undercapitalization, 74, 90
"Underrented" buildings, 90–91
Urban renewal, 36–39

V

Value of building, determining, 90
Visual aids, 41–43

W

Will, 279